us. What we become is our gift to God. —**ROGER H. C. DONLON** ✫ Real patriotism lies in the Te show love to God and love to man. My love for my fellow man led me to the Congressional Medal of Hono ✫ Don't hesitate to serve your country—your freedom depends on it. —**RUSSELL E. DUNHAM** ✫ The greatest experience of my life was serving my country, "One Nation Under God," the United States of America. —**WALTER D. EHLERS** ✫ Freedom is not free—more than 400,000 were killed during World War II, December 7, 1941, to September 2, 1945. —**HENRY E. ERWIN** ✫ Everything this country is, or hopes to be, is directly attributed to our veteran community. One enduring American principle guided their commitment to the nation no matter where or when they served—freedom! —**FREDERICK E. FERGUSON** ✫ I always remember the day I took the oath to support and defend the Constitution of the United States. That really meant something to me. —**JOHN W. FINN** ✫ We should follow our convictions in defense of this great country we live in, and defend it if needed. —**BERNARD F. FISHER** ✫ Everything for freedom! Find a way that works for you to serve God and country. —**MICHAEL J. FITZMAURICE** ✫ American service members are truly superb—they answer the call to duty for freedom, justice, and the American way. —**JAMES P. FLEMING** ✫ We don't have problems, just solutions. Drive yourself, lead others, and never offend. —**EUGENE B. FLUCKEY** ✫ If our actions are motivated by duty, honor, and country, we can promote goodness to achieve greatness. —**ROBERT F. FOLEY** ✫ There is only one way to go: full speed ahead for God and country. —**JOSEPH J. FOSS** ✫ One must have good character, solid principles, and high ethical standards to inspire others to follow. —**WESLEY L. FOX** ✫ Freedom is something the protected take for granted. —**ED W. FREEMAN** ✫ America—love it or leave it. Many have died to protect it. —**HAROLD A. FRITZ** ✫ With the help of God, we can accomplish any mission. —**ROBERT E. GALER** ✫ Everyone welcomes recognition, but the ones who truly deserve it most are those Americans who gave their lives for this country. —**SALVATORE A. GIUNTA** ✫ I have always tried to live by the "Golden Rule"—always do unto others as you would have them do unto you. —**NATHAN G. GORDON** ✫ In war I saw so many boys become men overnight. —**STEPHEN R. GREGG** ✫ Integrity is when you do the right thing when no one is watching. —**CHARLES C. HAGEMEISTER** ✫ When you're told it's time to go, you set your fears aside and go do it. —**BARNEY F. HAJIRO** ✫ To whom much is given, much is expected, so always strive to do what is right. —**SHIZUYA HAYASHI** ✫ I came when I was called and I did the best I could. —**JOHN D. HAWK** ✫ Do unto others as you would have them do for you. Love your family, friends, and God. —**JAMES R. HENDRIX** ✫ Love your enemy and bless those who curse you. —**RODOLFO P. HERNANDEZ** ✫ For God and country, we are united as one always. —**SILVESTRE S. HERRERA** ✫ Honor those who have served our country, especially those who made the ultimate sacrifice. Educate future generations about the price paid for the freedom we enjoy in America the beautiful. —**FREEMAN V. HORNER** ✫ It's a great privilege to be an American. And the greatest privilege of all is the right to choose. —**ROBERT L. HOWARD** ✫ Our freedom, envied the world over, was attained at great personal sacrifice—we cannot allow it to wither away through apathy. —**THOMAS J. HUDNER, JR.** ✫ The greatest gift I can leave to my children is their heritage. —**EINAR H. INGMAN** ✫ The reality of combat experience teaches life's greatest lesson—humility. —**ROBERT R. INGRAM** ✫ Duty, honor, country. As long as we believe in these words, our nation and our democracy will flourish. —**DANIEL K. INOUYE** ✫ Without discipline there can be no success in any endeavor. —**ARTHUR J. JACKSON** ✫ It's not only a person's privilege, but also his duty, to love his country. Have the courage to defend it with honor, integrity, and your life if necessary. —**JOE M. JACKSON** ✫ Freedom is purchased with the lives of those magnificent people who value American liberty above all. —**JACK H. JACOBS** ✫ Sometime you'll find yourself in the wrong place at the wrong time—deal with it the best you can. —**DON JENKINS** ✫ Make the world a better place by being more mindful of your children, thoughtful of the elderly, charitable to those less fortunate, and open to opposing views. —**LEONARD B. KELLER** ✫ Moral courage—doing what has to be done because it is the right thing to do—is the mark of a true hero. —**THOMAS G. KELLEY** ✫ When it comes to war, I'd rather fight on the enemy's court than the home court. —**ALLAN J. KELLOGG, JR.** ✫ Your character is built on one decision and one choice at a time. And what you build will determine whether you find happiness. —**JOSEPH R. KERREY** ✫ *(continued on back endpapers)*

Medal of Honor

Medal of Honor

PORTRAITS OF VALOR BEYOND THE CALL OF DUTY

FOREWORD Brian Williams

ESSAYS Tom Brokaw, Victor Davis Hanson, Senator John McCain

PHOTOGRAPHS Nick Del Calzo TEXT Peter Collier

Published by Artisan
A division of Workman Publishing Company, Inc.
225 Varick Street, New York, NY 10014-4381
www.artisanbooks.com

Published simultaneously in Canada by Thomas Allen & Son, Limited

The Library of Congress has cataloged the first edition as follows:

Library of Congress Cataloging-in-Publication Data

Collier, Peter, 1939–
    Medal of Honor : portraits of valor beyond the call of duty / photography by Nick Del Calzo ; text by Peter Collier ; Congressional Medal of Honor Foundation.
        p. cm.
    ISBN: 1-57965-240-9 (1st ed.)
1. Medal of Honor—Biography. 2. United States—Armed Forces—Biography.
I. Del Calzo, Nick. II. Congressional Medal of Honor Foundation. III. Title.

UB433.C64 2003
355.1'342—dc21 [B]   202300

ISBN 978-1-57965-462-7 (3rd ed.)

Printed in Singapore

First edition, 2003
Second edition, 2006
Third edition, November 2011

10 9 8 7 6 5 4 3 2 1

Book design by Nicholas Caruso

Medal of Honor is published in collaboration with the Congressional Medal of Honor Foundation.

To fallen friends, mothers and fathers, brothers and sisters, sons and daughters
who answered their nation's call and gave their lives that others may live in freedom.
We reflect on what their lives might have been, but never will be.
Their sacrifice is our mandate; our challenge is to remember.

Each of the Medal of Honor recipients featured in this book, many in the twilight of their years, agreed to sit for a photograph and to recount his story one more time for the benefit of future generations. Sadly, some of them have passed away since the photographer and the author were privileged to work with them. Yet together, these recipients, living or dead, help us put a face on the meaning of hero and understand what their heroism represents for us all.

Contents

BRIAN WILLIAMS

Foreword

I was profoundly honored to be asked to write this introduction to the third edition of *Medal of Honor: Portraits of Valor Beyond the Call of Duty*, which has been published to coincide with the 150th anniversary of the establishment of the Medal of Honor by an act of Congress, signed into law by President Abraham Lincoln back in 1861. This milestone celebrates the heroism and sacrifice of all those who have fought and died to defend the freedoms we enjoy as Americans.

As a member of the Congressional Medal of Honor Foundation board, I have had the staggering privilege of meeting and getting to know many of the recipients of this high honor who are still with us. I have listened to their conversations, heard their remarkable war stories, and marveled at their reflections on what the medal means to them. To a man, they insist they were just doing their job and were inspired to action by the plight of their fellow soldiers. Theirs is a bond that those of us who have not faced the horrors of combat can only imagine. They did what they did for their buddies, on their right and their left, whose very lives were held in the balance. They will tell you they wear the medal for their fellow soldiers, and for those who didn't come home. Their modesty and humility are breathtaking. They are living reminders that our culture of self-celebration has not yet affected everyone. As I wrote this foreword, we heard about the demise of the world's number one terrorist, Osama bin Laden. I couldn't help but reflect on those brave men and women who quietly go about their business without fanfare, willing to brave incredible risk on our behalf. It is why I believe that those serving today do so with the same spirit of courage and sacrifice as those of previous generations, as Peter Collier points out so poignantly in "The Mission Continues" (page 328).

Sadly, time and fate have taken a toll. As of this writing, there are fewer than eighty-five recipients still alive to carry on the Medal of Honor's rich legacy of courage and sacrifice, manifested in the most extreme situations. I have said many times: If you take the time to read their stories—or even just one story of one recipient—you'll never have a bad day again. These men represent the very best our country has to offer, and we can learn from their experience and their strength of character. They did the right thing when the chips were down and when things seemed hopeless. They thought of others before themselves, and risked life and limb to make a difference. And so can we—in our civilian lives on any particular day. As one recipient put it, "The Medal of Honor is proof that ordinary men and women have within them the potential to challenge fate and literally change the course of history—it only requires the courage to try."

As President of the United States, I am afforded no greater privilege than serving as Commander-in-Chief of the finest military the world has ever known. With this responsibility comes the distinction of bestowing military decorations upon our Nation's most valiant service members, and no award is higher than the Medal of Honor.

In 1861, President Abraham Lincoln began acknowledging individuals for their gallantry and intrepidity in action at the risk of life above and beyond the call of duty. In the century and a half since then, fewer than 3,500 brave patriots have received the Medal of Honor, each recipient embodying the virtues and values Americans hold dear: duty, honor, service, humility, and heroism.

This medal reflects the gratitude of our entire Nation, and we remain forever indebted to the women and men of our Armed Forces and their families for their service and sacrifice. May God bless and protect all those who serve, and may God bless the United States of America.

Sincerely,

GEORGE W. BUSH

Laura and I are proud to join our fellow Americans in observing the 150th anniversary of the Medal of Honor and in honoring the outstanding patriots who have received it.

The Medal of Honor is the nation's highest military distinction and the greatest award for bravery a President can bestow. It is given for gallantry above and beyond the call of duty, and for valor beyond anything that duty could require. For any President, presenting the Medal of Honor is a high privilege. I awarded the Medal to twelve brave Americans. Their stories—which spanned World War II, Korea, Vietnam, and today's conflicts in Afghanistan and Iraq—are awe-inspiring.

Since World War II, more than half of those who have been awarded this medal gave their lives in the action that earned it. Though many of these Americans never lived to wear the medal, they will always be honored in the annals of our country's history. By risking their own lives to save others, they exemplified the highest ideals of military service.

I commend the Congressional Medal of Honor Foundation for its work to preserve the history of those who have received this high award. On this anniversary, Laura and I extend our deepest gratitude to all the men and women of our Armed Forces and their families who have sacrificed so much to defend the freedoms we hold dear. We salute our Medal of Honor recipients for their unmatched bravery and heroism. And we ask for God's blessings on all who wear the uniform of the United States.

WILLIAM JEFFERSON CLINTON

In both peacetime and in war, the United States' achievements as a free nation have been built upon the sacrifices of our men and women in uniform. For the past 150 years, following a tradition established by President Lincoln in 1861, we have recognized our service members' most extraordinary acts of courage and valor with our country's highest military award, the Congressional Medal of Honor.

More than 3,400 Medals of Honor have been bestowed upon members of the United States Armed Forces since the Civil War. Hundreds of these medals were awarded posthumously to men who lost their lives as they heroically went above and beyond the call of duty to protect their comrades, defend our freedoms, and uphold our national security. Scores more were conferred upon individuals decades after the conflicts in which they fought, often in an effort to right history's wrongs by recognizing the individuals of every race and creed who risked or gave their lives for our country. Finally, the soldiers, sailors, airmen, Marines, and Coast Guardsmen who lived to receive their Medals of Honor in person have done so with profound humility and reverence for their fallen brothers and sisters. For their selflessness and their patriotism, we owe them all a debt of gratitude.

Though these men entered into military duty as ordinary people from all walks of life, together in their gallantry and as Medal of Honor recipients, they comprise an elite circle of America's most distinguished heroes. This publication celebrates their exceptional determination, resolve, and love of country. Their sacrifices remind us that whether or not the United States is at war, the members of our Armed Forces defend our liberties despite great peril to their own safety; jeopardizing—and sometimes losing—their lives in places where comforts are few and dangers are many.

All Americans have a profound responsibility to honor those who wear our nation's uniform, their extraordinary service, and the security they provide to the rest of us. It is also vital that we maintain the memory and understand the significance of those who have served and sacrificed for more than two hundred years. This book fulfills that mission by paying tribute to America's very bravest and best—its Medal of Honor recipients.

Sincerely,

Bill Clinton

The Medal of Honor epitomizes the very best of what America stands for and honors the gallant individuals who have received it. These special people represent the very heart and soul of America. They come from all walks of life and nearly every state in our great nation. They truly reflect the ethnic, cultural, economic, and educational diversity of America, but they have one common bond: They are the recipients of the Medal of Honor, the highest award for military heroism.

Of the more than 3,400 recipients, fewer than 85 remain with us today. This commemorative book is a tribute to them and to the thousands of others who are no longer with us. I encourage you, the reader, to absorb the power of each story so that these men can serve as role models, especially to our young men and women.

The Medal of Honor pays homage to comrades who have given their lives for this great country. These gallant souls, in their heroism and their humility, epitomize the nobility of service to country and of service above self.

A nation can be judged in part by how well it honors its heroes. This book tells more than one hundred stories. Each remarkable story goes well beyond the stirring words of the Medal of Honor citation. Each profile is unique, yet each one has a common theme—the willingness of someone to take great personal risks to protect endangered comrades and to accomplish an extremely dangerous mission.

Medal of Honor is an inspiring photographic and biographical tribute to those Americans who—by choice or by chance—left our shores to assure that our country would remain free of tyranny. Their legacy is carried on today by the valiant men and women who serve with the same spirit of commitment and sacrifice as those who preceded them.

Americans for all times will treasure the gifts that these brave warriors have given to all of us so selflessly.

Sincerely,

G Bush

JIMMY CARTER

Rosalynn joins me in expressing our gratitude to the men and women of our military on this 150th anniversary of the Medal of Honor. This award, the highest that can be given to our troops, was instituted during the Civil War and through the years has been presented for valor above and beyond the call of duty.

These brave individuals, ordinary Americans who have performed extraordinary deeds, are the finest example of selfless service for their country.

I join a grateful nation in paying tribute to these American heroes.

I have had the honor of awarding this medal on more than one occasion during my time as President and have personally found the recipients to be humble, selfless, patriotic Americans who are often reluctant to accept such an honor for themselves.

I warmly extend my thanks and gratitude to the Medal of Honor recipients for their service, their sacrifice, and their example.

May God Bless them, and God Bless America.

Sincerely,

Jimmy Carter

From the Civil War to Today: A 150-Year History

When the Civil War erupted, Joshua Chamberlain was a thirty-four-year-old professor of modern languages at Maine's Bowdoin College. He could have avoided serving, but two of his great-grandfathers had fought in the Revolutionary War, and Chamberlain felt honor bound to keep the nation they helped build from coming apart. By the time of the Battle of Gettysburg, he was a colonel in the 20th Maine Regiment. As the fighting raged, his commanding officer ordered Chamberlain to "hold the line at all costs" at a hill called Little Round Top to keep the Union Army from being flanked and possibly routed. The 20th Maine beat back two assaults from the Southern forces. But the regiment had taken so many casualties and was so low on ammunition that Chamberlain feared his men would have to use their rifles as clubs when the next attack came. So he gave the order to fix bayonets and led a charge down the hill, putting the Confederates on the defensive and changing the outcome of the battle and, according to some historians, the Civil War itself. For his "daring heroism and great tenacity" at Gettysburg in July 1863, Joshua Chamberlain received the Medal of Honor.

When Chamberlain had his rendezvous with destiny, the medal was new; it is now 150 years old. Its stature has grown over time, and it is one of the few American institutions that has remained immune to the doubt and cynicism that are so great a part of contemporary culture. Unique in every way, it is the only military medal worn around the neck; its recipients are the only individuals the president of the United States salutes as a matter of custom. Out of an estimated 40 million men and women who have served in the U.S. military since the Civil War, fewer than 3,500 have received the medal. Although serving in the armed forces of a democracy, these recipients have emerged from the fog of war as an aristocracy of valor.

General George Patton once remarked, "I'd give my immortal soul for that Medal." Harry Truman, a former artilleryman in World War I and colonel in the Army Reserves who personally awarded 113 medals, more than any other chief executive, said, "I would much rather have that Medal around my neck than to be President of the United States."

Recipients of the Medal of Honor have included privates and seamen, admirals and generals; teachers, businessmen, laborers, and professionals; blue bloods, members of minorities, and immigrants. (Seven hundred forty-six of them came to America from other countries.*) Coming from every walk of American life, they recapitulate the sprawling, diverse story of American nationhood itself. One early recipient (in 1869) was a Pawnee Indian Army scout named Co-Rux-Te-Cod-Ish.

---

* Ron Owens's *Medal of Honor* (Turner Publishing, 2004) is an important source for crucial facts and figures regarding the medal and its recipients.

The first black serviceman to be awarded the medal was an escaped slave, Richard Blake, who distinguished himself during the Civil War in an action on the Stono River in South Carolina aboard the U.S. Navy gunboat *Marblehead.* The only woman ever to receive it was Mary Walker, a surgeon during the Civil War. Tom Custer, who died with his brother George Armstrong Custer at the Little Bighorn, was one of nineteen men to receive two Medals of Honor—in his case for acts of valor in the Civil War—although the awarding of multiple medals, always rare, was formally discontinued in 1919.

Willie Johnson, a thirteen-year-old drummer boy who served in the Union Army's Peninsular Campaign of 1862, was the youngest to receive the Medal of Honor. At sixty-two, General Douglas MacArthur, commander of the U.S. forces in the Pacific in World War II, was the oldest. He and his father, Arthur MacArthur, who served in the Civil War, are one of a pair of fathers and sons to be awarded the medal. The other is Theodore Roosevelt and his son Theodore, Jr., who received their medals, respectively, for bravery at San Juan Hill in the Spanish-American War and on Utah Beach during the D-Day invasion.

In the great conflicts that have defined modern America—World War II, Korea, Vietnam, and now the War on Terror—over 60 percent of all medals have been awarded posthumously. The recipients who survived have gone on to lead lives that are different in every regard, except for their common belief that they did not "win" the medal for themselves, but merely hold it in trust for their comrades who never came home.

Some recipients have had great success after returning to the civilian world. Joshua Chamberlain himself, for instance, served four terms as governor of Maine. Audie Murphy, the most decorated serviceman of World War II, became a film star. Joe Foss, an air ace in the Pacific, served as the first commissioner of the American Football League. Bob Kerrey returned from a shattering wound in Vietnam to serve as governor of Nebraska and a U.S. senator for two terms. But most have simply gone back to the roles of son, husband, and father; wage earner, entrepreneur, and citizen—everyday Americans except for the transformative moment that will always make them stand for something larger than themselves. Almost all feel that it is harder to wear the medal than to have earned it in the first place. One recipient, Army Staff Sergeant Charles Morris, who was wounded several times while keeping his platoon together in an eight-hour firefight in Vietnam in 1966, spoke for most of the others when he said, "I've found that holding the medal is a humbling experience because it is so much bigger than I will ever be."

In its 150-year history, the Medal of Honor has reinforced the great lessons of human experience: that character is destiny; that the individual, not impersonal forces beyond his control, makes history. And whether awarded for an action at Little Round Top or in Kunar Province in northeastern Afghanistan, the medal has extracted moral lessons from the bloody chaos of war, teaching us about "daring heroism and great tenacity" and about the indomitability of the human spirit.

DEFINING THE MEANING OF THE MEDAL OF HONOR over the last century and a half has been a journey in self-inquiry for America. Until Senator James Grimes of Iowa introduced a bill in 1861 to create a medal for bravery, there had been no systematic effort to honor the heroism of American fighting men. In part, this was because most of the military actions during the first decades of U.S. history had been skirmishes taking place on the distant frontier out of the sight of most citizens. It was also true that the new nation had been ambivalent about badges and ribbons since its founding, associating them with the pomp and pretense of European military castes rather than the unassuming patriotism of citizen soldiers in a democracy. But the Civil War was a new kind of war—brother fighting brother in the neighborhoods of America, where citizens could not help but witness carnage that would not be equaled again until the trench warfare of World War I more than half a century later. A medal was needed, Senator Grimes and others believed, to provide an incentive for troops deserting in large numbers and for civilians reluctant to volunteer in the face of this bloodshed, and to exalt the sacrifice that would be required if the Union were to be saved.

Senator Grimes's bill established a medal for the Navy and was signed into law by President Abraham Lincoln on December 21, 1861. Shortly afterward, a resolution was introduced for an Army medal and signed by the President on July 12, 1862. Both the Navy and Army versions were called the Medal of Honor, to be awarded to those who "most distinguish themselves by their gallantry in action and other soldier-like qualities." The design provided by the U.S. Mint showed an inverted five-pointed star at whose center was the helmeted figure of Minerva, goddess of righteous war, representing America, repelling a crouching male figure holding snakes and representing "the foul spirit of secession." The Navy version of the medal was suspended from an anchor and attached to a red, white, and blue ribbon. The Army version was suspended from the figure of an eagle with cannons and cannonballs in its talons. The first medals struck by the Mint cost about $1.90 apiece.

A medal should not be awarded for "the simple discharge of duty," but rather for "such acts beyond this that if omitted or refused to be done, should not justly subject the person to censure as a shortcoming or failure."

At first, there were concerns that the troops, caught up in a fight that was far more brutal than any had imagined, might regard the new decoration as irrelevant. But as the horrors of the war mounted and the Medal of Honor came to symbolize the enormous sacrifice exhibited on the battlefield, it proved, if anything, too popular. In the absence of clear criteria for when and why it should be awarded, soldiers began to apply for the medal. Sometimes the award was nakedly political. When the enlistment of the 27th Maine Volunteer Infantry Regiment was due to expire on July 1, 1863, the eve of the decisive Battle of Gettysburg, for instance, the medal was presented to all 864 men in the unit as an inducement to reenlist, although only 310 actually did. Later on, the 29 men serving as an honor guard for Abraham Lincoln's body when it was sent home to Springfield for burial also received the medal.

The years after the Civil War offered no clearer sense of what the Medal of Honor should mean or of the circumstances under which it should be awarded. In 1876, Army officers reviewing the large number of recommendations resulting from the Battle of the Little Bighorn tried to make the requirements more stringent. A medal should not be awarded for "the simple discharge of duty," they noted, groping for a lasting definition, but rather for "such acts beyond this that if omitted or refused to be done, should not justly subject the person to censure as a shortcoming or failure."

The 1890s marked a low point in the history of the Medal of Honor because of the large number of Union veterans who personally lobbied members of Congress for the honor even though their reputed deeds of valor were now thirty years in the past. Many were rightly seeking delayed recognition for accomplishments that still burned brightly in their memories, even if the country as a whole had begun to forget. But other petitioners wanted the medal for more cynical purposes, such as using it to make a claim on a variety of public and private charities. Sometimes those seeking the medal merely sent a letter outlining their claim, and the secretary of war's office often granted the award without any attempt to verify the actions in question. More than five hundred medals were awarded retroactively between 1890 and 1897, many of them mailed out in the regular post with a terse note of congratulations.

In an effort to bring order and meaning to what had become a chaotic process, Secretary of War Russell Alger announced a new set of standards for the Medal of Honor on June 26, 1897. Under the more exacting criteria, individuals could no longer apply on their own behalf. Documentary evidence—official records and eyewitness testimony—would be required as evidence of valor, and recommendations for the medal would now have to be made within a year of the military action in which the individual had participated. One of the important by-products of this reform was that the official citations for the action, which had previously been a cursory sentence or two, would now give a more detailed description of the heroic act. Over time, these citations would become eloquent chapters in America's autobiography.

In the ongoing meditation about the Medal of Honor's meaning, attention was also paid to the setting in which it was awarded. During the Civil War, medals were most often distributed by commanding officers in front of military formations; in later years, they were sometimes simply handed to the recipient by low-ranking War Department personnel. Now, acting on a recommendation from the War Department, President Theodore Roosevelt ensured the award's prestige by a 1905 executive order stipulating that it should always be presented "with a formal and impressive ceremonial," if possible "by the President, as Commander in Chief, or by such representative as the President may designate."

Another key moment in the medal's evolution came a few years later, in 1916. With the world embroiled in a global military conflict the United States would soon join, Congress established an "Army and Navy Medal of Honor Roll" that awarded a pension of $10 a month to recipients who had distinguished themselves "conspicuously by gallantry or intrepidity, at the risk of life, above and beyond the call of duty."* This language, particularly the key phrase "beyond the call of duty," would continue to define the Medal of Honor in the years to come.

The 1916 legislation also sought to buttress the integrity of the medal by ordering the War Department to appoint a board to review whether past awards had been issued "for any cause other than distinguished conduct involving actual conflict with an enemy. . . ." General Nelson Miles, one of the nation's most esteemed soldiers, was chosen to head it. A Medal of Honor recipient himself as a result of actions in the Civil War Battle of Chancellorsville and also a commander of U.S. forces during the Indian Wars of the 1870s, Miles assembled a team of officers to reconsider each of the 2,625 medals so far awarded by the Army. In a report released in February 1917, this board called for the honor to be withdrawn from 910 of these recipients, including the 864 men of the 27th Maine who had received it en masse and the honor guard accompanying President Lincoln's body home after his assassination.

---

* The pension would rise over the years and is today $1,000 a month, accompanied by other distinctive benefits such as the automatic right to burial in Arlington Cemetery.

Among the eighteen others stripped of the decoration—not necessarily because they had failed in bravery but because most had been civilians—were William "Buffalo Bill" Cody, who had been awarded the medal for "gallantry in action" in 1872 while serving as a scout for the 3rd Cavalry during the Indian Wars, and Civil War assistant surgeon Mary Walker. The only woman to receive the medal, Walker was a colorful figure who when criticized after the war for wearing trousers instead of more feminine clothing, replied tartly, "I have the right to dress as I please in free America on whose tented fields I have served for four years in the cause of human freedom." She refused to return her medal after the award had been rescinded, and defiantly continued to wear it every day until her death in 1919. Over half a century later, after a careful review, President Jimmy Carter restored the rescinded medal to Mary Walker's heirs in 1976. In 1989, President George H. W. Bush restored Buffalo Bill Cody's as well.

The reforms of the early twentieth century underwrote the uniqueness of the Medal of Honor by clarifying the criteria under which it would be awarded and by giving its presentation a solemn dignity. But if a better picture now existed of what defined America's highest honor—actions "beyond the call of duty"—a question still remained. What about acts of battlefield bravery that were significant but not quite up to that exacting standard? Three additional medals were established to commend degrees of bravery: the Distinguished Service Cross, the Distinguished Service Medal, and the Silver Star (and, for the Navy and the Marine Corps, the Navy Cross). This was the beginning of a Pyramid of Honor with the Medal of Honor at the top and the Purple Heart at the base that would ultimately define the range of American military valor.

AT THE BEGINNING OF THE TWENTIETH CENTURY, a few Medals of Honor were awarded to Americans who served in the Philippines in 1910, Veracruz in Mexico in 1914, and Haiti a year after in what a later era would define as "incursions." But it was America's entry into the Great War, as it was then called, that put the country and its military on the world stage and brought the medal closer to most Americans. One hundred twenty-four medals were awarded during World War I, all under the new, more stringent criteria established in preceding years. With primitive battlefront footage now appearing on silent-movie screens and human-interest stories about U.S. fighting men pumping the circulation of increasingly influential big-city newspapers, Medal of Honor recipients became national celebrities.

None more so than a Tennessee farmer named Alvin York, whose story acquired overnight the

who in some cases were forced to train initially with broomsticks could overcome the seasoned armies of dictators who had been fine-tuning their war machines in Nanking and Poland and other unlucky spots for several years. By the end of the war, the answer had been given by the more than 13 million men in uniform who had suffered nearly a million casualties while fighting and winning wars on two fronts continents away from each other. Four hundred sixty-four Medals of Honor were awarded during this war, 266 of them posthumously.

The medal was a central factor of U.S. involvement in World War II from the very first day of battle. Fifteen medals were awarded for heroism at Pearl Harbor, ten of them posthumously. One of these went to Peter Tomich, a Croatian born as Petar Herceg Tonic in the Austro-Hungarian empire in 1893. Having changed his name when he came to America as a young man, Tomich joined the Army in World War I. When his enlistment was over, he joined the Navy. He was a forty-eight-year-old chief water tender aboard the USS *Utah* on the morning of December 7, 1941, when the ship was mortally wounded by a torpedo shortly after the Japanese attack began. Tomich made sure that all the other men in the engine room got out and then returned to his post. He was last seen trying to secure the boilers to give his shipmates a few minutes more to escape.

The Medal of Honor he received went homeless for a time because he had no relatives in the United States. When a destroyer named in his honor was commissioned in 1943, the medal was awarded to the ship itself. After the USS *Tomich* was mothballed at the end of the war, the governor of Utah proclaimed Peter Tomich an honorary citizen and the state took over guardianship of the medal. Diligent efforts to locate his kin finally paid off in 2006, when the medal was presented to a distant cousin of Tomich's in a ceremony aboard the USS *Enterprise* in the Croatian port city of Split.

There was no such wait for the sacrifice of Douglas Munro to be acknowledged. On September 27, 1942, Munro, the only Coast Guardsman ever to receive the Medal of Honor, was the officer in charge of a group of five boats evacuating a battalion of Marines unable to establish a beachhead at Guadalcanal because of heavy enemy fire. When the last of the Marines seemed in danger of being trapped there, Munro positioned his boat to serve as cover for them and was fatally wounded. Douglas Munro's mother accepted the medal on his behalf and then enlisted in the Coast Guard herself, serving until the end of the war.

Some recipients of the Medal of Honor served their country twice—on the field of battle and then at home, boosting the morale of a populace that had been deeply shaken by Pearl Harbor.

Marine Gunnery Sergeant John Basilone was one of the first of these inspirational figures. When the two sections of machine guns he commanded came under attack at the Battle of Guadalcanal by a vastly superior force of Japanese soldiers on October 24, 1942, he fought constantly for the next two days, running through heavy fire to resupply the guns as they ran out of ammunition and returning to inflict a large number of casualties on the enemy. When relieved, only Sergeant Basilone and two other Marines were left standing.

When John Basilone was brought home to receive the Medal of Honor for this action, he appeared on the cover of *Life* and was interviewed on national radio. His hometown of Raritan, New Jersey, staged a parade for him that was filmed by Movietone News, which distributed the footage to theaters across the country as a newsreel. Basilone toured the United States for several months to help sell war bonds. He had recently married and could have stayed home with his wife for the duration, but he asked to rejoin the Marines battling their way through the Pacific. At first, his superiors, trying to protect him, denied the request and offered to make him an officer if he agreed to remain stateside. Basilone continued to press for a return to active duty. Finally, in 1945, he was reassigned to a combat unit in time for the invasion of Iwo Jima. In an action that would result in his being awarded a Navy Cross to go along with his Medal of Honor, he got his men off an exposed position on the beach, single-handedly destroyed a heavily fortified Japanese position with grenades and explosives, and was fighting his way toward an enemy airfield when he was killed by shrapnel from an enemy mortar.

Taken together, the citations of the Medal of Honor recipients of World War II read like episodes in a modern American *Iliad*. Like Homer's heroes, some of these men killed dozens of the enemy in epic hand-to-hand combat. Yet while they were implacable warriors on the battlefield, many of those who received the medal would later say that the first thing they did when the fighting was over was to find somewhere to pray—for the friends they had lost and also for the men they had been forced to kill. Medic Desmond Doss, a devout Seventh-day Adventist, saved dozens of GIs at Okinawa and became the first conscientious objector to receive the medal. Lieutenant Commander Joseph O'Callahan, a Catholic priest serving in the Pacific on board the USS *Franklin* when the ship was attacked by enemy aircraft on March 19, 1945, groped his way through exploding bombs and rockets on the flight deck to minister to the wounded and dying, led firefighting crews, and manned a hose by himself to cool armed bombs rolling over the listing deck. He became the first chaplain to receive the medal, "serving with courage and deep spiritual strength," as his citation noted, and inspiring the officers and men of the *Franklin* "to fight with profound faith in the face of almost certain death."

In their willingness to sacrifice themselves, the men who earned the Medal of Honor didn't stop to think about the price they were paying. Nor did they realize that their actions were creating ripples that would continue to lap against the shores of other lives for years to come. On February 2, 1944, during the U.S. invasion of the Marshall Islands, for instance, Marine Private Richard Sorenson saw a Japanese grenade land near his comrades and threw himself on it without hesitation. (Twenty-six Marines would do the same thing during World War II, but only Sorenson and three others survived.) Decades later he got a letter from a young woman he had never heard of. She was a college student and enclosed a copy of a paper she had just written on important people in her life. The last line read, "Richard Sorenson is a man I held in awe even before I learned his name because one of the men he saved is my dad."*

The World War II Medal of Honor recipients might have been treated as celebrities, but they knew that those who served more anonymously beside them were also capable of behaving with such valor. Indeed, some had, although their actions had not been witnessed. In *D-Day, June 6, 1944*, historian Stephen Ambrose quotes the remembrance of Private John Fitzgerald of the 101st Airborne, who landed far from his drop zone on D-Day at Sainte-Mère-Église. Walking into the town, Fitzgerald saw trees filled with the hanging bodies of U.S. paratroopers who had been killed by the Germans while tangled in their parachutes. He also saw the body of one trooper who had managed to get down and made an enemy foxhole "his own personal Alamo." Around this dead soldier lay the bodies of nine German soldiers he had killed before falling himself. This paratrooper's empty cartridge cases, spilled out onto the ground around him, and his broken rifle stock, which he had used as a club of last resort against the enemy, told a story. Remembering this scene, Private Fitzgerald provided the only citation this paratrooper would ever receive: "He fought alone, and like so many others that night, died alone."†

By World War II, the Medal of Honor was established as a national institution, and the men who had received it in the past were an inspiration for those now going into combat. Growing up in Foster City, Michigan, in the 1920s, for instance, Oscar Johnson read everything he could get his hands on about Eddie Rickenbacker, America's leading World War I ace and leader of the famed

---

* Cited in *Above and Beyond* (Boston Publishing Group, 1985), p. 235.

† Cited by Owens, *Medal of Honor*, p. 108.

> In their willingness to sacrifice themselves, the men who earned the Medal of Honor didn't stop to think about the price they were paying.

Of the 135
medals awarded
in Korea, 97
were to men
who didn't
come home,
the highest ratio
of posthumous
to living recipi-
ents of any
U.S. war.

"Hat-in-the-Ring" fighter squadron. After Pearl Harbor, Johnson went off to war himself. On September 16, 1944, he was a private first class in a company of the 91st Infantry assigned to break the German line in a battle near Scarperia, Italy. Johnson led a seven-man team trying to stop an enemy counterattack seeking to flank and surround the American force. After several hours, all the other men in his squad were either dead or wounded. Private First Class Johnson fought off the Germans single-handedly in an all-night battle that left twenty enemy dead in front of his position. As he fought, he thought about the example of Eddie Rickenbacker—and, like his hero, he earned a Medal of Honor for his bravery.*

WORLD WAR II WOULD ALWAYS BE "THE GOOD WAR"—the war whose cause was unequivocally just and whose stakes were always clear-cut; the war whose heroes, dead and alive, were seen by the American public as knights of the great democratic round-table. By contrast, the Korean War was a "police action," fought under the aegis of the United Nations for reasons many Americans didn't fully grasp in a place about which they knew very little. The GIs who slogged through that hostile environment were regarded less as conquering heroes than as unlucky participants in a murky cause whose objectives the country had difficulty appreciating.

The Medal of Honor shone brightly in the midst of this uncertainty. Of the 135 medals awarded in Korea, 97 were to men who didn't come home, the highest ratio of posthumous to living recipients of any U.S. war.

There were no battles on whose outcome the American public hung as it had during Iwo Jima or the D-Day landings at Normandy. But some of the actions in Korea made military history. In the battle at the Chosin Reservoir, for instance, Army soldiers and Marine personnel faced an enemy that outnumbered them ten to one and fought their way out of encirclement over a week of hellish combat in a frozen and unforgiving landscape. Twelve medals would be awarded for actions during this engagement alone, six of them posthumously.

The Air Force, part of the Army until 1947, when it was made a separate branch of the service, had four of its men honored with Medals of Honor in Korea. The first one went to Major Louis J. Sebille, a highly decorated pilot during World War II who was now commander of the 67th Fighter-Bomber Squadron. On August 5, 1950, he led a flight of F-51 Mustangs against

* Peter C. Lemon, *Beyond the Medal* (Fulcrum Publishing, 1997), p. 114.

Communist artillery and troop positions concentrated on the banks of a river near Hamchang, South Korea. On Major Sebille's first attack, one of his five-hundred-pound bombs did not release. As he turned to make a second run on the target, he was hit by enemy fire. Sebille radioed his wingman that he had been fatally wounded; then, despite entreaties that he try to return to base, he deliberately flew his F-51 into a Communist truck convoy below, firing his machine guns as he destroyed a large contingent of enemy troops.

IN 1963, CONGRESS DEFINITIVELY ESTABLISHED THE CRITERIA for receiving the Medal of Honor, specifying that it was an award for heroic action in combat and standardizing the basic criteria to be used by each branch of the armed services in making recommendations for an award. The act performed must be one of personal bravery or self-sacrifice so conspicuous as to clearly distinguish the individual from his comrades; it must involve risk of life; and it must be so outstanding that it clearly represents gallantry beyond the call of duty distinct from lesser forms of bravery. Next, the recommendation for the Medal of Honor must include incontestable evidence provided by at least two eyewitnesses. Finally, the approval process must be marked by painstaking review at all levels of command, up to and including the secretary of one branch of service, the chairman of the Joint Chiefs of Staff, the secretary of defense, and, ultimately, the president, who personally approves the awarding of the Medal of Honor.

These rules were in effect by the beginning of the war in Vietnam, where 247 medals were awarded, 155 of them posthumously. If the Korean War had been on the periphery of America's vision, prosecuted for reasons that were not always clear to the general public, Vietnam, fought on the nightly television news and occasionally in the nation's streets, as well as in the jungles of Southeast Asia, was a war whose objectives—containing the advance of international Communism—were questioned by a divided country and ultimately caused deep social unrest. While GIs in World War II knew that the American public was hanging on their every action and passionately involved in their struggle, many of the soldiers in Vietnam felt by comparison that the people back home didn't understand what they were experiencing and sometimes didn't care, and that their only real audience, therefore, was each other. More than in other wars, they fought with great heroism simply because they didn't want to let the men beside them down.

Marine Corporal William Morgan, for instance, was in Quang Tri Province on February 25, 1969, when his platoon was pinned down while attacking a North Vietnamese bunker complex.

Two Marines were hit in what became a no-man's-land and couldn't be reached by medics because of the heavy enemy fire. Corporal Morgan maneuvered through the dense jungle to get closer to the wounded men. He shouted words of encouragement to them as he initiated a bold one-man attack on the lead enemy bunker. He drew the attention of the North Vietnamese, who concentrated their fire on Morgan. He was mortally wounded, but he had given his comrades time to drag the two wounded Marines to safety.

The men who earned the Medal of Honor in Vietnam might not have become household names back home, as their predecessors were a generation earlier, but they taught other servicemen about courage and kept the ideals of patriotism alive in an era when America's goodness as a nation was called into question. After being shot down over North Vietnam on November 9, 1967, for instance, Air Force Captain Lance Sijan, though badly injured, survived in the jungle for six weeks, evading enemy patrols until he was finally captured. He continued the fight while imprisoned in the Hanoi Hilton. At one point, Captain Sijan managed to overpower a guard and escape. When he was recaptured a few hours later, he was brutally tortured. Savagely beaten over a period of weeks, he refused to cooperate with his torturers and kept looking for new ways to escape. By the time he finally died in the spring of 1968 of abuse and sickness, he had become an inspiration for the remaining POWs—because of his unyielding faith in his country and because he epitomized the "maximum resistance" they expected of each other as they continued to wage war even while locked up in an enemy hellhole far from home. After Sijan's passing, one of his comrades said that even though he had died in a filthy prison, he had never stopped being "a free man from a free country."

The Medal of Honor was never tarnished by the controversy that surrounded the war in Vietnam. In fact, as the national mood back home gradually shifted to a belated appreciation of the sacrifice and valor that had characterized that lonely conflict, what the men had done there to earn the medal helped light the veterans' way back home to the admiration of their countrymen.

AT THIS POINT IN ITS LONG AND DISTINGUISHED HISTORY, the Medal of Honor was defined in part by an ongoing process of review that had become an integral aspect of its basic identity—a sort of institutional rumination about valor and the way it manifested itself in battlefield situations. Acknowledging that the medal was about truth as well as bravery and that its integrity depended on "getting it right," the Department of Defense engaged in a comprehensive review at the beginning of the twenty-first century to remedy errors of omission or oversight that might have kept members of some minority groups from receiving the medals they had earned. On January 13, 1997, medals were awarded to seven African-American servicemen from World War II whose heroism had gone unacknowledged because of the social prejudices of the day. A little more than three years later, on June 21, 2000, medals were awarded retroactively to twenty-two Asian Americans, many of whom served in Europe as part of the famed 442nd Regimental Combat Team, whose motto was "Go for Broke!" Among them was Senator Daniel Inouye of Hawaii.

This look backward has encompassed overlooked individuals as well as overlooked groups and continues to this day. Several medals have been awarded in the last quarter century to men whose comrades made their heroism a cause and simply wouldn't take no for an answer. The case of Captain Benjamin Louis Salomon, a dentist who served as an Army surgeon, is an example of how, where the Medal of Honor is concerned, the power of memory often triumphs over the power of forgetting. Captain Salomon was giving medical care to U.S. soldiers during the 1944 Battle of Saipan when Japanese troops overran the American position. Dozens of wounded were carried to Salomon's tent, now serving as a field hospital. When one of the enemy entered the tent and tried to bayonet a wounded GI, Salomon put down his surgical instruments, picked up a gun, and killed him. He had returned to tending the wounded Americans when four more of the enemy appeared. Salomon killed two and disarmed the others. He then ordered bearers to transfer the wounded to the regimental aid station while he held off the enemy with a machine gun. Days later, when U.S. soldiers returned to the site, they found Captain Salomon's body slumped over the gun, with the bodies of ninety-eight enemy soldiers in front of his position.

Salomon was immediately recommended for a Medal of Honor, but the recommendation was denied because he was a surgeon, and therefore not technically a combat soldier. In 1951, Salomon's former commanding officer tried again, but in a catch-22 response, he was now told that the time limit for recommendations had lapsed. An effort to revive the issue once again in 1969 was ignored by the Defense Department. Then the recommendation was resubmitted one last time in 1998 by staff members of the University of Southern California's School of Dentistry, Salomon's alma mater, who had solicited a local congressman to help see justice done. Finally, on May 1, 2002, President George W. Bush presented Benjamin Salomon with a posthumous Medal of Honor, accepted on his behalf by USC's School of Dentistry, where it now resides.

The War on Terror under-taken in response to the attacks of September 11, 2001, has re-inforced the Medal of Honor's continuing relevance.

The future of the Medal of Honor, as well as its past, has also become an issue in the new century. There were approximately 275 living recipients in 1975 when the war in Vietnam ended. There are fewer than 85 alive as of this writing. As age and infirmity take these men from us, it sometimes seems that the national curriculum on heroism and sacrifice they have helped create with their deeds is in danger of disappearing, too.

This slow attrition takes place in part because the conventional wars in which our country fielded massive armies of citizen soldiers have become a thing of the past. In the post-Vietnam era, American servicemen and -women have seen combat in places such as Grenada, Panama, Bosnia, Panama, Kuwait, and Somalia—fighting smaller wars without the large-scale pitched battles that so often resulted in actions "beyond the call" in the past.

But the idea that bravery stopped when America's servicemen and -women became an all-volunteer force involved in "asymmetrical" conflicts was disproven by the battle that took place in 1993 between outnumbered American Rangers and Special Forces operators and the militias of Somali warlords in Mogadishu. The decision of two Delta Force sergeants, Randall Shugart and Gary Gordon, to rope down from a helicopter to save a wounded pilot with full knowledge that they would probably not survive, an action for which they were both posthumously awarded the Medal of Honor, was indistinguishable from similar deeds performed by earlier generations of soldiers while fighting in very dissimilar conflicts.

The War on Terror undertaken in response to the attacks of September 11, 2001, has reinforced the Medal of Honor's continuing relevance. As of this writing, eight medals have been awarded in Iraq and Afghanistan, seven of them posthumously. Like earlier Medal of Honor recipients at the Argonne Forest, Iwo Jima, the Chosin Reservoir, the Mekong Delta, and other places on foreign soil where American bravery made history, these men offered up their lives to save their comrades.

This was certainly the case for Special Forces Sergeant Robert J. Miller, who was leading a team of Afghan nationals and coalition soldiers in a combat reconnaissance patrol in the snowy remoteness of Afghanistan's Kunar Province on January 25, 2008, when they were ambushed by a large force of Taliban insurgents. They were immediately pinned down with no cover. Sergeant Miller radioed for backup; then, as the only Pashto speaker on his team, he organized the Afghan soldiers in a defensive position. But the enemy fire was overpowering. Miller ordered his team to fall back and advanced toward the insurgents to cover their retreat. For a long time, his comrades heard him firing his weapon and throwing grenades. Then he was silenced. Miller had died fighting, but his team survived.

Army Staff Sergeant Salvatore Giunta, the first living serviceman to receive the award during a conflict since the Vietnam War,* joins a select group of men who fought in World War II, Korea, and Vietnam. Each is old enough to be Staff Sergeant Giunta's father or even grandfather, but now they are all part of a band of brothers. Salvatore Giunta reached into the hearts of these older servicemen and spoke for them, as well as himself, when, after receiving his Medal of Honor from President Barack Obama, he said of the action in which he distinguished himself: "I lost two dear friends of mine. I would give this back in a second to have my friends with me right now."

Doing what most of us would regard as impossible in an effort to save their friends and serve their country has been the defining characteristic of recipients of the Medal of Honor during its evolution over the last 150 years. They have all, living and dead, sharpened our appreciation of the cost of freedom while writing unforgettable chapters in the unfinished book of our national heritage.

---

* Salvatore Giunta's profile and portrait can be found on pages 330–31.

Fallen Heroes

BEHIND THE MEN IN THIS BOOK—AND ALL THE MEN and women who have served our country—stands an army of fallen heroes who have died defending our country. We take their sacrifice for granted—just as we take for granted our liberty itself. We know that there always have been and always will be Americans who will give up all their tomorrows for our todays.

Most Medals of Honor—more than 60 percent since World War II—have been awarded to men who never came home. Their reward is sparse: the riderless horse, the lonely echo of a bugler's taps, the last salute of a rifle team's gunfire, the folded American flag handed to those who now have only memories to cherish.

A few of them become celebrated figures. On October 3, 1993, for instance, Delta Force Sergeants Randall Shugart and Gary Gordon were involved in an assault on a rebel force in the Somalian capital of Mogadishu when two Black Hawk helicopters went down. From their own helicopter, they were providing protective fire at the crash sites when they learned that U.S. ground forces would not be able to rescue one of the crews. Shugart and Gordon volunteered twice to go down and help protect the Americans. Their commanding officers denied the requests because they knew how great the odds were against the two men. Shugart and Gordon knew, too, but they insisted on going anyhow and were inserted near the site, each armed with only a sniper rifle and a pistol. As dramatized in the book and film *Black Hawk Down*, they fought their way through heavy fire to the downed helicopter and gave their lives saving the injured pilot.

Most posthumous recipients are more anonymous, earning only a brief mention in the news when they receive their medals from a grateful nation. Sergeant First Class Paul R. Smith, for instance, the first man to receive the medal in the War on Terror, was at the Baghdad airport on April 4, 2003, engaged in the construction of a prisoner-of-war holding area, when his small task force was attacked by an enemy numbering more than one hundred. Smith immediately organized a defense with grenades and antitank weapons and then directed the evacuation of three wounded Americans. Fearing that his unit would be overrun, Smith moved under withering fire to a .50-caliber machine gun mounted on a damaged armored personnel carrier and engaged the enemy, killing dozens of them before he himself was killed. Smith saved his unit.

These three men and all the others—more than five hundred since the beginning of World War II— who fell on grenades to save their buddies, single-handedly charged enemy machine guns, or fought on long after ordinary bravery should have been exhausted would not have suffered in the eyes of their comrades if they had decided to live to fight another day. But for reasons that are beyond our understanding—reasons having much to do with duty, country, and honor, and little to do with fame and glory—they made a different decision: to look unflinchingly into the face of death.

Each of them is now an inspiring story in America's Book of Deeds. As members of an army of fallen heroes, they protect us still by their legacy. What each of them did challenges us to continue to learn from their sacrifice. The lesson is as clear as it is compelling: We are the land of the free for one reason and one reason only— because we are also the home of the brave.

Portraits of Valor

WORLD WAR II

TOM BROKAW

A Special Category of Hero

When I was a young man in the 1950s, right after World War II, there was a special category of hero everyone in America recognized: the men who wore the distinctive ribbon and star of the Medal of Honor. In those years when the legacy of war and sacrifice, bravery and humility was a touchstone in every community, the very mention of the Medal of Honor was part of the secular liturgy, an ideal to be honored and always remembered.

Some of the men who earned the MOH in World War II were as familiar as baseball stars or movie stars. In fact, one, Audie Murphy, was both a Medal of Honor recipient and a movie star. The governor of my home state of South Dakota, Joe Foss, was another. He was a famed sportsman and the first commissioner of the American Football League. Jimmy Doolittle, who led the famous raid on Tokyo, flying B-25 bombers off an aircraft carrier, was a national celebrity wherever he went for many years after his daring feat.

Those who earned the MOH on the Korean peninsula may not have become so famous in large part because that war was caught in the backwater of World War II. Americans, even veterans, were so preoccupied with getting on with their lives that the bitter and bloody Korean conflict rarely received the public attention it deserved.

Then, as America was consumed by the assassination of John F. Kennedy, the social and political upheaval that followed, the bitter divide over Vietnam, and the constitutional crisis of Watergate, the place of the Medal of Honor began to fade from the public consciousness. But for the military men who went into harm's way on the ground, at sea, and in the air, it never lost its place as the highest rank of recognition for uncommon valor and selfless courage.

Now, once again, there is a broad and deep appreciation of the place of the Medal of Honor as America reflects on all that we owe the military forces who defend our national security and protect our constitutional heritage.

For me, the meaning of the MOH reentered my life in June 1984, when I went to Normandy to produce a documentary on the fortieth anniversary of D-Day. One of my subjects was Gino Merli, who landed at Omaha Beach with the Big Red One. I was aware that he later earned the Medal of Honor for heroic action in Belgium. But when we walked onto that Normandy beach together and he began to softly recount the horrors of that day and the days to come in combat, I began to have a much richer appreciation of all that we owed his generation and the generations of military men and women that followed.

In a way that I didn't fully understand at the time, that day with Gino Merli was the beginning of a personal odyssey that led me to write *The Greatest Generation*.

I have learned from the MOH recipients invaluable and common lessons. They have an enduring humility about their heroic acts, almost always saying, "I'd rather talk about my buddy who didn't come back." They represent the fundamental fabric of America ethnically, geographically, and economically. They come in all sizes. My friend Jack Jacobs, a Vietnam-era MOH recipient, is a bantamweight. The late Joe Foss looked as if he could be a middle linebacker until the day he died in his mid-eighties. Bob Bush lost an eye on Okinawa, but he sees reality twice as well as anyone I know.

Over the years I've been privileged to attend any number of big deals, from presidential summits to state dinners to royal weddings, World Series, Super Bowls, and Broadway openings, but nothing means as much to me as the time I've spent with the Medal of Honor recipients, many of whom you will read about in this book. They always make me laugh, make me cry, and, most of all, make me proud that we're fellow citizens.

"The Tornado from Texas"

LUCIAN ADAMS

STAFF SERGEANT, U.S. ARMY 30th Infantry, 3rd Infantry Division

BIOGRAPHY

BORN
October 26, 1922
Port Arthur, Texas

ENTERED SERVICE
Port Arthur, Texas

BRANCH
U.S. Army

DUTY
World War II

DIED
March 31, 2003
San Antonio, Texas

TWENTY-YEAR-OLD LUCIAN ADAMS JOINED THE Army in 1943 after spending two years in a wartime plant making landing craft—just like the ones that would carry him to the shores of Italy and then France in the American invasion of Europe.

In the summer of 1944, the 3rd Infantry Division landed near Saint-Tropez and began advancing into central France. By late October, Sergeant Adams's company was near the town of Saint-Dié in the Mortagne forest, moving down a country road to open a supply line to two assault companies of his battalion that were cut off by the Germans, when it was stopped by heavy enemy fire. Adams, sent forward to scout the German position, reported three enemy machine-gun nests to his company commander. "You go on out there and make a breakthrough to get those GIs," the captain ordered.

Carrying a borrowed Browning automatic rifle, Adams began walking with his men down the road, which was heavily wooded on both sides. They hadn't gone ten yards before the German machine guns started firing, killing three of the men immediately and wounding six others. The rest of his unit hit the dirt, but Adams pressed forward, shooting the Browning from the hip as he zigzagged from tree to tree. As fire from the first German machine gun tore off leaves right above his head, he killed the gunner with a grenade. When another German popped up from a foxhole a few feet away, Adams killed him with a burst from his automatic rifle. Charging into the fire of the second machine gun, he killed its gunner with another grenade and forced the two supporting infantrymen to surrender. Then he ran deeper into the woods, killing five more Germans. When he got within close range of the third machine gun and the

gunner began shooting, Adams thought, "Uh-oh, I'm a goner now." But the gunner missed, and Adams killed him, too. By the time he had finished his one-man rampage, he had cleared the woods entirely of enemy soldiers. His men started calling him the tornado from Texas.

Right after the action, Adams was told by a messenger that he was being recommended for the Medal of Honor. Since he had heard the same thing at Anzio, where he had single-handedly destroyed a German machine-gun position, he didn't pay much attention. For the next few months, he and his unit continued to fight their way into Germany. In the spring of 1945, after the Americans had reached Munich, he received a call from regimental headquarters telling him he was to go home to be awarded the medal by President Franklin D. Roosevelt. Before he left, however, news came that FDR had died. Adams received the medal from Lieutenant General Alexander Patch on April 23, 1945, in Nuremberg's Zeppelinfeld stadium. An American flag was draped over a huge swastika on top of the stadium; after the ceremony, American engineers removed the flag and blew up the swastika.

Leading from the Front

VERNON BAKER

FIRST LIEUTENANT, U.S. ARMY 370th Regiment, 92nd Infantry Division

BIOGRAPHY

BORN
December 17, 1919
Cheyenne, Wyoming

ENTERED SERVICE
Cheyenne, Wyoming

BRANCH
U.S. Army

DUTY
World War II

DIED
July 13, 2010
St. Maries, Idaho

IN NEED OF A JOB AND WANTING TO SERVE HIS country, Vernon Baker enlisted in the Army in June 1941. He was assigned to the segregated 370th Regiment of the 92nd Infantry Division; it was the first black unit to go into combat in World War II, although not until late in the fighting and then under the command primarily of white officers. In June 1944, the 370th landed at Naples and fought its way north into central Italy. One evening in the fall, Baker, on night patrol, ran into a German sentry. In the duel that followed, Baker killed the German but was wounded so badly himself that he had to be hospitalized for two months.

In the spring of 1945, Lieutenant Baker—the only black officer in his company—was in command of a weapons platoon made up of two light-machine-gun squads and two mortar squads. His unit was near Viareggio on April 5 when it was ordered to launch a dawn assault against Aghinolfi Castle, a mountain stronghold occupied by the Germans. Moving ahead of the other platoons, Baker and his men had reached a shallow ravine about 250 yards below the castle at about 10:00 A.M. when they encountered heavy fire. As they took cover, Baker spotted a pair of cylindrical objects pointing up out of a mound in a hill above him. At first he thought they were flash suppressors for machine guns, but as he slithered closer, he realized they were observation scopes. He stuck his rifle into the slit of the observation post and emptied the clip, killing the two Germans who had been directing fire from the castle.

Moving forward, Baker stumbled on a well-camouflaged machine-gun nest and shot and killed the two soldiers manning it. The next moment, as Company C's commanding officer joined Baker, a German soldier appeared in the ravine and tossed a potato masher grenade, which came to rest at their feet. Luckily, it turned out to be a dud, and Baker shot the German as he tried to run. Spying a dugout quarried into the hillside, he blasted open the fortified entrance with a grenade, shot one enemy sniper who emerged after the explosion, then entered the dugout and killed two more.

By afternoon, German fire began to inflict heavy casualties on Baker's platoon. His captain ordered a withdrawal and left with his radioman as Baker covered their retreat. Then Baker and his men—the six remaining of the twenty-five he had led into battle earlier—began to make their way back down to the American lines. They ran into two more German machine-gun positions that had been bypassed during the assault; Baker used hand grenades to destroy them.

The next day, Baker volunteered to lead a battalion assault on Aghinolfi Castle. On the way up the hill, he saw the bodies of the nineteen men he had lost the day before, all of them barefoot because the Germans had taken their shoes and socks during the chilly night. Picking their way through minefields and heavy fire, the Americans finally routed the Germans and secured the position at the top of the mountain.

Vernon Baker was awarded the Distinguished Service Cross in July 1945, and remained in the military until 1968. In March 1996, more than fifty years after the assault on Aghinolfi Castle, he received a telephone call from a man working on a federal grant to reevaluate the heroism of blacks in World War II. Extensively interviewed about the events of April 5 and April 6, 1945, he then learned that he was to be awarded the Medal of Honor. When President Bill Clinton presented him with the medal on January 13, 1997, Vernon Baker became the only living black serviceman from World War II to receive this honor.

Minefield Warrior

VAN T. BARFOOT

TECHNICAL SERGEANT, U.S. ARMY 157th Infantry, 45th Infantry Division

BIOGRAPHY

BORN
June 15, 1919
Edinburg, Mississippi

ENTERED SERVICE
Carthage, Mississippi

BRANCH
U.S. Army

DUTY
World War II

CURRENT RESIDENCE
Virginia

LATER IN HIS LIFE, VAN BARFOOT WOULD BE HAILED as one of the most significant Native American heroes of World War II. His grandmother was a full-blooded Choctaw, but his mother failed to enroll him with the government as a member of that tribe, so Barfoot grew up aware only that he had American Indian blood, not that he was an "official" Choctaw.

He enlisted in the Army in 1940, before the new selective service law authorizing the peacetime draft was passed by Congress, and was assigned to the 1st Infantry Division. After his training, he participated in maneuvers in Louisiana and Puerto Rico. In December 1941, he was promoted to sergeant and assigned to the newly activated Headquarters Amphibious Force Atlantic Fleet at Quantico, Virginia. When the unit was inactivated in 1943, he was reassigned to the 157th Infantry.

Technical Sergeant Barfoot took part in the landings at Sicily in July 1943 and at Salerno two months later. In late January 1944, the 157th landed at Anzio and began moving inland rapidly. But counterattacking German reinforcements stopped the Allied advance, even forcing some withdrawals. By May, Barfoot's unit had been in a defensive position near the town of Carano for several weeks, during which time Barfoot conducted day and night patrols to probe the German lines, mentally mapping out the terrain and the minefields in front of the enemy positions.

Early on the morning of May 23, his company was ordered to attack. As the lead squads approached the German minefields, they came under heavy fire. Because he knew the lanes through the minefields so well, Barfoot asked for permission to head a squad. Moving through depressions in the terrain and shallow ditches, he advanced to within a few yards of an enemy machine gun on the right flank and destroyed it with a grenade. Then, following the German trench line, he moved to the next gun emplacement, where he killed two soldiers with his submachine gun and wounded and captured three others. When he approached the Germans manning a third gun, they surrendered. In all, he captured seventeen of the enemy.

Later in the day, after he had consolidated the newly captured position, Barfoot, seeing three German tanks advancing in a counteroffensive, grabbed a bazooka and destroyed the track of the leading tank, causing the two other tanks to change direction. As the crew of the disabled tank jumped out, Barfoot killed three of them, then continued into enemy territory and destroyed a German fieldpiece with a demolition charge. He ended the day by helping two seriously wounded men from his squad walk nearly a mile to safety.

Not long after this action, Barfoot was promoted to lieutenant. Four months later, his unit was in France's Rhône valley when he was ordered to division headquarters and informed that he had been awarded the Medal of Honor. Given the choice of returning to the United States for the ceremony or receiving the medal in the field, Barfoot chose the latter so that his men could be present. Lieutenant General Alexander Patch awarded him the medal in Épinal, France, on September 28, 1944.

Scout on a Mission

MELVIN E. BIDDLE

PRIVATE FIRST CLASS, U.S. ARMY Company B, 517th Parachute Infantry Regiment

BIOGRAPHY

BORN
November 28, 1923
Daleville, Indiana

ENTERED SERVICE
Anderson, Indiana

BRANCH
U.S. Army

DUTY
World War II

DIED
December 16, 2010
Anderson, Indiana

AFTER PARACHUTING INTO SOUTHERN FRANCE TWO months after D-Day, Melvin Biddle fought with the 517th Infantry Regiment as it made its way toward Germany. Enemy resistance appeared to be collapsing, and members of the 517th had begun practicing the victory parades they expected to be having back home, when on December 16, 1944, the German army suddenly launched the counterattack that initiated the Battle of the Bulge.

On the morning of December 23, Private First Class Biddle's battalion was near the Belgian town of Soy, trying to rescue a company made up primarily of cooks and clerks that had been encircled by the German advance. Things got off to a very bad start. The two lead scouts of the battalion were injured and taken out of action when one of them stepped on a mine. The commanding officer then pointed at Biddle and barked, "You! Out front!" Crawling through the snowy underbrush of a densely wooded area, Biddle ran into a German outpost. He killed three snipers who appeared one after the other, then moved forward until he saw an enemy machine-gun nest, which he took out with hand grenades. Signaling his company to advance, he destroyed two more German machine-gun positions.

After he returned to his position, his commanding officer instructed Biddle to go back behind enemy lines to try to take a prisoner. As he was moving through a field, he heard a large number of German soldiers approaching and hid in a drainage ditch until they had passed by. Then—it seemed almost a dream—he saw a lone German officer all dressed up in a hat with a shiny bill, a greatcoat, and polished jackboots, looking as if he was about to attend an official review. Biddle

stood and pointed his rifle at the man in hopes of capturing him, but the officer pulled out a Luger, fired a wild volley, and ran off.

Biddle continued to scout enemy positions, then returned to his unit and hunkered down for the night, so cold that he feared that his finger would freeze on the trigger of his rifle. Sometime after midnight, he heard a roar above him and saw flashes of light as an American P-38 night fighter shot down a Junkers bomber. The following morning, Christmas Eve, he found the dead pilot and copilot of the downed German plane frozen in their cockpit.

Shortly afterward, he heard the command again: "Biddle, out front!" When he had advanced several hundred yards into enemy territory, he saw thirteen German soldiers running hunched over across a field right in front of him. He opened fire and killed them all. Then moving forward, he saw a boy, perhaps fourteen years old, in a German uniform. He had been tied to a tree to keep him from retreating, and there were hand grenades and a rifle at his feet. Another GI who had come up behind Biddle yelled at him to shoot; instead, Biddle took the boy prisoner.

A week later, in the middle of another battle, Biddle was hit in the neck by a piece of shrapnel, which narrowly missed his jugular. He was sent to England to recuperate. Several weeks later, on a train headed back to his outfit, he read in *Stars and Stripes* that he would be receiving the Medal of Honor.

On October 12, 1945, when President Harry Truman presented the medal to Biddle, he whispered to him, "People don't believe me when I tell them that I'd rather have one of these than be president."

Closing the Aachen Gap

JAMES M. BURT

CAPTAIN, U.S. ARMY Company B, 66th Armored Regiment, 2nd Armored Division

BIOGRAPHY

BORN
August 18, 1917
Hinsdale, Massachusetts

ENTERED SERVICE
Lee, Massachusetts

BRANCH
U.S. Army

DUTY
World War II

DIED
February 15, 2006
Wyomissing, Pennsylvania

IN THE WEEKS AFTER THE ALLIED BREAKOUT AT Normandy, Captain James Burt was commanding a tank company in the 66th Armored Regiment. As his tanks, which had already seen heavy action in Morocco, Tunisia, and Sicily, made their way across France and Belgium toward Germany, it occurred to him that he was traversing many of the World War I battlefields on the Western front.

In mid-October of 1944, as they crossed the Belgian border and approached the German city of Aachen, they suddenly encountered unexpected and ferocious resistance. The retreating Germans had committed a regiment to keep the Americans from closing the Aachen gap, the only spot on the front where the Allied advance was stalled.

When an infantry battalion to which Burt's tank company was attached began a coordinated attack on the large German garrison on October 13, the Americans ran into murderous small-arms and mortar shelling. Burt's tanks were positioned behind it, giving fire support. Visibility was poor; to get a better sense of the battlefield, Burt dismounted from his command tank and began moving forward on foot to the front lines two hundred yards away. An artillery round hit in front of him with a tremendous blast that threw him back into a shell crater. He was unconscious for a few moments, then got up and continued to move ahead until he reached a vantage point from which he could use hand signals to motion his tanks into better firing positions.

As the stalled American attack was finally regaining momentum, Burt returned to his tank and directed the action from its rear deck for the next several hours. Sometime in the afternoon, he saw members of a German antiaircraft crew methodically crank down their gun so that it was aimed directly at him. The German shell exploded against the armor of his tank, sending more than one hundred tiny fragments into his face and chest. Refusing treatment, he kept his company in position, his tank often taking point-blank fire from enemy guns until American artillery knocked them out.

The Germans counterattacked the next morning. Burt again left his tank and ran through heavy fire to consult with the infantry battalion commander, but the officer was hit just as he arrived. Burt dragged him to safety. Then, realizing that all the other infantry officers were dead or wounded, he took command of the entire operation.

On October 15, hoping to achieve a breakthrough, he took his tank three hundred yards into enemy-held territory, then dismounted so that he could direct American artillery fire by walkie-talkie. At one point, he was rushed by two German soldiers; he killed them both with his .45-caliber pistol.

For the next six days, through miserable weather and relentless enemy bombardment, and in constant pain from his wounds, Burt held the combined American forces together. On two occasions, the tank in which he was riding was knocked out by enemy fire; each time he commandeered another one to use as a command post.

By October 21, the Germans were in retreat, and the Aachen gap was closed by the American advance. Burt's tank company moved forward once again, meeting up with its Soviet counterparts at the Elbe River a few months later and finally moving into Berlin.

The Medal of Honor was awarded to James Burt by President Harry Truman on October 12, 1945. Afterward, one of his buddies asked him if he was surprised. "After what we've seen the last few years, there are no surprises left," he answered.

Corpsman Fires Back

ROBERT E. BUSH

HOSPITAL APPRENTICE FIRST CLASS, U.S. NAVY 2nd Battalion, 5th Marines, 1st Marine Division

BIOGRAPHY

BORN
October 4, 1926
Tacoma, Washington

ENTERED SERVICE
Washington State

BRANCH
U.S. Navy

DUTY
World War II

DIED
November 8, 2005
Olympia, Washington

ROBERT BUSH WAS JUST SEVENTEEN IN THE FALL OF 1943, and beginning his junior year in high school, when he got his mother's permission to join the Navy. He was selected for training as a medical corpsman. It was a natural assignment for him: His mother ran the local hospital in Raymond, Washington, where he and his sister had spent a lot of time with the doctors and patients. There were many accidents involving axes and saws in that logging community, and one of the jobs Bush's mother had given him when he was growing up was disposing of limbs amputated in the hospital.

The day he turned eighteen—the minimum age for going into combat—Bush was told that he was shipping out to the Russell Islands in the Pacific with a Marine rifle company.

On May 2, 1945, in the middle of a Marine advance against dug-in Japanese forces on Okinawa, Bush's company was preparing to assault a hill held by the enemy. Shortly after dawn, as the company lieutenant and nineteen men were reconnoitering the area, Japanese soldiers suddenly sprang up out of camouflaged foxholes. Eleven Marines were killed or wounded in the first few minutes of the fighting; the lieutenant was among those who went down. With enemy machine guns kicking up dirt at his feet and mortar shells crashing all around him, Bush went from one fallen Marine to another. When he got to his lieutenant and saw that his pupils were dilating, he immediately began a flow of plasma, working desperately to revive him.

Just as the lieutenant began to stir, the Japanese rushed them. Holding the plasma bottle to maintain the flow, Bush fired his pistol with his other hand until he was out of ammunition. Several grenades went off near him, piercing his body with shrapnel and blinding him in one eye. By that time, the wounded lieutenant was able to withdraw under his own power. To cover him, Bush grabbed the officer's carbine and began firing at Japanese soldiers whenever they raised their heads.

When the carbine ran out of ammunition, Bush picked up a discarded M-1, skirted the Japanese position to get behind it, and began methodically shooting at the machine-gun crews from their rear. The noise of battle was so loud that they couldn't locate him. Advancing within twenty feet of them, he killed the entire opposing force in the space of a few minutes. When the Marines joined up with him, he resumed caring for the wounded. And although he had lost an eye, he refused treatment for himself until the wounded men he had been tending to were evacuated.

After being hospitalized for nearly two months, Bush was sent home in late June 1945. That fall he reenrolled in high school and began seeing his childhood sweetheart again. Not long after, he got a call from Secretary of the Navy James Forrestal informing him that he had been awarded the Medal of Honor. At first, Bush suspected a hoax. Forrestal finally convinced him that the call was genuine, but Bush argued with him about whether he actually deserved the honor. He finally agreed to go to Washington for the award ceremony, and made arrangements to get married earlier than he'd originally planned so the trip could double as a honeymoon. President Harry Truman presented the medal to him on October 5, 1945, the day after he turned nineteen.

Native Son

ERNEST CHILDERS
SECOND LIEUTENANT, U.S. ARMY   45th Infantry Division

BIOGRAPHY

BORN
February 1, 1918
Broken Arrow, Oklahoma

ENTERED SERVICE
Tulsa, Oklahoma

BRANCH
U.S. Army

DUTY
World War II

DIED
March 16, 2005
Coweta, Oklahoma

IT WAS STILL PITCH BLACK ON THE MORNING OF September 22, 1943, when Ernest Childers moved his platoon toward a dug-in enemy position near Oliveto, Italy. Crossing an asphalt road, he stumbled and fell into a shell crater, breaking a bone in his foot. Childers made his way back to an aid station. As dawn broke, he could see his men being raked by heavy fire from machine guns entrenched behind the wall of an old cemetery up on a rise.

Good God, they're killing all those Indian boys! he thought. He was a full-blooded Creek who had grown up on the prairie near Broken Arrow, Oklahoma, and had attended Chilocco Indian School, a government boarding school on the Oklahoma-Kansas border. Chilocco, which had students from all tribes, was the only Indian school in the country with a military cadet corps. Childers became a student officer of the corps, and after graduation went into the Oklahoma National Guard. When the corps was mobilized in 1940, his classmates were formed into an all-Indian company and he was made first sergeant. He led them through North Africa and Sicily, where he was given a battlefield commission. Now these same soldiers, some of whom he had known since school days, were getting hit by enemy fire, and he felt he had to try to save them.

Collecting eight other unattached GIs, Childers moved toward the firing, looping around the hill so he could come up behind the German position. He ordered the men behind him to lay down a base fire as he crawled up the hill toward a cemetery where the Germans were hiding. As he approached a small building near the rise of the hill, a pair of snipers jumped out with their guns leveled at him. He quickly killed them both.

One of two Germans manning a machine-gun emplacement inside the cemetery walls saw him and turned the gun around to fire. As bullets sprayed dirt in his face, Childers shot them both, then moved toward a second machine-gun nest about thirty yards away. The two soldiers in it ducked down below the top of the foxhole. Frustrated, Childers picked up a baseball-size stone and lobbed it at them. Probably thinking it was a grenade, both jumped up. Childers killed one, and a GI behind him killed the other.

Childers continued up the hill to another house from which an enemy mortar observer was directing enemy fire. He got the gunner in his sights and pulled the trigger, only to find he was out of ammunition. He approached the house shouting "Surrender!" with such authority that the German came out and threw down his gun and helmet in a gesture of defeat.

Childers's foot was so badly broken that he was evacuated on a hospital ship bound for North Africa. After several weeks, he returned to his unit in Italy. He was wounded again, at Anzio, and sent to Naples to convalesce. On April 22, 1944, he was given a fresh uniform and escorted outside to an impromptu parade at a replacement center. Surrounded by the colors, he was told to face a large group of men standing at attention. Then Lieutenant General Jacob Devers appeared, read some words Childers didn't quite catch because of the poor acoustics, and put a medal around his neck. After the brief ceremony was over and everyone had started to disperse, Childers picked up the medal from his chest and tried to read the inscription upside down. "What is this?" he asked a sergeant who was watching him. "Why, that's the Congressional Medal of Honor, sir!" the man replied in an awestruck voice.

Stopping for No One

MIKE COLALILLO

PRIVATE FIRST CLASS, U.S. ARMY Company C, 398th Infantry, 100th Infantry Division

MIKE COLALILLO, ONE OF NINE CHILDREN, WAS born shortly after his parents emigrated from Italy. He grew up in a tough neighborhood in Duluth, Minnesota, and left high school without graduating. Drafted in 1944, he was an eighteen-year-old private when he landed with the 100th Army Infantry Division at Marseille that October. His unit was engaged in constant combat over the next few months as it pushed up through central France and into Germany. Through the heartbreak of losing his comrades killed in the fighting, Colalillo hung on to memories of the rare funny moments as well: stealing chickens from a run-down farm, smoking cigars from a captured cigar factory.

The Germans had blown all the bridges leading into the Fatherland, so the Americans crossed the Rhine on pontoons. For his part in the bloody skirmishes that were almost daily occurrences, Colalillo was ultimately awarded the Silver Star and the Bronze Star.

On April 7, 1945, Colalillo's company was pinned down during an attack against enemy positions in the vicinity of Untergriesheim, Germany. Although enemy artillery and machine-gun fire made it dangerous even to raise one's head, when he saw an American tank unit moving through the lines toward the enemy position, Colalillo stood up and shouted at the other men to follow him. He ran forward, firing the grease gun he'd found on the battlefield and had been carrying for several weeks. When a random piece of shrapnel destroyed the weapon, Colalillo scrambled onto the turret of an American tank and, fully exposed to shelling from a German gun emplacement, began firing its machine gun. He killed or wounded ten enemy soldiers and destroyed the machine-gun nest. With bullets glancing off the tank's shell, he kept firing as the tank moved forward toward the German line. He took out another machine-gun emplacement, killing at least three more Germans.

When the machine gun jammed, Colalillo pounded on the hatch of the tank and had one of the men inside hand him up a tommy gun, then jumped down and continued the attack on foot. Even after the tanks had exhausted their ammunition and were ordered to withdraw, he stayed behind to help a wounded GI, carrying the man over several hundred yards of open terrain in the midst of a German artillery and mortar barrage.

Colalillo was fighting on the line a few weeks later when a pair of MPs appeared and told him that his commanding officer wanted to see him. Naturally, Colalillo wondered what he had done to get arrested, but when he arrived at company headquarters, his captain told him that he'd been recommended for the Medal of Honor. He was ordered to stay around division headquarters for the next few months so that nothing would happen to him before the presentation. He was sent home after the bombing of Hiroshima and honored by President Harry Truman at the White House on December 18, 1945.

BIOGRAPHY

BORN
December 1, 1925
Hibbing, Minnesota

ENTERED SERVICE
Duluth, Minnesota

BRANCH
U.S. Army

DUTY
World War II

CURRENT RESIDENCE
Minnesota

No Surrender

CHARLES H. COOLIDGE
TECHNICAL SERGEANT, U.S. ARMY Company M, 141st Infantry, 36th Infantry Division

THE BLOODIEST COMBAT CHARLES COOLIDGE experienced was in 1943, after he went ashore at Salerno. Coolidge's unit went up the boot of Italy and crossed the Rapido River to engage the Germans at Monte Cassino. There were surreal moments as well as violent ones: capturing sheep from the countryside and forcing them at bayonet point to cross enemy minefields. In all, the fighting was brutal and the American losses heavy, far worse than anything Coolidge would encounter later on.

By mid-1944, after the landing at Anzio and the capture of Rome, Coolidge, now a technical sergeant with a machine-gun platoon, was back in Naples, preparing with his unit to go into France. They landed at Cannes on August 15, then chased the retreating Germans up the center of the country. Moving fast, they covered more than five hundred miles in sixty days.

On October 24, Coolidge took his machine gunners to the crest of Hill 623 near Belmont-sur-Buttant and dug in. As he and another sergeant were reconnoitering a heavily wooded area to the right of the hill to establish positions from which they could coordinate the guns' fire, they ran into a handful of enemy soldiers. Coolidge told the other man, who spoke German, to approach some of the men and demand their surrender, but the bluff didn't work. One German soldier raised his rifle, and Coolidge shot him, then shot another before running back to his men.

With no officer present, Coolidge assumed command of his unit, now augmented by some riflemen. Exposed to enemy guns, he walked up and down the position, encouraging the men and directing their fire as the Germans advanced. They were able to throw back the initial attack, and over the next three days fought desperately to hold their position.

On October 27, German infantry, supported by tanks, threatened to overrun Coolidge's unit. One of the tanks came so close that its commander, standing up in the open turret, was able to call out to Coolidge—in perfect English—to demand that he surrender. "Sorry, Mac, you'll have to come and get me," Coolidge yelled back. The German tank commander whirled the turret around, trying to shoot Coolidge as he took cover behind the trees. Coolidge grabbed a bazooka and aimed at the tank, but the weapon failed. Gathering all the grenades he could find, he crawled forward, throwing them at the German infantrymen huddled around the tank. He and his men killed twenty-six and wounded sixty, according to a later Associated Press report, but because of the Germans' superior numbers and armor, he was finally forced to evacuate his men.

When he was told that he was to receive the Medal of Honor, Coolidge knew what it was only because the famous Sergeant Alvin York, a recipient in World War I, was from a town about one hundred miles from his hometown of Signal Mountain, Tennessee. The ceremony took place on June 18, 1945, at a bombed-out airfield near Dornstadt, Germany, where gaping craters had been repaired by American bulldozers. The medal was presented by General Frederick Haislip.

BIOGRAPHY
BORN
August 4, 1921
Signal Mountain, Tennessee
ENTERED SERVICE
Signal Mountain, Tennessee
BRANCH
U.S. Army
DUTY
World War II
CURRENT RESIDENCE
Tennessee

Taking the Initiative

WILLIAM J. CRAWFORD

PRIVATE, U.S. ARMY 36th Infantry Division

BIOGRAPHY

BORN
May 19, 1918
Pueblo, Colorado

ENTERED SERVICE
Pueblo, Colorado

BRANCH
U.S. Army

DUTY
World War II

DIED
March 15, 2000
Palmer Lake, Colorado

GROWING UP IN PUEBLO, COLORADO, WILLIAM Crawford was on his own as a boy. He took up boxing and fought in the Golden Gloves; he might have gotten in the ring as a professional if not for the war.

Crawford was a private when his company attacked a German position near Altavilla, Italy, on September 13, 1943. He was the scout for his platoon, which found itself pinned down by intense machine-gun fire as it reached the crest of a hill. As the men scrambled for cover, he saw that one of the enemy machine guns was dug into a terrace on the next hill over. On his own initiative and under heavy enemy fire, he immediately moved toward the gun emplacement. He got to within a few yards, then took it out with a grenade, killing the three Germans manning it.

The platoon was now able to move forward. When it joined up with Crawford, the Germans opened fire once more. Crawford moved ahead into the fire from two more machine-gun nests dug into terraced ground above him. Charging at the one on his left, he killed the crew with a hand grenade. Then he turned toward the remaining gun, which was concentrating its fire on him. Shooting point-blank with his rifle, he killed one of the Germans. As the others jumped out of the emplacement and tried to flee, he seized their machine gun and fired on them while his company advanced behind him.

During another battle that took place a few days later, Crawford was captured and was thought to be dead. The Medal of Honor he was awarded was presented "posthumously" to his father by General Thomas Allen on February 26, 1944. Two months later, his family found out that he was alive, and word arrived at the German prison camp where he was interned that he was a Medal of Honor recipient. Crawford's poor treatment—a German guard tried to beat him; Crawford knocked him down—improved after that.

In the spring of 1945, Crawford and his fellow prisoners were liberated, and he returned home. He reenlisted in the Army in 1947, retired in 1967 as a master sergeant, and took a job as a janitor at the Air Force Academy in 1970. The cadets, unaware of his past, largely ignored him—until one of them came across his name in a book about World War II. When questioned, Crawford acknowledged that he had indeed been awarded the Medal of Honor. From that moment on, he was a celebrity. On many occasions, Air Force Academy cadets would invite him to special dinners, called Dining Ins. Crawford would always be introduced by the president of the mess, and the entire squadron of cadets would give him a standing ovation.

Over the years, Crawford mentioned to acquaintances at the Academy that he wished he had received his medal from a president, as most recipients do. In 1984, he got his wish: Ronald Reagan, speaking at the Air Force Academy graduation, re-presented Crawford with his medal and extolled his heroism in front of the cheering cadets.

Old Enough to Be a Hero

FRANCIS S. CURREY

PRIVATE FIRST CLASS, U.S. ARMY Company K, 120th Infantry, 30th Infantry Division

BIOGRAPHY

BORN
June 29, 1925
Loch Sheldrake, New York

ENTERED SERVICE
Hurleyville, New York

BRANCH
U.S. Army

DUTY
World War II

CURRENT RESIDENCE
New York

AN ORPHAN WHO HAD GROWN UP IN A FOSTER HOME in upstate New York, Francis Currey enlisted in the Army in the summer of 1943, one week after he graduated from high school. Though he completed the Officer Candidate School course, his superior officers decided he was "too immature" to receive a commission.

After another eight months of training with the 75th Infantry Division, Currey headed for England in the spring of 1944 as an infantry replacement. As a result of the public furor over the deaths of the five Sullivan brothers aboard a U.S. Navy combat ship, President Roosevelt had issued an executive order preventing American servicemen from going abroad until they were nineteen. Currey had to wait until his birthday at the end of June to ship out. He eventually landed at Omaha Beach, but it wasn't until several weeks after D-Day. He joined the 120th Infantry in the Netherlands in September 1944.

In the winter of 1944, Private First Class Currey's infantry squad was fighting the Germans in the Belgian town of Malmédy to help contain the German counteroffensive in the Battle of the Bulge. Before dawn on December 21, Currey's unit was defending a strongpoint when a sudden German armored advance overran American antitank guns and caused a general withdrawal. Currey and five other soldiers—the oldest was twenty-one—were cut off and surrounded by several German tanks and a large number of infantrymen. They began a daylong effort to survive.

The six GIs withdrew into an abandoned factory, where they found a bazooka left behind by American troops. Currey knew how to operate one, thanks to his time in Officer Candidate School, but this one had no ammunition. From the window of the factory, he saw that an abandoned half-track across the street contained rockets. Under intense enemy fire, he ran to the half-track, loaded the bazooka, and fired at the nearest tank. By what he would later call a miracle, the rocket hit the exact spot where the turret joined the chassis and disabled the vehicle.

Moving to another position, Currey saw three Germans in the doorway of an enemy-held house and shot all of them with his Browning automatic rifle. He then picked up the bazooka again and advanced, alone, to within fifty yards of the house. He fired a shot that collapsed one of its walls, scattering the remaining German soldiers inside. From this forward position, he saw five more GIs who had been cut off during the American withdrawal and were now under fire from three nearby German tanks. With antitank grenades he'd collected from the half-track, he forced the crews to abandon the tanks. Next, finding a machine gun whose crew had been killed, he opened fire on the retreating Germans, allowing the five trapped Americans to escape.

At nightfall, as Currey and his squad, including two seriously wounded men, tried to find their way back to the American lines, they came across an abandoned Army jeep fitted out with stretcher mounts. They loaded the wounded onto it, and Currey, perched on the jeep's spare wheel with a Browning in his hand, rode shotgun back to the American lines.

Six months later, after the war in Europe had officially ended, Currey wasn't surprised when he learned he had been awarded the Medal of Honor—the news had been leaked to a newspaper in his hometown, and a friend had already sent him the clipping. Major General Leland Hobbs made the presentation on July 27, 1945, at a division parade in France.

A Familiar Smell of Potatoes

EDWARD C. DAHLGREN

SERGEANT, U.S. ARMY 3rd Platoon, Company E, 2nd Battalion, 142nd Infantry, 36th Infantry Division

EDWARD DAHLGREN'S FAMILY EMIGRATED FROM Sweden and became potato farmers in Maine. Dahlgren grew up speaking Swedish at home and attended a one-room schoolhouse. He left high school after his junior year to work on a potato farm near his home. Agriculture was always his first love, but because he wanted to help the war effort, in 1942 he took a job in a Massachusetts machine shop doing defense-related work. He was drafted into the Army early in 1943.

As part of the 36th Infantry Division, Dahlgren was shipped to North Africa that summer and trained for the upcoming invasion of Italy. In September, his unit hit the beach at Salerno and for months fought its way to Monte Cassino, where early in 1944 Dahlgren was shot in the shoulder. He returned from the hospital that summer just as his unit was being redeployed to France. The 36th Infantry Division landed near Marseille on August 15, and then slowly fought its way north.

On February 11, 1945, Dahlgren, now a sergeant, was leading his men toward another American platoon pinned down near the town of Oberhoffen, in the Alsace-Lorraine region of France. They were proceeding down a narrow street when Dahlgren saw several German soldiers cross through some pastureland about a hundred yards away. From his cover in a nearby barn, he killed six and wounded several others with his Thompson submachine gun. Then, through heavy enemy fire, he led his men to the besieged American platoon. In the midst of the fighting, he noticed a familiar smell and realized that it came from potatoes planted in the field.

Putting the rescued unit under his command, Dahlgren advanced into Oberhoffen. When he came under fire from an enemy-held house, he ran to the building, tossed in a grenade, and entered firing. Eight enemy soldiers immediately surrendered. Coming under machine-gun fire as he approached the house next door, he used rifle grenades to take out the position, killing two more of the enemy. When German soldiers began shooting at him from a barn across the street, he rushed their position, throwing grenades and firing his submachine gun. Five more Germans surrendered.

Sergeant Dahlgren then entered another house through a window, trapping several soldiers in the cellar. He opened a trapdoor and tossed a grenade down the stairs, wounding several and forcing ten more Germans to surrender.

At the end of the block, Dahlgren entered a fourth house, which seemed deserted; but then he heard German being spoken in hushed tones in the cellar. He kicked open the cellar door and fired several bursts down the stairway. Sixteen men hiding there filed out with their hands up.

After this engagement in which Dahlgren single-handedly killed at least eight of the enemy and forced thirty-nine others to surrender, Dahlgren's men asked their commanding officer to recommend him for the Medal of Honor. The unit continued to fight its way into Germany, where Dahlgren received a battlefield commission as a second lieutenant in March 1945. After the enemy surrendered, he realized that he had been in combat for 340 days.

Edward Dahlgren received the Medal of Honor from President Harry Truman on August 23, 1945. Afterward, he went home to Maine, where he worked for the Maine Department of Agriculture as a seed potato inspector for the next thirty-seven years.

BIOGRAPHY

BORN
March 14, 1916
Perham, Maine

ENTERED SERVICE
Fort Devens, Massachusetts

BRANCH
U.S. Army

DUTY
World War II

DIED
May 31, 2006
Mars Hill, Maine

Distinguished Father and Son

MICHAEL J. DALY

FIRST LIEUTENANT, U.S. ARMY Company A, 15th Infantry, 3rd Infantry Division

BIOGRAPHY

BORN
September 15, 1924
New York, New York

ENTERED SERVICE
Southport, Connecticut

BRANCH
U.S. Army

DUTY
World War II

DIED
July 25, 2008
Fairfield, Connecticut

MICHAEL DALY ENTERED WEST POINT IN 1942, BUT he left after one year to enlist as a private in the infantry. He trained in England and waded ashore on Omaha Beach on D-Day with the 1st Infantry Division, known as "the Big Red One." After moving through France and into Germany, Daly was wounded near Aachen; he recuperated in England, then returned to action assigned to the 3rd Infantry Division and was given a battlefield commission as a second lieutenant.

Early on the morning of April 18, 1945, First Lieutenant Daly was in command of an infantry company moving through the rubble on the outskirts of Nuremberg, where bombed-out houses provided good cover for German snipers. As the Americans were going down the city's main thoroughfare, an enemy machine gun suddenly opened up from across a city square. As his men fell all around him, Daly charged the German position and killed the three-man crew with his carbine. Continuing on ahead of his unit, he came upon an enemy patrol armed with rocket launchers entrenched in the shell of a house and ready to ambush American tanks. He again opened fire with his carbine. Though the Germans responded by firing rockets, he held his ground and kept shooting until he had killed all six members of the patrol.

As he continued to move ahead of his company, Daly entered what had been a city park. A German machine gun began firing from close range. When one of his men was killed, he picked up the soldier's rifle and used it to shoot both enemy gunners. In all, he killed fifteen Germans that afternoon and took out three machine-gun positions.

The next day, as he was leading his company into action, Daly was shot in the face; the bullet entered at one ear and exited the opposite cheek. Falling to the ground, he felt that he might drown in his own blood until one of his men cleared his throat.

Daly received medical treatment in England and in the States until mid-1946 but was well enough to travel to the White House on August 23, 1945, to receive the Medal of Honor from President Harry Truman. The next day, he was back home in Connecticut, riding in a motorcade. Alongside him was his father, Paul Daly, a World War I recipient of the Distinguished Service Cross who had twice been recommended for the Medal of Honor. The elder Daly had reentered the Army after Pearl Harbor, was severely wounded while serving as a regimental commander in northern France, and was sent back to the States to recuperate. Sitting next to him that day, Michael wished his father had received the medal he was wearing around his neck.

The Medal Fifty-six Years Later

RUDOLPH B. DAVILA

STAFF SERGEANT, U.S. ARMY Company H, 7th Infantry

THE COUNTRY WAS DEEP IN THE DEPRESSION IN 1939, with jobs hard to find, when Rudolph Davila enlisted in the Army. By late 1942, he was a buck sergeant, training in a new division formed for jungle fighting, but he became impatient for action and put his name in for combat. Because his mother was Filipino (his father was Hispanic), he hoped to be sent to the Pacific, but instead found himself headed to Europe with the 7th Infantry.

Early in 1944, Davila's unit—a machine-gun squad—landed with advance elements at Anzio. Facing little initial opposition, it quickly moved into the mountain pass leading to Rome, the ultimate objective. But when supply lines became overextended, the men were ordered back to the beachhead to regroup. The Germans moved in artillery and began firing down on the American position. Anzio became a bloody battleground for several weeks before U.S. forces finally broke out of the German containment.

By the end of May 1944, Davila's squad had advanced back up into the mountains. On May 28, the rifle company it was supporting was suddenly ambushed by Germans dug into high ground. With tracers from enemy machine guns cutting through the top of the high grass, Staff Sergeant Davila scrambled up toward the crest of the hill. He yelled for his men to follow, but they continued to hug the ground, unwilling to move forward in the face of German fire. He ordered them to pass him a tripod, a machine gun, and ammunition. Lying on his back to lessen his chances of being hit, he assembled the weapon, set it upright, got to his knees, and began firing, raking the enemy position until he had used up several 250-round ammo containers.

Seeing a disabled American tank smoking from a direct hit and thinking that its .50-caliber machine gun might still work, Davila ran through heavy fire and climbed up to the turret. But the machine gun had been removed. He saw German snipers in the second story of a stone house to his left. He yelled for one of his men to toss him a rifle and began to shoot back. When the snipers ducked, he jumped down from the tank and ran toward the house, tossing two grenades into the second-floor window. He entered the house and found the snipers dead upstairs. He then began to shoot at the two German machine-gun emplacements across the road. He quickly took the guns out and killed the Germans manning them before they figured out where he was.

After the battle, the company captain told Davila that he was writing a recommendation for the Medal of Honor. "If you hadn't done this, I think we all would have been slaughtered," he said.

Davila received a battlefield commission as a lieutenant, but he didn't hear anything further about the medal. Several months later, not long after D-Day, his unit landed at Marseille and began to fight its way up the gut of France. By November, Davila and his men had reached Strasbourg. During a battle for the city, a German tank began to stalk them. As they took cover under a tree, the tank fired. A large piece of shrapnel ricocheted off the tree trunk and hit Davila in the chest, piercing his lung and severing nerves on his left side. Despite six years in a military hospital and thirteen operations, he never regained the use of his left arm.

In the late 1990s, U.S. Senator Daniel Akaka took up the cause of minority soldiers whose heroism might have been overlooked. As a result, on June 21, 2000, fifty-six years after the engagement in the mountains above Anzio, President Bill Clinton finally awarded Rudolph Davila the Medal of Honor.

BIOGRAPHY

BORN
April 27, 1916
El Paso, Texas

ENTERED SERVICE
Los Angeles, California

BRANCH
U.S. Army

DUTY
World War II

DIED
January 26, 2002
Vista, California

Island-Hopping Ace

JEFFERSON J. DeBLANC

CAPTAIN, U.S. MARINE CORPS RESERVE Marine Fighter Squadron 112

BIOGRAPHY

BORN
February 15, 1921
Lockport, Louisiana

ENTERED SERVICE
Louisiana

BRANCH
U.S. Marine Corps

DUTY
World War II

DIED
November 22, 2007
Saint Martinville, Louisiana

IN 1938, JEFFERSON DeBLANC WAS WORKING AS A bench chemist in the sugarcane industry to earn enough money to attend college. The Civilian Pilot Training program, which the federal government had initiated in universities, seemed perfect for him—he had been fascinated by aviation ever since a U.S. Mail pilot had made a forced landing near his home and allowed him to get into the cockpit. He signed up for the program and learned to fly in Piper Cubs, then entered the Naval Aviation Cadet Reserve program and became a Marine fighter pilot. At the time he was sent to the Pacific in the fall of 1942, he had only ten hours in a Grumman F4F-3 Wildcat fighter.

On January 31, 1943, DeBlanc already had three kills in air combat when his section took off to escort a strike force of dive-bombers and torpedo planes whose mission was to attack Japanese ships lying off Kolombangara Island in the Solomons. Two of the planes had to turn back because of mechanical failure. DeBlanc's own auxiliary fuel tank malfunctioned; he knew that if he completed the mission, he wouldn't have enough fuel to return to base, but he radioed the other pilots that he was proceeding.

As the American planes reached the rendezvous point, a large number of Japanese Zeros appeared. DeBlanc's section instantly engaged, driving them away from the American bombers. Then, seeing that Japanese float planes had intercepted U.S. dive-bombers beginning their attack, DeBlanc descended and quickly shot down two of them. As the U.S. attack force completed its run and turned for home, twelve Zeros came out of the setting sun and pounced on the four Wildcats. The Americans tried desperately to get altitude to defend themselves. DeBlanc shot down one

Zero, then lined up another head-on, firing steadily. The Zero exploded; DeBlanc flew through its debris. With still another enemy plane on his tail, he chopped the throttle and dropped his flaps. As his plane slowed suddenly, the Zero pilot, overanxious for the kill, flew by, and DeBlanc shot him down.

Just then, bullets shattered his cockpit—one came so close that it sheared off his wristwatch. As his instrument panel caught fire, he bailed out. After releasing from his parachute early, DeBlanc hit the water hard. Using his life jacket for support, he swam many hours to reach the shore of Kolombangara. He had heard of U.S. airmen captured by natives being handed over to the Japanese for execution, but he felt he had a good chance of surviving because he had grown up in the Cajun swamps of Louisiana.

He slept in a tree the first night. The next day he wandered until he came upon a native hut in a clearing. Hearing birds singing, he knew from his time in bayou country that this probably meant there were no people around. He spent the second night in the hut; when he awoke the next morning, there were no birds singing. Outside there were five natives, armed with machetes. The natives traded him for a ten-pound sack of rice to an islander who was working with the Australian coast watchers. The coast watchers returned him to the U.S. military.

With eight kills, DeBlanc was an ace. After spending six months back home working as a flight instructor, he returned to the Pacific. He shot down one more enemy plane, a kamikaze, during the Battle of Okinawa.

Captain DeBlanc was awarded the Medal of Honor at the White House by President Harry Truman on December 6, 1946.

Healing Seven Days a Week

DESMOND T. DOSS

PRIVATE FIRST CLASS, U.S. ARMY Medical Detachment, 307th Infantry, 77th Infantry Division

BIOGRAPHY

BORN
February 1, 1919
Lynchburg, Virginia

ENTERED SERVICE
Lynchburg, Virginia

BRANCH
U.S. Army

DUTY
World War II

DIED
March 23, 2006
Piedmont, Alabama

DESMOND DOSS QUIT SCHOOL AFTER THE EIGHTH grade in the middle of the Depression to help support his family. He was working in the shipyards in Newport News, Virginia, when he was drafted into the Army in April 1942. He wanted to serve his country, but as a devout Seventh-day Adventist he chose not to bear arms, so he joined the Army's Medical Corps. In basic training, the other recruits considered him strange because of his deep religious convictions—so much so that they threatened and harassed him and tried to get him transferred out of their unit. Doss successfully fought efforts to discharge him.

Private Doss served as a medic with the 77th Division in campaigns on Guam and Leyte in 1944, where the lingering suspicions the other men had about him were dispelled by his bravery under fire. On Okinawa, in the late spring of 1945, his battalion was assaulting a jagged escarpment rising up four hundred feet whose summit was commanded by well-entrenched Japanese forces. It was a battle that began on April 29 when the Americans took the position and continued on for nearly three weeks as the Japanese fought back from caves and tunnels. At one point, he treated four men who had been cut down while assaulting a strongly defended cave. Only a few yards away from Japanese guns, he dressed each of their wounds and made four trips to drag them to safety.

On May 5, a Saturday and Doss's Sabbath, he was the only medic available as the ongoing assault on the escarpment met heavy resistance. Telling himself that Christ had healed seven days a week, he advanced with the rest of the men. They seemed on the verge of finally taking the position when the enemy concentrated massive artillery, mortar, and machine-gun fire on them, driving most of them back down the face of the escarpment and leaving dozens of casualties behind.

Doss alone stayed with the fallen soldiers. Under constant fire, he tended the wounded, then dragged them to the edge of the escarpment and lowered them down in a rope sling. Each time he got one of them to safety, he prayed, "Dear God, let me get just one more man." By nightfall, he had rescued seventy-five GIs.

Several days later, after American forces were advancing slowly against strong resistance, Doss was seriously wounded in the leg by a grenade. He treated himself, then waited five hours to be rescued. As he was being carried back to an aid station on a stretcher, the enemy counterattacked. Along the way, Doss insisted on giving his stretcher to a badly injured GI.

Another soldier who was slightly wounded came along and suggested to Doss that the two of them try to reach the aid station together. As they were making their way, a sniper's bullet struck Doss in the arm, entering at his wrist and traveling to his upper arm. He improvised a splint out of a rifle stock, and he and the other wounded man eventually made it to the aid station.

In the meantime, the litter bearers had returned for Doss. When they couldn't find him, they assumed he was dead. The news made the front page of his hometown newspaper in Lynchburg, Virginia. Doss, now at a field hospital, had a nurse help him write a letter to his mother to let her know that reports of his death had been greatly exaggerated.

The bullet in Doss's arm was removed at the Woodrow Wilson Hospital in Waynesboro, Virginia. After the operation, he was told he was being taken to Washington, D.C., in the company commander's car to receive the Medal of Honor. President Harry Truman placed it around his neck on October 12, 1945.

Daring Escape

RUSSELL E. DUNHAM

TECHNICAL SERGEANT, U.S. ARMY Company I, 30th Infantry, 3rd Infantry Division

BIOGRAPHY

BORN
February 23, 1920
East Carondelet, Illinois

ENTERED SERVICE
Brighton, Illinois

BRANCH
U.S. Army

DUTY
World War II

DIED
April 6, 2009
Jerseyville, Illinois

IN MID-1940, RUSSELL DUNHAM, UNABLE TO FIND a job, joined the Army. After the war started, he saw action in North Africa, Sicily, and Anzio as part of the 3rd Infantry Division. In August 1944, his unit landed at Toulon in the south of France and fought its way toward Alsace-Lorraine. Five months later, Sergeant Dunham's company was facing a significant German force at the small town of Kaysersberg, France.

On the morning of January 8, 1945, the men were issued white mattress covers to camouflage them in the deep snow and ordered on patrol. Heavily armed with carbine magazines and a dozen grenades hooked into his belt, Dunham scrambled through the snow up a hill where three German machine guns were dug in. The first gun was in a bunker made of logs; Dunham took it out with a grenade. He advanced toward the second gun and had turned to call up his squad when a bullet hit him in the back and knocked him fifteen yards down the hill. As he got back on his feet, a grenade hit nearby; he kicked it away. He then crawled to the machine gun and threw his own grenade into the bunker, killing two of the Germans and taking a third prisoner. With blood staining his white wrapper, he ran fifty yards to the third machine-gun emplacement and took it out with a grenade, killing its three crew members. As German infantrymen began to jump out of the foxholes the machine guns had been protecting, he fired down on them. Chasing them down the back side of the hill, Dunham and his brother Ralph, who was in the same unit, came upon a fourth machine gun, and Ralph took it out with another grenade. Suddenly, an enemy rifleman appeared out of the trees and shot point-blank at him; he missed Dunham but killed a GI behind him. Dunham immediately shot the German

with his carbine. By the end of the action, he had killed nine enemy soldiers.

Dunham's back wound had not yet fully healed when he was on the line again. On January 22, his battalion was surrounded by German tanks at the town of Holtzwihr. Most of the men were forced to surrender and were eventually sent to Germany, but Dunham managed to hide in a sauerkraut barrel right outside a barn. The next morning, as he was about to make his escape, two German soldiers took him prisoner. While they were patting him down, they found a pack of cigarettes in his pocket and began to fight over it. As a result, they never finished searching him and missed a pistol snuggled up under his arm in a shoulder holster. They held him in the barn all day; late in the afternoon, they drove him toward the German lines.

After going a few miles, the driver stopped at a roadside bar. When the other guard's attention wandered, Dunham drew his pistol and shot him in the head, then sprinted back in the direction from which they had come. He located the barn where he had hidden earlier in order to orient himself, then struck out for the American lines at night.

He hid the next day, resuming his journey at nightfall; his feet and ears were frozen. Then he was spotted by American engineers working on a bridge over the Ill River. They took him to the battalion field hospital, where doctors worked feverishly to save his feet from amputation. One of the medics treating him reported that the commanding officer had intended to recommend him for a Distinguished Service Cross but was now changing it to a Medal of Honor.

Lieutenant General Alexander Patch presented the medal to Dunham on April 23, 1945, in Nuremberg.

The Bond of Brothers

WALTER D. EHLERS

STAFF SERGEANT, U.S. ARMY 18th Infantry, 1st Infantry Division

BIOGRAPHY

BORN
May 7, 1921
Junction City, Kansas

ENTERED SERVICE
Manhattan, Kansas

BRANCH
U.S. Army

DUTY
World War II

CURRENT RESIDENCE
California

WALTER EHLERS'S OLDER BROTHER, ROLAND, HAD bullied and protected him throughout their childhood in Kansas. By D-Day, the two had already fought their way through North Africa and Sicily in the same unit. While training for the Normandy landing, Walter was made a squad leader and transferred to a different company. The brothers wished each other luck and promised to "meet up on the beach."

The first wave was pinned down on the beach. Ehlers's squad, along with about two hundred other soldiers, were on an LCI (landing craft, infantry) scheduled to be in the second wave. Orders were quickly changed. Ehlers and his squad were transferred to a Higgins boat and sent to the beach three hours ahead of the second wave. They were not prepared for the chaos that they found on the beach.

By June 9, Ehlers's unit had worked its way about eight miles inland, near the small town of Goville. The French countryside was checkerboarded with thick hedgerows several feet high, which provided cover for German units fighting desperate rearguard actions. As it moved ahead through the dense brush, Sergeant Ehlers's platoon suddenly came under heavy fire from machine guns and mortars. Ehlers climbed up a hedgerow and called on his men to follow. He spotted a German patrol coming up from the other side and killed four of the enemy. Ordering his men to fix bayonets, and firing from the hip, he destroyed a machine-gun nest and scattered a mortar crew. Next he attacked a second machine-gun nest, killing three more soldiers.

The platoon moved out the next morning, but it came under intense fire from both sides. When the company commander ordered a withdrawal, Ehlers realized that if someone didn't provide cover, the Americans would be picked off one by one. Motioning to his automatic rifleman to follow him, he scrambled to the top of a mound of earth that provided a vantage point on enemy positions. Then the two men began to shoot at German machine guns and mortars, drawing fire on themselves as the rest of the platoon headed for cover. Ehlers was hit in the back but managed to kill the sniper who shot him. When his automatic rifleman was badly wounded, Ehlers dragged him to safety despite his own injuries.

Ehlers was treated at a field station. The bullet that hit him had actually entered his side, ricocheted off a rib, and exited through his back into his pack—where it pierced a picture of his mother, a bar of soap, and his entrenching tool. He insisted on returning to action; unable to wear a backpack, he strapped on two bandoliers of ammunition, picked up a rifle, and went to find his men.

A month later, on July 14, Ehlers encountered his brother's company commander, who told him that Roland had died at Omaha Beach when an enemy mortar round hit his landing craft. Ehlers saluted the officer who had brought the bad news, then found a private place where, for the only time during the war, he "went to pieces."

In December 1944, on a train headed back to the front after recuperating from another wound, Ehlers read in *Stars and Stripes* that he had been awarded the Medal of Honor. Before he could react, the soldier sitting next to him saw the news, too. Knowing Ehlers only by his last name and knowing that he had a brother, he said, "Hey, I see that your brother just got the medal." Without looking up, Ehlers replied, "Yes, I read that, too," saying to himself that Roland certainly deserved it.

On December 19, 1944, Lieutenant General John H. C. Lee presented the Medal of Honor to Walter Ehlers.

Aboard *The City of Los Angeles*

HENRY E. ERWIN

STAFF SERGEANT, U.S. ARMY AIR CORPS 52nd Bombardment Squadron, 29th Bombardment Group, 20th Air Force

THE CREW OF *THE CITY OF LOS ANGELES* HAD completed eleven missions in the Pacific by the spring of 1945. At dawn on April 12, the B-29 took off from Guam as the lead bomber in the 52nd Bombardment Squadron's attack on Koriyama, Japan.

As the lead aircraft, *The City of Los Angeles* was responsible for signaling the squadron to assemble into attack formation. It was the job of Henry "Red" Erwin, the plane's radio operator, to drop a marker, a twenty-pound white phosphorus canister with a six-second fuse, through a tube in the belly of the craft when the plane reached the assembly area over enemy territory. A gregarious Alabamian who had once hoped to fly fighter planes, Staff Sergeant Erwin positioned the canister in the launching chute, then pulled the pin at the pilot's orders. But the flare flew back up the tube. It exploded in Erwin's face and fell into the belly of the plane, spewing flames just feet away from the payload of tons of incendiary bombs.

Erwin felt his hair catch fire and the skin on his nose begin to melt. Billowing white smoke filled the aircraft. The pilot and copilot were momentarily blinded, and the plane went into a steep dive.

Erwin dropped to his hands and knees, feeling for the canister. Although it was burning at thirteen hundred degrees Fahrenheit, he picked it up and cradled it to his body with his forearm, then began crawling toward the cockpit.

His entire upper body burning, Erwin groped his way forward to the cockpit. He yelled to the copilot to open the window and threw the burning flare out into the sky. Then he fell back, his clothing on fire and his face charred beyond recognition. After the pilot pulled the plane out of its dive, the crew turned the fire extinguisher on Erwin and began to administer first aid. They injected him with morphine to ease the excruciating pain.

When the B-29 landed at Iwo Jima to get urgently needed medical assistance, Erwin's body was so rigid that he had to be removed from the plane through a window. The doctors, sure he was going to die, had him transferred to a hospital on Guam, where Air Corps Major General Curtis LeMay arranged to fly Erwin's brother, a Marine, to be with him.

LeMay recommended Erwin for the Medal of Honor and got authorities in Washington to expedite the award so that it could be presented before he died. But there was only one medal in the Pacific, on display in a locked glass case in Honolulu. On the morning of April 18, an officer there, not able to find the key, smashed the case, grabbed the medal, and hustled it onto a plane. The next day, just one week after the attack on Koriyama, General LeMay presented it to Erwin at a bedside ceremony with the crew of *The City of Los Angeles* standing by.

Erwin surprised his doctors by surviving. A few weeks after receiving the medal, he was flown home to Alabama, where he was hospitalized for two and a half years, undergoing repeated reconstructive operations and learning to use what was left of his hands and to deal with his badly disfigured face.

In 1948, not long after he was finally released from the hospital, Erwin and his wife were flown to the SAC air base in Omaha to attend the premiere of *The Wild Blue Yonder,* a film about the air war in the Pacific that dramatized his determined struggle to save his plane that April morning in the skies over Japan.

BIOGRAPHY

BORN
May 8, 1921
Adamsville, Alabama

ENTERED SERVICE
Bessemer, Alabama

BRANCH
U.S. Army

DUTY
World War II

DIED
January 16, 2002
Leeds, Alabama

Fighting Back on December 7

JOHN W. FINN

AVIATION ORDNANCE CHIEF, U.S. NAVY

JOHN FINN DROPPED OUT OF SCHOOL AFTER THE seventh grade and worked at various jobs until a few days before his seventeenth birthday, when he joined the Navy. It was 1926, and the world seemed permanently at peace, without even a rumor of war. What Finn wanted was to travel. Over the next few years, he got his wish, serving on a variety of ships that took him up through the Panama Canal and six hundred miles up the Yangtze River.

In December 1941, he was stationed at the Naval Air Station in Kanoehe Bay, Hawaii. He had moved rapidly through the ranks during his years in the Navy and was now a chief petty officer in charge of a twenty-man ordnance crew whose primary duty was maintaining the weapons of a squadron of PBY naval patrol planes. On the morning of December 7, he and his wife were in their quarters about a mile from the aircraft hangars when he was awakened by a popping noise. His first irritated thought was that some fool had decided to do gunnery practice on a Sunday morning. Then he heard planes passing overhead and shouting in the street, followed by a loud knock on his door. It was the wife of one of his men. When he asked her what was wrong, she just pointed up in the air and ran off.

Still not aware of what was causing all the confusion, Finn jumped in his car and headed for the hangars. He was observing the base's strictly enforced speed limit of twenty miles an hour until a fighter plane came roaring down out of the sky above him. He watched it with curiosity for a moment until he saw the "red meatball" of the Japanese insignia, then he rammed the car into second gear and stomped on the accelerator.

He came to a skidding stop at the launching ramps where the amphibious patrol planes were towed back and forth between the water and their hangars and found total chaos. Most of the thirty-six PBYs were already on fire. (Only three would be left at the end of the day because they happened to be on antisubmarine patrol when the Japanese attacked.) Some of his men were inside the burning planes trying to fire at the enemy from the PBYs' machine guns. Others were struggling to get the guns out of the damaged planes; there were no stationary gun mounts to hold them, and the sailors were trying to improvise using pipe from the machine shop and other materials.

Finn found a mobile instruction stand on which guns were sometimes mounted to teach gunnery. Although enemy planes continued to strafe the position, he moved the stand into a parking area where he would have clear visibility. Then he set a .50-caliber machine gun on it and began to shoot. He held his position for the next two hours. The Japanese fighters went by too quickly to track with the gun. He did hit some of the slower-moving bombers, although they quickly disappeared over the tree line so he couldn't know if any crashed. He didn't stop firing until all the enemy planes had gone and it was quiet again.

Finn had been hit by shrapnel in twenty-one places; several were serious wounds. His left arm was numb, and a bullet had passed through one foot. Following medical treatment, he returned to the squadron area and supervised the rearming of the remaining American planes.

Nine months later, Finn was awaiting sea duty when he was informed that he was to receive the Medal of Honor. It was presented to him by Admiral Chester Nimitz on September 14, 1942, on board the USS *Enterprise* in Pearl Harbor.

BIOGRAPHY

BORN
July 24, 1909
Los Angeles, California

ENTERED SERVICE
California

BRANCH
U.S. Navy

DUTY
World War II

DIED
May 27, 2010
Pine Valley, California

Making His Own Luck

EUGENE B. FLUCKEY

COMMANDER, U.S. NAVY Commanding Officer, USS *Barb*

AS ONE OF THE MOST SUCCESSFUL U.S. SUBMARINE commanders in World War II, Eugene Fluckey would be called "Lucky" to rhyme with his last name. But his naval career hardly began with good fortune: On the day he graduated from the Naval Academy in 1935, his parents were involved in a car crash on their way to the ceremonies. His mother was killed and his father was left an invalid.

Fluckey entered submarine school in 1938, then served aboard the USS *S-2* and USS *Bonita*. In April 1944, he assumed command of the USS *Barb*. Early in 1945, the *Barb* was moving along the China coast, looking for targets of opportunity. On January 8, it sank a large Japanese ammunition ship it had been stalking for hours. Believing a larger group of enemy ships was in the area, by January 25 Fluckey had located this "mother lode," as he called it: a convoy of more than thirty Japanese ships anchored in Mamkwan Harbor. The harbor was shallow and heavily mined, with threatening rock formations. It was clear that if the *Barb* got close enough to attack, it would require a nearly impossible run at full speed through uncharted mine- and rock-obstructed waters to make a successful escape. Fluckey immediately ordered an attack anyway.

He managed to penetrate the perimeter of frigates designed to protect the anchored ships from submarines. In water only thirty feet deep, he maneuvered to within range and launched four torpedoes from the forward tubes, then fired four more from the rear tubes. After watching eight direct hits on six main targets—including another ammunition ship whose explosion damaged craft all around it—he turned the *Barb* about and headed for open sea. With Japanese shells hitting all around it,

the *Barb* had to stay on the surface for almost an hour before reaching waters deep enough for it to dive.

When the submarine returned to Pearl Harbor, President Franklin D. Roosevelt was there, conferring with General Douglas MacArthur and Admiral Chester Nimitz. All three men congratulated Fluckey, and on March 23, 1945, he received the Medal of Honor from Secretary of the Navy James Forrestal.

In July 1945, Fluckey led the *Barb* on its twelfth patrol. After sinking an enemy frigate, he landed a shore party on the Japanese coast, which set an explosive device on a railroad track that destroyed a sixteen-car military train. This was the only combat operation on the Japanese mainland during the war.

Fluckey ended his career in 1972 as a rear admiral. With four Navy Crosses in addition to the Medal of Honor, he is one of the most highly decorated servicemen in American history. Fluckey is the author of *Thunder Below: The USS* Barb *Revolutionizes Submarine Warfare in World War II*, which was published in 1992. In 2003, he received the Distinguished Graduate Award from the United States Naval Academy.

BIOGRAPHY

BORN
October 5, 1913
Washington, D.C.

ENTERED SERVICE
Illinois

BRANCH
U.S. Navy

DUTY
World War II

DIED
June 28, 2007
Annapolis, Maryland

Pacific Ace

JOSEPH J. FOSS

CAPTAIN, U.S. MARINE CORPS Marine Fighting Squadron 121, 1st Marine Aircraft Wing

BIOGRAPHY

BORN
April 17, 1915
Sioux Falls, South Dakota

ENTERED SERVICE
South Dakota

BRANCH
U.S. Marine Corps

DUTY
World War II

DIED
January 1, 2003
Scottsdale, Arizona

JOE FOSS WAS CRAZY ABOUT AIRPLANES FROM THE time he was eleven, when he saw Charles Lindbergh in an airport near his home in Sioux Falls, South Dakota. A few years later, he himself flew, this time with a barnstormer who put his biplane into a series of extreme aerobatics to see if he could make the boy sick. Foss loved the sensation and began to save his money to get a pilot's license.

In 1940, he enlisted in the Marine Corps, but when he graduated from fighter pilot school at twenty-six, he was considered too old for combat and was made a flight instructor at the Navy's Pensacola Training Center. He kept lobbying to get into action, until he finally got himself assigned to the South Pacific. After several weeks flying photoreconnaissance missions, he was made the executive officer of the Marine Fighting Squadron 121 in time for the battle of Guadalcanal.

In early October 1942, Japanese ships lying off shore were shelling American positions on the island. Large numbers of Japanese aircraft made daily raids, focusing on Henderson Field in order to neutralize the beleaguered U.S. air forces, which at one point had only seven airplanes left.

Between October 9 and November 19, Foss led daily attacks against the Japanese bombers. He shot down twenty-three Japanese planes and damaged several others so severely ("smokers" in pilot slang) that they probably went down. He himself was shot down four times in the five-week battle. Once, in a driving rainstorm, after hitting a hundred yards off the beach, he was in the water for five hours as the tide carried him a mile out to sea. When he saw dorsal fins, he emptied a packet of shark repellent and hoped for the best. He was saved only because a native had seen his

plane crash and had run to a Catholic mission with the information. The missionaries, looking for Foss in an outrigger canoe in the gathering darkness, almost ran over him as he bobbed in the water.

On January 23, 1943, as the battle for Guadalcanal was nearing its end, Captain Foss led a group of twelve American planes against a superior force of Japanese bombers and fighter escorts. His squadron took down four enemy Zeros—Foss himself accounting for three of them—and forced the bombers to turn back without dropping a bomb. By the time he was ordered back to the United States early in the spring, he had twenty-six confirmed kills—equaling Eddie Rickenbacker's World War I record—along with fourteen smokers. His squad had shot down 280 enemy planes and lost only a few dozen of their own.

Foss was stationed in San Diego awaiting orders when he got a call inviting him to Washington to receive the Medal of Honor. When he arrived at the White House on May 18, 1943, President Roosevelt's secretary immediately invited him into the Oval Office. Although the secretary of state and chief of naval operations were waiting in the corridor for a meeting, FDR chatted alone with Foss for nearly an hour after presenting him with the medal. The President wanted to know all about the war in the Pacific; Foss later realized it was because two of his sons were serving there.

A photographer snapped Foss's picture as he emerged from the Oval Office wearing the medal. A week later it appeared on the cover of *Life* magazine.

After the war, Foss served in the legislature of South Dakota and was elected governor of the state in 1954. He later became the first commissioner of the American Football League.

The Cactus Air Force

ROBERT E. GALER

MAJOR, U.S. MARINE CORPS Marine Fighter Squadron 244

BIOGRAPHY

BORN
October 23, 1913
Seattle, Washington

ENTERED SERVICE
Seattle, Washington

BRANCH
U.S. Marine Corps

DUTY
World War II

DIED
June 27, 2005
Dallas, Texas

WHEN HE WAS A BOY, ROBERT GALER'S IMAGINATION had been so galvanized by Charles Lindbergh's flight across the Atlantic that when the commanding officer in his college Navy ROTC unit spoke to him about Marine Corps aviation, he eagerly joined up after his graduation in 1935.

He was stationed at Pearl Harbor in 1941. After the Japanese attacked, he jumped into his car and rushed to the field in hopes of getting in the air, but when he reached the base, all the American planes were on fire. All he and the other pilots could do was to take cover in a nearby swimming pool that was under construction and ineffectually fire back at attacking Zeros with rifles.

When his squadron was deployed to Wake Island, he was ordered to remain behind, being the only landing signal officer in the Pacific capable of supervising aircraft carrier takeoffs and landings. Just before the Battle of Midway, however, Galer, now a captain, was given command of the 244th Marine Fighter Squadron and sent to Guadalcanal after American forces established a beachhead there in August 1942.

The Japanese sent bombers and fighter escorts to hit the Americans every day in September. And every day, Galer and his men went up to intercept them. Since the Marines had only six or seven planes able to fly out of two squadrons based on Guadalcanal, several carrier-based Navy planes were pressed into duty as part of this "cactus air force" that took off every day from a desertlike landing strip. On most days, the badly outnumbered Americans faced an average of forty Japanese planes; their only advantage was advance information about enemy takeoffs radioed ahead by Australian coast watchers.

During a twenty-nine-day period in September, Galer's squadron shot down twenty-seven Japanese planes, Galer personally accounting for eleven of these kills. (In all, he brought down fourteen enemy planes in the course of the war.) He himself was shot down three times. After one crash landing, he swam to shore and was picked up by Australian coast watchers. On another occasion, two Marines swam out to help him. Galer lost a third plane when he was forced to make a crash landing on an island.

In the spring of 1943, Galer was attending the Army Command and Staff College in Fort Leavenworth, Kansas, when he received a message from headquarters that he was to go to Washington to receive the Medal of Honor from President Franklin D. Roosevelt. He took his mother to the March 24 ceremony because she idolized FDR.

A few months later, he was back in Hawaii, stationed at the Ewa air base. One afternoon, he was told that someone would be staying in his quarters for a couple of nights. It turned out to be his boyhood hero, Charles Lindbergh, who was finishing a tour of the Pacific for a consortium of commercial air carriers. The Lone Eagle didn't talk much, but he did admit to Galer that during his tour, even though he was a civilian, he had secretly flown a combat mission against the Japanese in a "borrowed" P-38.

During the Korean War, Galer, by then a colonel, flew in combat with Marine Air Group 12. Shot down by antiaircraft in June 1952, one hundred miles behind enemy lines, he was picked up by a Navy helicopter in a daring rescue. He was subsequently promoted to brigadier general and worked on guided missile development before retiring in 1957.

Back-to-Back Rescues

NATHAN G. GORDON

LIEUTENANT JUNIOR GRADE, U.S. NAVY Commander of Catalina patrol plane

NATHAN GORDON HAD PRACTICED LAW FOR TWO years when he decided to enlist in the Navy in 1941. He had always wanted to fly, and he figured that it would be more interesting to see the war he was sure the United States would become involved in from the air than on the ground.

At the end of training, young aviators had some say in the kinds of aircraft they wanted to fly. Many of Gordon's buddies chose the glamorous fighter planes, but he preferred the ungainly PBY patrol planes. He joined a squadron in Norfolk, Virginia, and later went to the Caribbean, where he flew a Catalina PBY on night missions searching for the German U-boats preying on Allied convoys. Then he was sent to Hawaii, Midway, and Perth, Australia, before being ordered to Samarai, a small island off the southeastern tip of New Guinea, from which he flew bombing and torpedo missions against Japanese merchant shipping in the Bismarck Sea.

On February 15, 1944, a large force of American bombers attacked the strongly defended Japanese air-field at Kavieng, New Ireland, a stepping-stone to the Admiralty Islands. In the daylong battle, several were hit by antiaircraft fire. When they could, the pilots circled back and went down in Kavieng Harbor to avoid crashing in enemy-held territory, and the PBYs went to their rescue.

Over the radio, Gordon heard that a B-25 had gone down and flew to the position where he was told the crew had ditched. Seeing the yellow dye marker in the water, he made a risky landing in fifteen-foot swells, hitting with such force that his plane popped rivets and developed several cracks. He found wreckage, including a deflated life raft, but no survivors, and after taxiing for several minutes to make sure that no one was still alive, he got the plane airborne again.

Shortly afterward, Gordon was guided to another downed bomber by a B-25 that had just finished its bombing run. This time he saw six American fliers, several of them badly injured, in a life raft. He made another difficult landing, and while his crew tried to plug the leaks in the plane, he taxied toward the raft as Japanese artillery on shore opened fire. After several abortive attempts to reach the airmen in the rolling seas, Gordon had to cut the engines and stop, making the plane a sitting target—only its erratic bobbing in the waves prevented the PBY from being hit by Japanese guns. Finally, he got the airmen aboard, restarted the engines, and positioned the plane for takeoff by forcing the nose up to keep from being capsized by the high swells.

Just as he was airborne, he received a call about another downed B-25, this one much closer to shore. To rescue the crew, he would have to fly directly over enemy guns at three hundred feet and land close to them. His crew pulled in another three American fliers as fire from the enemy shore batteries bracketed his plane.

Gordon got airborne again and was headed for home when he received yet another call. He made another risky landing and picked up six more airmen. After the last rescue, with the plane leaking badly as he crashed through the high waves on takeoff, he managed to return to base with his precious cargo of fifteen airmen.

Several months later, Gordon found out he was to be awarded the Medal of Honor. Great! he thought. I guess that means I'll get to go back to Washington. Instead, he was ordered to Brisbane, Australia, where Admiral Thomas Kincaid, the senior U.S. Navy officer on General Douglas MacArthur's staff, presented the medal to him on July 13, 1944. Later that same day, he was in the air again, flying a fifteen-hour patrol.

BIOGRAPHY

BORN
September 14, 1916
Morrilton, Arkansas

ENTERED SERVICE
Arkansas

BRANCH
U.S. Navy

DUTY
World War II

DIED
September 9, 2008
Morrilton, Arkansas

The "Old Man" Takes Charge

STEPHEN R. GREGG

TECHNICAL SERGEANT, U.S. ARMY 143rd Infantry, 36th Infantry Division

BIOGRAPHY

BORN
September 1, 1914
New York, New York

ENTERED SERVICE
Bayonne, New Jersey

BRANCH
U.S. Army

DUTY
World War II

DIED
February 4, 2005
Bayonne, New Jersey

UNTIL DECEMBER 7, 1941, STEPHEN GREGG WORKED in the New Jersey shipyards building destroyers for the Navy. It was a job that would have deferred him from military service, but after Pearl Harbor he decided that he had to get into the fight, and he joined the Army.

He fought through North Africa, then landed at Salerno with the 143rd Infantry. At the age of twenty-nine, he was among the oldest men in his unit; the recruits sometimes called him Pops. He was wounded in the leg during the Battle of the Rapido River and took part in the landing at Anzio and the capture of Rome. But his memories of Italy were mostly of the monotony, not the horror, of war. It rained constantly during the eleven months he was there, often in muddy foxholes watching German and American artillery duels overhead.

At the beginning of August 1944, two months after D-Day, the 143rd Infantry, along with units of the Free French, invaded southern France near Nice. On August 27, Technical Sergeant Gregg's platoon was advancing through picturesque hill country toward the town of Montélimar when a German force on a rise opened fire. They wounded and killed several GIs, then started firing at the medics who tried to reach them. Hearing the wounded crying out, Gregg, the "old man" in a platoon whose officers had been killed, knew he had to act. Saying to himself, Okay, what the hell, so I'm never coming back, he picked up a .30-caliber machine gun and moved toward the German positions, firing from the hip. A medic fell in behind him.

Gregg stood his ground, raking enemy positions while the medic dragged seven wounded soldiers to safety. When he ran out of ammunition, he found himself surrounded by four enemy soldiers who screamed at him to put his hands up. At that moment, the shrill sound of an incoming artillery round caused everyone to hit the dirt. One of the Germans dropped his machine pistol in the confusion; Gregg grabbed it and shot at his captors, killing one and wounding another; the other two got away. Then he sprinted back to an American machine-gun position and opened fire. His platoon was able to advance up the hill.

The next morning, the Germans, supported by Tiger tanks, counterattacked in an effort to dislodge the Americans from high ground. Gregg directed his unit's mortar fire by walkie-talkie, but by the afternoon his communications had been knocked out, so he began to trace the wires to find the place where they had been cut. When he was within a hundred yards of what he thought was the U.S. mortar position, one of his men rushed up to report that the mortar section had been overrun by the Germans. Crawling closer to the guns, Gregg and two riflemen saw five Germans using the American mortars to fire at American positions. "Take down as many as you can before they get you," Gregg told his men. He threw a grenade and charged the Germans, killing one and injuring two. After taking the remaining two soldiers prisoner, he regained command of the mortars and began firing them at the Germans.

Gregg received a field commission as a second lieutenant. Six months later, his unit was in northern France when he was informed that he was to receive the Medal of Honor. It was awarded to him at battalion headquarters on March 14, 1945, by General Alexander Patch. After the brief ceremony, Gregg stuffed the medal in his back pocket and climbed into a truck heading toward the Siegfried Line. He fought for two more weeks before receiving orders to go home.

Proof of Allegiance

BARNEY F. HAJIRO

PRIVATE, U.S. ARMY Company I, 442nd Regimental Combat Team

BARNEY HAJIRO WAS BORN IN 1916, THE SECOND of nine children, two of whom died in infancy. His parents had emigrated from Hiroshima to the Hawaiian island of Maui during World War I. As the eldest son, Barney had to forgo high school and went to work instead at ten cents an hour on a sugarcane plantation to help support the family. Money was scarce. Barney and his brothers and sisters looked forward to New Year's Day because it was the only time they got a bottle of soda.

Hajiro moved to Honolulu, where he found work as a stevedore. Not long after the Japanese attacked Pearl Harbor, he was drafted and assigned to an engineering battalion that performed menial labor. In March 1943, Hajiro and the rest of his battalion volunteered to form the all-Nisei 442nd ("Go for Broke!") Regimental Combat Team, made up of Japanese Americans from Hawaii and the mainland.

The 442nd landed in Italy in May 1944 and went into action north of Rome, pushing the Germans back along the Arno River. Then it was redeployed to France. On October 19, while acting as a sentry on top of an embankment near the town of Bruyères, Private Hajiro left himself vulnerable to enemy fire in order to direct Allied troops attacking an enemy strongpoint; he killed two snipers with his Browning automatic rifle. Three days later, he and his ammo carrier for the BAR ambushed an eighteen-man German patrol, killing two of the enemy and taking the rest prisoner. Soon after that, the 442nd was ordered to go to the rescue of the Texas 36th Division's "Lost Battalion," which, for more than a week, had been cut off and surrounded by the Germans in the Vosges forest.

On October 29, in a wooded area in the vicinity of Biffontaine, France, Hajiro's unit was pinned down, getting picked off one by one by Germans occupying the high ground approximately one hundred yards above them. When the order to attack finally came, Hajiro rose, his BAR cradled in his arms, and charged up the hill toward the heavily fortified enemy positions. Halfway uphill, he killed three Germans in a machine-gun nest. Then, when an enemy rifleman fired at him and missed, Hajiro turned and killed him. Later, he destroyed another emplacement, killing two more enemy gunners and a sniper guarding it. Nearing the top of the hill, he took aim at a third machine-gun nest and was hit in the shoulder at point-blank range. Another bullet entered his wrist, severing a nerve. Finally, a medic came up and forced him to go back to an aid station.

After treatment at a field hospital, he rejoined the 442nd at Monte Carlo and remained with his buddies, even though his left arm was partially paralyzed and he was barred from combat duty.

Hajiro recovered at a Michigan hospital, then received the Distinguished Service Cross, was discharged, and returned to Hawaii. In 1948, the British government awarded him the British Military Medal for rescuing the Lost Battalion; in 2004, France awarded him its highest medal, the Légion d'honneur. In the spring of 2000, Hajiro was told that he would receive the Medal of Honor. On June 21, it was presented to him by President Bill Clinton. The high point of his trip to Washington, D.C., was visiting the Tomb of the Unknowns at Arlington Cemetery because it reminded him of all the servicemen who had fought with him and died and whose bravery was never acknowledged.

BIOGRAPHY

BORN
September 16, 1916
Puunene, Hawaii

ENTERED SERVICE
Honolulu, Hawaii

BRANCH
U.S. Army

DUTY
World War II

DIED
January 21, 2011
Pearl City, Hawaii

Tank Destroyer

JOHN D. HAWK

SERGEANT, U.S. ARMY Company E, 359th Infantry, 90th Infantry Division

BIOGRAPHY

BORN
May 30, 1924
San Francisco, California

ENTERED SERVICE
Bremerton, Washington

BRANCH
U.S. Army

DUTY
World War II

CURRENT RESIDENCE
Washington State

JOHN HAWK, DRAFTED RIGHT OUT OF HIGH SCHOOL in 1943, was a private first class when he landed at Normandy in a C-47 transport plane a few weeks after the Allied invasion. As his infantry company fought its way to the town of Chambois, he received what his buddies called a "bang promotion" when he was chosen to replace his wounded sergeant.

Americans advancing from the south and English troops from the north had encircled German troops in what became known as the Falaise Pocket. The Germans were trying desperately to fight their way out toward the east to get their armor and other heavy equipment back to defend their homeland. At dawn on August 20, 1944, the machine-gun squad Hawk commanded was dug in on the edge of an apple orchard when the enemy counterattack began. With the smell of dead farm animals heavy in the air, Hawk saw a pair of German Tiger tanks lumber into his sector, followed by enemy infantry. His badly outnumbered gunners repelled the soldiers but couldn't effectively oppose the tanks. German explosive rounds took out one of Hawk's guns, and a tank ran over another one. Hawk took cover behind an apple tree, but a German machine-gun shell penetrated it and hit him in the right thigh.

He limped to a drainage ditch, where he found an American soldier with a bazooka but with no one to load it for him. The two men, working together, began firing at the German tanks, stalking them through the orchard until they withdrew. Hawk then reorganized his scattered machine gunners into one squad and directed them to assemble one workable weapon from the parts of two damaged machine guns.

Later in the day, Hawk saw more Tiger tanks massing for another attempted breakout. Two American tank destroyers on the other side of the orchard were ready to open fire, but they couldn't see the tanks because of the tree cover. Hawk called in a description of their position, then moved to an exposed position facing the Germans and, using arm signals, directed the American tank destroyers against the unseen German tanks. Next he ran back to the tank destroyers and helped them correct the range, then returned to the hill so the Americans could again use him to aim their guns. As a result, two enemy tanks were destroyed, and the rest were driven off. Eventually, five thousand Germans surrendered because the battle in the apple orchard had kept part of the Falaise Pocket closed.

Hawk was treated for his leg wound, but he was unwilling to become separated from his unit and refused to be hospitalized. He made it into Germany just before the Battle of the Bulge, where he was wounded again.

Hawk was back home in Washington State when he learned that he would receive the Medal of Honor. Not wanting to travel to Washington, D.C., he called a childhood friend, U.S. Senator Warren Magnuson, for help. When Magnuson learned that President Truman was planning to attend an international conference in San Francisco, he asked Truman to come to the state capitol in Olympia. After putting the medal around Hawk's neck in Olympia on June 21, 1945, the President turned his attention to Hawk's father, who he had discovered was an old World War I artilleryman like himself.

After attending college for seven years, Hawk graduated. He dedicated the next thirty-one years of his life to the education of young children. He not only taught elementary school for all of those years, he also served for a time as an elementary school principal.

Purple Heart Battalion

SHIZUYA HAYASHI

PRIVATE, U.S. ARMY, Company A, 100th Infantry Battalion

BIOGRAPHY

BORN
November 28, 1917
Waialua, Oahu, Hawaii

ENTERED SERVICE
Schofield Barracks, Hawaii

BRANCH
U.S. Army

DUTY
World War II

DIED
March 12, 2008
Pearl City, Hawaii

SHIZUYA HAYASHI WAS SERVING IN THE 65TH Engineers in Hawaii when Pearl Harbor was bombed. After the attack, there was uncertainty about what to do with the Japanese Americans in this unit, and for a time they were ordered to work on plantations and to clean trash off the roads. Then in June 1942, Hayashi and 1,400 other Nisei soldiers were sent to Camp McCoy in Wisconsin, where they formed the 100th Infantry Battalion, the first combat unit in the history of the U.S. Army made up mainly of Japanese Americans. After more than a year of instruction, the 100th became the most intensively trained unit in the Army, with each man qualified as an expert in several different weapons. It received its colors and the motto it had requested: "Remember Pearl Harbor."

In September 1943, the 100th landed at Salerno, Italy, where the Germans were amazed to see Japanese Americans fighting against them. During the next two months, the unit crossed the waist-deep waters of the winding Volturno River three times in a running engagement with the enemy and suffered the kinds of losses that would eventually earn it the nickname "Purple Heart Battalion."

Late on the afternoon of November 29, 1943, Private Hayashi's platoon was attacking the Germans on a hill near the town of Cerasuolo. The Germans were firing their 88 mm artillery, called screaming mimis by the GIs because of the shrill and disorienting sound the artillery rounds made before hitting the ground. In an effort to find cover, the Americans stumbled through a minefield, setting off deadly explosions. A bullet grazed Hayashi in the neck; his commanding officer was shot in the back.

As night fell, Hayashi and two other GIs were separated from the rest of the platoon. After waiting all night to be rescued, Hayashi sent his two comrades to look for help at daybreak. Drawn by their loud conversation, the Germans opened fire and advanced on them. One German, looking for the two men, came within three feet of Hayashi, then fired at point-blank range. He missed, and Hayashi killed him. In the face of grenades and rifle and machine-gun fire, Hayashi rose, alone, and, shooting his automatic rifle from the hip, charged a German machine-gun position, killing nine of the enemy. When his platoon tried to advance, and an enemy antiaircraft gun began to lob shells at them, Hayashi returned fire, killing nine more Germans. Then he came upon a boy, perhaps thirteen years old, in uniform, curled up and crying. Hayashi couldn't shoot—he took the boy prisoner, along with three other Germans.

The 100th fought several engagements through Italy. The night before it was scheduled to go into action at Anzio, Hayashi was summoned to battalion headquarters and presented with the Distinguished Service Cross. In 1998, almost fifty-five years later, he received a call from the secretary of the army informing him that this award had been upgraded to the Medal of Honor as a result of a comprehensive review of the contributions of Asian-American servicemen during World War II. President Bill Clinton presented the medal to him in a ceremony on June 21, 2000, at the White House.

"Second Miracle of This World"

JAMES R. HENDRIX

PRIVATE, U.S ARMY Company C, 53rd Armored Infantry Battalion, 4th Armored Division

JAMES HENDRIX HAD GONE ONLY AS FAR AS THE third grade before quitting school to help his sharecropper father. He had never been more than a few miles away from his hometown of Lepanto, Arkansas, in his entire life, but in 1944, at the age of eighteen, he was drafted into the Army, sent to Florida for basic training, and dispatched to England on a British ship.

Hendrix's armored infantry battalion remained anchored in the English Channel for the first days of the Normandy invasion; the seasickness the troops experienced made the perils of combat seem almost welcome. Once the beachhead was secured, his unit landed and joined General George Patton's Third Army as it pushed through France into Belgium. Hendrix was a bazooka man specializing in antitank warfare. Part of a "headquarters squad," he served wherever he was needed, responding to the call "Bazooka man up front!"

On the night of December 26, 1944, as the Battle of the Bulge raged, Hendrix was part of the leading element of American troops engaged in the final thrust to break through to the besieged American garrison in the Belgian city of Bastogne. Near the town of Assenois, a few miles from the surrounded Americans, the advance stalled, much to General Patton's surprise and concern. Private Hendrix dismounted from his half-track and started to move forward with his bazooka, only to find a German Tiger blocking the road. He ran into a building flanking the tank and from a second-floor window fired the bazooka, hitting the tank in the turret and disabling it.

He returned to the half-track as the U.S. column started to move again. Suddenly, a fierce German artillery barrage began. When his half-track was hit, Hendrix jumped out and took cover in a hedgerow, carrying only a rifle. From there, he saw two German 88 mm field guns set up on the road to block the Americans on their way to Bastogne. As the artillery shells continued to explode all around him, he moved forward—more to keep from getting hit than anything else. Suddenly, he found himself behind the German guns. When the shelling let up, he moved out from his cover and yelled at the enemy gunners in their foxholes—he counted fourteen of them—to come out with their hands up. Thirteen surrendered; he shot and killed the one who didn't.

After turning over his prisoners, Hendrix returned to the column. But again the advance toward Bastogne stalled because of heavy enemy fire. Given cover by an American tank, Hendrix took out the two German machine guns blocking the road. As he was returning to his unit, he saw an American half-track on fire. He jumped in to try to help the men trapped in it—one of them was burned over his entire body, his skin the color of charcoal. In the midst of enemy sniper fire and exploding ammunition in the vehicle, Hendrix pulled the man out and extinguished his burning clothing. He could tell the soldier was alive only because he was screaming.

Hendrix was recommended for the Medal of Honor by General Patton and received it on August 23, 1945, from President Harry Truman. His path crossed the President's again a few years later. He had decided to become a career soldier and was taking airborne training, but in his first practice jump, his parachute failed to open and he fell more than a thousand feet. He somehow managed not only to survive but to escape serious injury. Truman happened to be reviewing the troops when he heard about this incident and contacted Hendrix. "That was the second miracle of this world," the President told him. Hendrix asked what the first one was. "That I ever got elected president," Truman replied.

BIOGRAPHY

BORN
August 20, 1925
Lepanto, Arkansas

ENTERED SERVICE
Lepanto, Arkansas

BRANCH
U.S. Army

DUTY
World War II

DIED
November 14, 2002
Davenport, Florida

Deadly Crossfire

SILVESTRE S. HERRERA

PRIVATE FIRST CLASS, U.S. ARMY Company E, 142nd Infantry, 36th Infantry Division

BIOGRAPHY

BORN
July 17, 1917
El Paso, Texas

ENTERED SERVICE
Phoenix, Arizona

BRANCH
U.S. Army

DUTY
World War II

DIED
November 26, 2007
Glendale, Arizona

SILVESTRE HERRERA WAS TWENTY-SEVEN YEARS OLD, married with three children, and working in his hometown of Phoenix, Arizona, when he was drafted into the Army early in 1944. Men with families were no longer exempt from the service—in basic training, he met another draftee who said he was the father of eight.

Private First Class Herrera's company landed in Italy, by this time largely under Allied control, as part of the 142nd Infantry in the summer of 1944. That fall they invaded France at Marseille and took a troop train to the front. By the end of the year, as his unit reached France, it began to encounter resistance from the retreating Germans. When the fighting became heavy by the spring of 1945, Herrera had to concede a grudging respect for the enemy, regarding them as *"muy macho."*

On March 15, Herrera's platoon was advancing along a wooded road near the French town of Mertzwiller when it ran into two German machine-gun emplacements. Caught in a deadly crossfire between the two guns, the GIs dived for cover. Fearing that his comrades would be cut to pieces, Herrera stood up and ran toward the closest enemy position, firing his rifle from the hip. He tossed two grenades at the machine-gun nest; the concussion knocked the Germans down. Then he was on them, and all eight soldiers threw down their weapons and surrendered to him.

Herrera turned his prisoners over to men in his squad, then started crawling toward the other machine gun, firing as he went. ("My M-1 was talking, and the Germans understood what it was saying," he commented later.) The position was protected by a minefield; GIs were throwing rocks into the area in an effort to explode the mines. Herrera got up and charged the Germans anyway, but as he neared the machine-

gun nest, he stepped on a mine. He was thrown to the ground, both of his feet blown off at the ankle. Though bleeding heavily, he lay on his stomach and fired at the Germans, forcing them to stay down and thus enabling his squad to skirt the minefield, flank the enemy, and move in for the kill.

Herrera remained conscious for the next few hours. At the aid station, he said to the examining doctor, "Just try to save my knees, Doc." After two months in an Army field hospital, he was sent to the Army Amputation Center in Utah. During a ninety-day furlough to Phoenix, he was notified that he was to receive the Medal of Honor and traveled to Washington with an uncle who was given time off from his job to help him make the trip. In time, Silvestre Herrera would be fitted with new prosthetic feet, but on August 23, 1945, at the White House, President Harry Truman bent over his wheelchair to present him with the Medal of Honor.

Seemingly Invulnerable

FREEMAN V. HORNER

STAFF SERGEANT, U.S. ARMY Company K, 119th Infantry, 30th Infantry Division

BECAUSE HIS MOTHER WAS UNABLE TO TAKE CARE of him after he was born, Freeman Horner went to live with his grandparents in Traverton, Pennsylvania. After his grandmother died, neighbors helped his grandfather raise him. They gave him adventure books to read, and when they asked what he wanted to be when he grew up, he always replied, "A soldier of fortune." Instead, he just became a soldier, enlisting in the Army right after Pearl Harbor.

After a variety of postings in the United States in the first years of the war, Horner, then a staff sergeant with the 119th Infantry, was sent to England in the spring of 1944 to train for the invasion of Europe. He landed at Normandy the week after D-Day. His unit fought through France, Belgium, and Holland on its way to Germany. On November 16, 1944, his platoon was moving forward through an open field near Würselen, Germany, when it ran into a hornet's nest of German machine-gun fire. As the GIs lay pinned down in a flat, exposed area, enemy artillery gunners began to shell them, causing serious casualties.

Seeing that his men would be slaughtered if they stayed where they were, Horner jumped up and charged the Germans, carrying a heavy load of ammunition, several grenades, and a tommy gun he had taken off a dead American tank driver earlier. As he rushed into concentrated fire coming from two gun emplacements in a farmhouse, he was shot at from the side by a third gun that had been silent until then. He turned toward it and, firing the tommy gun, killed the German gunners. Then, hunching down, he zigzagged fifty yards toward the two remaining machine-gun nests in the farmhouse. Both guns appeared to have him squarely in their sights, but

neither was able to hit him. Demoralized by Horner's apparent invulnerability, the Germans abandoned their guns and ran into the cellar as Horner smashed through the front door. He tossed two grenades down the stairs as he called for them to surrender. One German was killed; four others came up with their hands in the air.

Horner's unit continued its advance into Germany after this action and was on its way to Berlin when the war ended. In October 1945, Horner was back home in Pennsylvania when the call came informing him that he was to receive the Medal of Honor.

In awarding it on October 12, President Harry Truman said, as he did to other medal winners, "I'd rather have one of these than be president." Horner smiled as he repressed the reply running through his head: "I'd rather be president!"

BIOGRAPHY

BORN
June 7, 1922
Marion Heights,
Pennsylvania

ENTERED SERVICE
Shamokin, Pennsylvania

BRANCH
U.S. Army

DUTY
World War II

DIED
December 1, 2005
Columbus, Georgia

Going for Broke

DANIEL K. INOUYE

SECOND LIEUTENANT, U.S. ARMY Company E, 442nd Regimental Combat Team

BIOGRAPHY

BORN
September 7, 1924
Honolulu, Hawaii

ENTERED SERVICE
Honolulu, Hawaii

BRANCH
U.S. Army

DUTY
World War II

CURRENT RESIDENCE
Hawaii and
Washington, D.C.

DANIEL K. INOUYE WAS A SENIOR IN HIGH SCHOOL in Honolulu when Pearl Harbor was bombed. He remembered standing outside his house with his father as Japanese planes swooped down on the U.S. fleet, both of them, as Japanese Americans, sharing a special sense of horror at this event. Inouye, who had been teaching first aid to local community groups, spent the first day of the war working at a Red Cross station.

The next September, he enrolled in the University of Hawaii, with plans to become a doctor. Then the War Department, which had refused to accept Japanese-American volunteers after Pearl Harbor, reversed itself, so Inouye quit school and enlisted. He was assigned to the 442nd Regimental Combat Team; during training in Mississippi, the unit found its motto: "Go for Broke!"

When the 442nd shipped out for Naples in May 1944, Inouye was a sergeant and squad leader. Its casualty rate was so high that it eventually took 12,000 men to fill the original 4,500 places in the regiment. The unit began fighting in June 1944 north of Rome, pushing the Germans back along the Arno River. Later in the summer, it spent several months fighting in France's Rhône valley, where Inouye was given a battlefield commission as a second lieutenant. The 442nd then returned to Italy.

On April 21, 1945, with the European war nearing its end, Inouye's company was ordered to attack a heavily defended ridge guarding an important road in the vicinity of San Terenzo. His platoon wiped out an enemy patrol and mortar observation post and reached the main line of resistance before the rest of the American force. As the troops continued up the hill, three German machine guns focused their fire on them,

pinning them down. Inouye worked his way toward the first bunker. Pulling out a grenade, he felt something hit him in his side but paid no attention and threw the grenade into the machine-gun nest. After it exploded, he advanced and killed the crew. He didn't realize he'd been shot until one of his men told him he was bleeding.

Although he felt weak, Inouye continued up the hill, throwing two more grenades into the second gun emplacement and destroying it before he fell. His men, trying to take the third bunker, were forced back. He dragged himself toward it, then stood up and was about to pull the pin on his last grenade when a German appeared in the bunker and fired a rifle grenade. It hit Inouye in the right elbow and virtually tore off his arm. He pried the grenade out of his dead right fist with his other hand and threw it at the third bunker, then lurched toward it, firing his tommy gun left-handed. A German bullet hit him in the leg. A medic reached him and gave him a shot of morphine, but Inouye didn't allow himself to be evacuated until the position was secured. In the hospital, the remnants of his right arm were amputated.

After leaving the Army and going through a long period of recuperation, Inouye finished college. Forced to give up his dream of practicing medicine, he decided to study law. He was elected to the U.S. House of Representatives from Hawaii in 1954—Congress's first Japanese American—and to the Senate in 1962.

On June 21, 2000, as part of a reevaluation of the military accomplishments of Asian Americans in World War II, Senator Inouye was presented with the Medal of Honor by President Bill Clinton for his heroism in Italy more than half a century earlier.

Explosive Charge

ARTHUR J. JACKSON

PRIVATE FIRST CLASS, U.S. MARINE CORPS 3rd Battalion, 7th Marines, 1st Marine Division

ARTHUR JACKSON GRADUATED FROM HIGH SCHOOL in 1942, then got a job as a laborer at the Naval Air Station in Sitka, Alaska. That December, he traveled down to Portland, Oregon, to enroll in the Navy's flight training program, but was turned down because of poor vision in one eye. The Navy recruiter suggested that he consider the Marine Corps. He signed up in January 1943.

He eventually joined the 17th Replacement Battalion and was sent to Australia. In Melbourne, he was assigned to the 7th Marines and served in the machine-gun section of a weapons platoon, which took part in the invasion of New Britain in December. The 7th Marines then went on to the Russell Islands to prepare for the landing on Peleliu. At his request, Jackson was moved into a rifle platoon, where he became an automatic rifleman.

Jackson's unit landed on Peleliu on September 15, 1944, in temperatures topping 110 degrees. For three days, the 7th Marines moved across the island. On the fourth day, Jackson's company was held up by sniper and machine-gun fire. His commander asked him if he thought he could make it to a shallow trench system that connected the enemy bunkers. Jackson's answer was yes. He lightened his load by removing his helmet, pack, and leggings; then, carrying a twenty-pound Browning automatic rifle and several magazines weighing one pound each, he headed directly toward the Japanese as his platoon laid down covering fire. Each time he got to an enemy position, he unloaded a full twenty-round magazine at it. By the time he finally reached the largest bunker, which held approximately thirty-five Japanese soldiers, his squad leader had brought up more ammunition and grenades, as well as a combat pack containing about forty pounds of explosives. Together he and Jackson prepared the charge. With his rifle, Jackson killed the two enemy soldiers guarding the bunker, then carried the charge of explosives to the aperture of the bunker and shoved it in, running for cover to a bomb crater about fifty yards away.

When all the debris from the explosion, including the huge coconut logs framing the bunker, had fallen to the ground around him, Jackson got up and took out the remaining enemy positions. In all, he accounted for the destruction of twelve pillboxes and fifty soldiers.

Four nights after this one-man assault, Jackson and his assistant automatic rifleman were in a defensive position when an enemy soldier lobbed a grenade into their foxhole. Jackson reached down and felt for it in the dark. When he stood up and tossed it back, killing two Japanese, he was hit in the neck by a stray .45-caliber bullet from a GI on the line. The slug came within a hair of his jugular vein. He was evacuated to a hospital ship bound for New Caledonia. After recuperating, he returned to his unit, eventually taking part in the invasion of Okinawa. A platoon sergeant by then, he was again wounded in action.

On October 5, 1945, Jackson received the Medal of Honor from President Harry Truman along with thirteen other men, including fighter ace Gregory "Pappy" Boyington of the Black Sheep Squadron and future Marine Corps Commandant Louis Wilson. The next day the group went to New York City for a ticker-tape parade in honor of Admiral Chester Nimitz.

BIOGRAPHY

BORN
October 18, 1924
Cleveland, Ohio

ENTERED SERVICE
Oregon

BRANCH
U.S. Marine Corps

DUTY
World War II

CURRENT RESIDENCE
Idaho

One Determined Defender

ALTON W. KNAPPENBERGER

PRIVATE FIRST CLASS, U.S. ARMY Company C, 30th Infantry, 3rd Infantry Division

ALTON KNAPPENBERGER WAS WORKING ON A Pennsylvania pig farm when he was drafted in 1943 at the age of nineteen. He landed at Anzio, on the Italian coast, on January 22, 1944, as part of the Army's 3rd Infantry Division, and although he did not know it at the time, he was about to become engaged in one of the toughest combat actions of World War II. "Knappie," as his friends called him, was surprised by how little resistance the Germans initially offered. But as his unit slowly pushed inland over the next few days, he could sense that the enemy was regrouping. It rained constantly. He never forgot the mud; it was so thick and viscous that he worried it might suck off his boots.

On February 1, as Private First Class Knappenberger's battalion neared the small town of Cisterna di Littoria, the Germans launched a strong counterattack with tanks and artillery that nearly overwhelmed the U.S. force. It was the Germans' intent to push the Americans into the sea. With American soldiers taking heavy casualties all around him, Knappenberger crawled to a rise so that he could see the enemy. A German machine gun about eighty yards away opened fire, its slugs hitting right in front of Knappenberger and kicking mud into his face. He scrambled to a Browning automatic rifle lying beside one of his dead comrades, stood up, and aimed a burst at the machine gun, killing the three Germans operating it. Two Germans crawled to a point within twenty yards of Knappenberger's knoll and threw potato masher grenades at him. Knappenberger wheeled and killed them both with one burst from his automatic rifle.

He was moving forward when a second German machine gun opened fire from a range of a hundred yards. Knappenberger silenced it with the BAR. Shortly afterward, a German 20 mm antiaircraft gun directed fire at his unit. He took out the German position with his BAR. For the next two hours, Knappenberger single-handedly held off the enemy infantry, which was threatening the efforts of the U.S. force to organize a defense. When he ran low on ammunition, he crawled through heavy fire to the body of another fallen American and grabbed clips from his pack. He resumed firing and repelled a German platoon armed with automatic weapons. Despite heavy fire, shells bursting within fifteen yards of him, he held his precarious position while continuing to fire at the enemy. Finally, his ammunition supply completely exhausted, he rejoined his company, having disrupted the enemy attack for more than two hours. Only six men out of his company of two hundred had not been killed or wounded.

Over the next few weeks, the breakout from Anzio stalled and developed into a stalemate between Allied and German forces as each regrouped. Knappenberger was in a foxhole not far from where the February action had occurred when he was informed that he was to receive the Medal of Honor. It was presented to him on June 8, 1944, by General Mark Clark, commander of the Fifth Army, with American troops looking on and the regimental band playing. Soon therafter, Knappenberger was sent home and traveled around the country telling his story as part of a war bond drive. After the war, he returned home to Pennsylvania and worked as a truck driver and as the supervisor of an asphalting crew.

BIOGRAPHY

BORN
December 31, 1923
Coopersburg, Pennsylvania

ENTERED SERVICE
Spring Mount, Pennsylvania

BRANCH
U.S. Army

DUTY
World War II

DIED
June 9, 2008
Boyertown, Pennsylvania

NEAR KRINKELT, BELGIUM, 1944

Building a Line of Defense

JOSE M. LOPEZ

SERGEANT, U.S. ARMY 23rd Infantry, 2nd Infantry Division

JOSE LOPEZ WORKED FOR YEARS AS A DECKHAND on passenger liners, visiting exotic places like Tahiti. On December 3, 1941, his ship left Hawaii for San Francisco; he was on board when he learned by radio about the attack on Pearl Harbor. When the ship docked, however, he was arrested as a Japanese agent because of confusion caused by his Hispanic features and held until he convinced federal officials that he was actually a Mexican American.

Drafted into the Army early in 1942, Lopez volunteered for Airborne and made one jump before he was relieved of that hazardous duty because he was married and had a child. When informing him of this decision, his commanding officer told him, "Don't worry. Everything will be fine. We're going to put you in the infantry."

Lopez was a sergeant when he landed on Omaha Beach on D-Day and began to fight toward Germany. On December 17, 1944, a bitterly cold day, his unit was in a heavily forested area near Krinkelt, Belgium, struggling to advance through knee-deep snow when German tanks and infantry suddenly appeared and threatened to roll over them. Their part of the Battle of the Bulge had begun.

Lopez grabbed his heavy machine gun and carried it to the company's left flank, which was in danger of being overrun. With enemy bullets slicing into the snow all around him, he held his ground, praying all the time to the Virgin of Guadalupe. He then jumped into a shallow hole offering no protection above the waist and cut down a group of ten German soldiers, after which he killed twenty-five more who were trying to turn his flank. Dazed from the artillery fire all around him, he carried his gun back to a position at the right rear of his sector and opened fire again. When the concussion of an enemy shell knocked him down, he got up, reset his gun, and continued to shoot.

Seeing that he was about to be surrounded, Lopez again loaded the machine gun on his back and ran to where several GIs were trying to set up another defense. He fired from this position until he had used up all his ammunition, then picked up his gun and worked his way back to the town.

Lopez's action, in which he single-handedly killed more than one hundred Germans, kept his company from being overwhelmed and allowed reserve troops time to build a line that would repel the German drive.

When his commanding officer offered to make him an officer through a field commission, Lopez declined, saying he preferred to be a sergeant. His unit continued to drive through Germany and was in Czechoslovakia when the war ended. It was there that Lopez, sleeping on the floor of an abandoned building, was awakened by a buddy one morning and told that he was being taken back to Germany, where he would be awarded the Medal of Honor. It was presented by Major General James Van Fleet III in Nuremberg on June 18, 1945.

BIOGRAPHY

BORN
June 1, 1912
Mission, Texas

ENTERED SERVICE
Brownsville, Texas

BRANCH
U.S. Army

DUTY
World War II

DIED
May 16, 2005
San Antonio, Texas

The Youngest Recipient

JACK H. LUCAS

PRIVATE FIRST CLASS, U.S. MARINE CORPS 1st Battalion, 26th Marines, 5th Marine Division

BIOGRAPHY

BORN
February 14, 1928
Plymouth, North Carolina

ENTERED SERVICE
Norfolk, Virginia

BRANCH
U.S. Marine Corps

DUTY
World War II

DIED
June 5, 2008
Hattiesburg, Mississippi

JACK LUCAS WAS A CADET CAPTAIN IN THE MILITARY school where his mother had enrolled him after his father's death when he heard radio reports of the Japanese attack on Pearl Harbor. The next day he promised his mother that if she let him enlist, he would come home after the war and finish his education—but he wound up forging her signature on the consent form because she would have had to lie for him. Lucas, big for his age, told the Marine recruiters he was seventeen. Shortly before being sent to the training center at Parris Island, South Carolina, he turned fourteen.

Troops were moving out to Hawaii, but because of his experience in military school, Lucas was ordered to stay behind and drill new recruits. He knew his buddies were ultimately headed for combat, so he hopped onto the train with them—in effect going AWOL to get into the war. Once in Hawaii, he managed to convince officers that he was there because of a clerical error.

He was almost drummed out of the Corps when a censor read a letter to his girlfriend that mentioned his real age, fifteen by then. He managed to talk his way out of trouble again and was assigned a job driving a truck on the base.

A year later, when a large number of troops were being ferried out to ships in Pearl Harbor heading into action, Lucas stowed away on the USS *Deuel*, in effect going AWOL a second time. He slept on deck and scrounged meals from other men. When the ship was well out to sea, he turned himself in for fear of being classified as a deserter, and a sympathetic colonel decided that instead of punishing him, he would finally grant Lucas his wish of being assigned to a combat unit.

Not long after, the *Deuel* approached Iwo Jima. On February 19, 1945, five days after he turned seventeen,

Lucas hit the beach with forty thousand other Marines, five thousand of whom would become casualties that first day of combat. The next morning, his unit destroyed a Japanese pillbox, then took cover in a Japanese escape trench, where eleven Japanese soldiers surprised them. The Marines and the Japanese started firing at each other at point-blank range. Lucas shot one soldier in the forehead before his rifle jammed. As he was trying to get it to work, he saw two Japanese grenades land near the Marine next to him. He dove down into the soft volcanic ash, covering the grenades with his body. One failed to go off, but the explosion of the second one flipped him over on his back and inflicted large wounds on his arm, chest, and thigh. His chin was sliced open, and one eye was forced out of its socket. He had internal injuries and was bleeding heavily from his nose and mouth.

A Marine from a following unit, reaching down to take off Lucas's dog tags, saw Lucas's hand wiggle. He was given a shot of morphine, carried back to the beach on a stretcher, and transferred to a hospital ship. At one point he was almost given up for dead, but the doctors kept working on him.

After hospitalizations in Guam and San Francisco, and several of the twenty-two surgeries he would undergo, he was discharged in September 1945. On October 5, at the age of seventeen, he received the Medal of Honor from President Harry Truman, making him the youngest recipient since the Civil War. Then, as he had promised his mother years before, he went back to school—a ninth grader wearing the Medal of Honor around his neck. He later graduated from high school and earned a college degree. His book, *Indestructible*, was published in 2006.

Wire Man

ROBERT D. MAXWELL

TECHNICIAN FIFTH GRADE, U.S. ARMY 7th Infantry, 3rd Infantry Division

BIOGRAPHY

BORN
October 26, 1920
Boise, Idaho

ENTERED SERVICE
Larimar County, Colorado

BRANCH
U.S. Army

DUTY
World War II

CURRENT RESIDENCE
Oregon

ROBERT MAXWELL WAS THE "WIRE MAN" TO HIS army buddies—a lineman in charge of stringing up the field phone connections for his battalion's communications. When he landed in North Africa with the 7th Infantry as a technician fifth grade, he carried an M-1 rifle along with his wire and tools. But the load was so heavy that he was reclassified as a noncombatant, which allowed him to carry only a .45-caliber pistol.

After the North African campaign, Maxwell's division invaded Sicily in July 1943, then raced north to Palermo and east to Messina, helping to capture the island in thirty-eight days. The division next moved to the newly established Salerno beachhead and fought its way north through the mountains near Monte Cassino. In early January 1944, a few days after it landed on the beaches of Anzio, Maxwell was wounded. Hospitalized in Naples for several months, he rejoined his outfit before the invasion of southern France that summer.

On September 7, Maxwell's battalion was part of the assault on the town of Besançon. His job was to string communications wire to connect the front lines with the American command post, which was set up in a shell-pocked farmhouse surrounded by a four-foot stone wall. Along the top of this wall was a mesh-wire fence. Shortly after midnight, as Maxwell was standing guard in the courtyard of the house, a German platoon that had infiltrated the American battalion's forward companies opened fire with machine guns and 20 mm antiaircraft weapons. In the dark, he could see the advancing Germans as they were briefly illuminated by gunfire and hear the twang of their grenades bouncing off the mesh wire above the wall. They came within ten yards of the command post, trying to take out

the officers inside. Maxwell fought them off with his .45 as three other soldiers, also armed only with pistols, joined him.

After several minutes of chaos, an enemy grenade cleared the wire. Maxwell heard it hit in the courtyard a few feet away from the door of the command post. Fearing that it would injure the officers, he moved to grab it and toss it back at the enemy. But he realized there wasn't time, so he smothered it with his body, then lost consciousness.

When he came to, he was alone. He had large shrapnel wounds in his head and arms, and part of his right foot was blown away. His platoon leader appeared, picked Maxwell up, and helped him walk out the back door of the farmhouse. Just as they reached the road, another German grenade hit behind them, knocking them both down.

When a chaplain in the Naples hospital where Maxwell was recuperating told him that he had been recommended for the Medal of Honor, Maxwell assumed it was just talk. But on May 12, 1945, at the Camp Carson Convalescent Hospital in Colorado, he received the medal from camp commander General C. W. Danielson in a ceremony attended by all the medical personnel.

Surviving a Kamikaze Attack

RICHARD M. McCOOL, JR.

LIEUTENANT, U.S. NAVY USS Landing Craft Support (L) (3) 122

RICHARD McCOOL WAS FIFTEEN YEARS OLD WHEN HE finished high school and nineteen when he graduated from the University of Oklahoma. He received an appointment to the Naval Academy as a member of the class of 1945, but because of the war the course was compressed into three years, and the class of 1945 graduated early.

Shortly before graduation, McCool attended a presentation given by a captain recruiting officers for amphibious craft. This kind of duty didn't have the tradition or romance of the deep-water navy, but the midshipmen were offered the possibility of commanding their own ship instead of being junior officers on a large vessel. Midshipman McCool signed up. After graduation, he picked up his ship in Boston. It was an LCS, similar in looks to the landing craft that brought soldiers ashore in invasions, but instead of a blunt bow with troop ramps, it had a sharp bow and was heavily armed with 40 mm and 20 mm guns, .50-caliber machine guns, and 120 preloaded 4.5-inch rockets. It carried a crew of seventy, including six officers.

McCool sailed for San Diego through the Panama Canal in December 1944. By June 1945, his ship was in Okinawa, part of a unit made up of four LCS ships and three destroyers patrolling for Japanese kamikazes. Behind the LCS picket line, the destroyers picked up enemy aircraft on their radar and radioed the information to McCool and the other LCS commanders, who attempted to shoot down the planes as they passed overhead.

On June 10, one of the Japanese planes got through and hit one of the destroyers. McCool's ship was the closest and rushed to help the sinking ship. Along with another LCS, McCool picked up the destroyer's surviving crew members and transferred them to another American ship.

There were many radar sightings the next day. Then, suddenly, kamikazes dived down through the overcast sky. Instead of heading for the destroyers, the first pilot pointed his plane at McCool's LCS. McCool's gunners opened fire and knocked the plane down, but another kamikaze was right behind it. Their guns hit the second plane as well, but it crashed into the ship's conning tower. McCool, suffering chest wounds and burns, was knocked unconscious. When he came to, the conning tower was on fire. He managed to get down to the main deck, and acting instinctively—he would remember almost nothing of the ensuing events—he rallied his crew to fight the fire that threatened to engulf the ship. When he heard that several men were trapped in the burning deckhouse, he went in to try to rescue them and half-carried one badly wounded man to safety despite his own burns. He continued to command his ship until help was on the way. Then one of his lungs collapsed and he passed out again.

After two months in a hospital in Guam, where he was one of the first servicemen to be treated with massive doses of the new drug penicillin, McCool was transferred to the Oak Knoll Naval Hospital in California and then back home to Norman, Oklahoma. He received the Medal of Honor from President Harry Truman on December 18, 1945.

McCool was well enough to go back on active duty in mid-1946. After serving in the Korean and Vietnam wars, he retired as a Navy captain in 1974.

BIOGRAPHY

BORN
January 4, 1922
Tishomingo, Oklahoma

ENTERED SERVICE
Oklahoma

BRANCH
U.S. Navy

DUTY
World War II

DIED
March 5, 2008
Bainbridge Island,
Washington

Playing Dead

GINO J. MERLI
PRIVATE FIRST CLASS, U.S. ARMY 18th Infantry, 1st Infantry Division

GINO MERLI NEVER MADE IT TO HIS SENIOR YEAR IN high school. Instead, he joined the Army in 1943 and was sent to Scotland early in 1944 after basic training as a machine gunner. That spring he joined the 1st Infantry, which was in England preparing for D-Day. He waded ashore at Omaha Beach and fought from the sand embankment below Pointe du Hoc as the U.S. Ranger battalion made its famous climb up those steep cliffs.

Two months later, Private First Class Merli's company was dug in at a roadblock near Sars-la-Bruyère, Belgium, trying to cut off enemy units as they attempted to retreat to Germany. Even though villagers warned the Americans that there were "*beaucoup de Boches*" in the area, Merli's commanding officer ordered the unit to hold its ground "come hell or high water."

At nightfall on September 4, 1944, a numerically superior German force attacked with fixed bayonets. In intense and chaotic fighting, Merli's machine-gun position was overrun and his assistant gunner was killed. U.S. riflemen retreated; Merli, still at his machine gun, could see the shadowy shapes of the German soldiers passing around him. At about 9:00 P.M., his position was finally captured. Eight members of his squad put their hands up and surrendered, but Merli slumped down beside his assistant gunner and played dead. He heard Germans talking above him as they jabbed bayonets into his backside; it took everything in his power not to cry out. After they moved off, taking the captured GIs with them, he went back to his gun and started firing again. After about half an hour, another enemy patrol overran his position, and again he feigned death. As he silently recited the Our Father, the same scene played out: He heard the Germans talking among themselves as they kicked at the lifeless bodies of

American soldiers lying near him. Then they moved on, and once again he went back to his gun and continued to fight. His fear evaporated as he began to feel that he was involved in a sort of game. He started wondering: How long can I get away with this?

By daybreak the next morning, American forces had succeeded in their counteroffensive, and the Germans asked for a truce. The American negotiating party, moving into German-occupied ground, found Merli still at his machine gun. There were fifty-two enemy dead sprawled around the position he had never given up. He asked for permission to go to a nearby chapel and pray for all the soldiers—on both sides— killed that night.

Two months later, Merli was hit by grenade fragments in his leg and wrist in the Battle of the Bulge. He was hospitalized in England for several weeks, then sent home to Atlantic City on a troopship. After surgery to remove shrapnel, he was given a ten-day furlough. Midway through it, he was picked up by two military policemen; he couldn't imagine what he had done wrong. The MPs finally told him that he had been ordered to go to the White House to receive the Medal of Honor. President Harry Truman placed it around his neck on June 15, 1945.

BIOGRAPHY

BORN
May 12, 1924
Scranton, Pennsylvania

ENTERED SERVICE
Peckville, Pennsylvania

BRANCH
U.S. Army

DUTY
World War II

DIED
June 11, 2002
Peckville, Pennsylvania

Stand on the Rhine

CHARLES P. MURRAY, JR.

FIRST LIEUTENANT, U.S. ARMY Company C, 30th Infantry, 3rd Infantry Division

BIOGRAPHY

BORN
September 26, 1921
Baltimore, Maryland

ENTERED SERVICE
Wilmington, North Carolina

BRANCH
U.S. Army

DUTY
World War II

CURRENT RESIDENCE
South Carolina

BECAUSE HE HAD ALREADY FINISHED THREE YEARS at the University of North Carolina when he was drafted into the Army in the fall of 1942, Charles Murray was selected for Officer Candidate School. He was commissioned a second lieutenant in the spring of 1943 and was sent to England in the summer of 1944 as a replacement officer. After landing on Omaha Beach several weeks after D-Day, he was assigned to the 3rd Infantry Division.

As the division fought through the Vosges mountains and reached the Rhine River at Strasbourg, Lieutenant Murray served as rifle platoon leader and company executive officer before he was put in command of the company. Early on the morning of December 16, Murray's battalion slipped through the outskirts of the town of Kaysersberg to occupy positions on a commanding hill to the south. Lieutenant Murray decided to accompany one of his platoons down a narrow, winding mountain trail leading to the valley below in an attempt to deny that route to the enemy.

Shortly after they set out, the lead scout stopped the column and called for Murray. He had spotted a large German force—later estimated at two hundred men—partially hidden in a sunken road at the bottom of the hill and in a position to move against the Americans above. Murray crawled to a vantage point from which he could see the exact location of the enemy and called in artillery. The first round was off target. He adjusted the range and was calling for another when his radio went dead. Using a borrowed rifle with a grenade launcher, he fired the platoon's supply of grenades down on the enemy. When the Germans responded with small-arms and mortar fire, he repeatedly fired a Browning automatic rifle from his

exposed spot on the trail, stopping a German truck that was pulling out from the enemy position.

When a mortar arrived from his company, Murray took over as gunner, firing until all the rounds were gone. With the Germans at this point in full retreat, he stood up, drew his pistol, and led the charge down the trail, yelling, "Okay, let's go!" Near the bottom, he came upon a German soldier dug into a position above the road. The soldier put up his hands as if to surrender but then threw a grenade, which knocked Murray down. Although wounded by shrapnel, he got to his feet, took the German prisoner, and continued down the trail. All that was left of the fleeing German force was its wounded. A company sergeant counted fifty German dead and reported that the truck Murray destroyed with the Browning had been carrying three heavy mortars.

After seeing that his troops were properly deployed to hold the position, Murray went back up the hill, turned his command over to his executive officer, and walked to the battalion aid station. He was hospitalized until after Christmas. Eager to get back to his men, he "borrowed" a uniform, hitched rides in U.S. vehicles, and rejoined them on the hill where he had left them.

Murray learned that he was to receive the Medal of Honor when his wife sent him a clipping from their hometown newspaper. General Geoffrey Keyes made the presentation on July 5, 1945, at the Salzburg airport. The entire fifteen-thousand-man 3rd Division, which had received a presidential citation, passed by the reviewing stand.

Charles Murray continued on active duty until his retirement as a colonel in 1973. His last combat duty was as an infantry brigade commander in Vietnam, where both of his sons also served.

Assault on Leyte

ROBERT B. NETT

FIRST LIEUTENANT, U.S. ARMY Company E, 305th Infantry, 77th Infantry Division

IN EARLY 1940, SEVENTEEN-YEAR-OLD ROBERT NETT, already in the Connecticut National Guard, petitioned to leave high school and go on active duty with the Army. The board of education gave him permission to leave school because he had sufficient credits to graduate with his class. He was sent to Camp Blanding, Florida.

In the spring of 1942, Nett was part of the 102nd Infantry, which became the first American unit sent to the South Pacific in anticipation of war with Japan. His battalion wound up on Christmas Island, part of the British Ellice Islands group. After eight and a half months there and serving as an acting platoon sergeant, he was recommended for Officer Candidate School. He returned to Fort Benning, Georgia. After graduating from OCS in 1942, he joined the 77th Infantry Division.

The 77th landed with the Marines on Guam in July 1944. Nett became company commander only two hours before the invasion when his captain was transferred to battalion headquarters. After Guam was secured, the 77th was ordered to New Hebrides, but the American assault on Leyte had suffered a setback and the ship that Nett was on was rerouted to the Philippines.

On the morning of December 14, a week after landing behind enemy lines, Nett's company attacked a Japanese battalion holding up an American advance into the heart of Leyte. As the assault wavered, Nett moved forward to lead the charge. The Japanese had concentrated their defense around a heavily fortified three-story municipal building flanked by bunkers constructed of coconut logs. Nett directed his soldiers to use bangalore torpedoes to make way for the advance, then ordered the heavy use of flamethrowers. As he was moving toward the objective, he and his men engaged in a fierce hand-to-hand struggle with the Japanese defenders. Nett shot five of them, and when his M-1 ran out of ammunition, he bayoneted two more.

As the Americans charged the building in a final assault, a rifle round grazed Nett's neck, just missing his jugular vein. He grabbed at the wound to stop the bleeding, and a medic bandaged him. Then a bullet hit him in the chest, collapsing a lung and blowing one of his ribs out through his back. Still, he continued to direct his troops until the building was secured, then moved his forces up to attack a road junction beyond the structure. He knew that he had lost too much blood to continue, so he turned his command over to one of his lieutenants and moved to the rear for medical aid.

Nett underwent several long operations in a field hospital, then was sent to Hawaii for two months of convalescence. When he returned to Leyte, he served as a courier carrying top secret maps of the planned Okinawa invasion, in which he also participated.

In January 1946, Nett was stationed at Fort Bragg, North Carolina, where he was informed that he was to receive the Medal of Honor from President Harry Truman in Nett's birthplace, New Haven, Connecticut. But when the President was called to San Francisco at the last moment to resolve a crisis threatening the founding of the United Nations, Lieutenant General Oscar Griswold presented the award on February 8, 1946, on the President's behalf.

Nett served in the Korean War as a company commander training South Korean soldiers and was later detailed as an inspector general. During the Vietnam War, he was an adviser to the Vietnamese 2nd Infantry Division and was awarded the Air Medal, the Bronze Star, and his second Combat Infantryman's Badge. He retired as a colonel in 1973.

BIOGRAPHY

BORN
June 13, 1922
New Haven, Connecticut

ENTERED SERVICE
New Haven, Connecticut

BRANCH
U.S. Army

DUTY
World War II

DIED
October 19, 2008
Columbus, Georgia

All the Points He Needed

NICHOLAS ORESKO

MASTER SERGEANT, U.S. ARMY Company C, 302nd Infantry, 94th Infantry Division

BIOGRAPHY

BORN
January 18, 1917
Bayonne, New Jersey

ENTERED SERVICE
Bayonne, New Jersey

BRANCH
U.S. Army

DUTY
World War II

CURRENT RESIDENCE
New Jersey

NICHOLAS ORESKO, A PLATOON LEADER WITH THE 302nd Infantry, landed in France in August 1944, two months after the Normandy invasion. There were still pockets of German troops in northern France that had been bypassed by the swift Allied advance after D-Day, and Master Sergeant Oresko's unit spent several weeks working to contain them. In December, his unit was suddenly rushed to support American troops that had been forced to retreat during the Battle of the Bulge.

In late January 1945, Oresko's company began to attack strong enemy positions near Tettington, Germany. For two days, the Americans tried to break through; each time, the assault stalled and they were pushed back. Then on the afternoon of January 23, the word came down to make another push. Pointing at the bunkers containing the German machine guns that had kept his unit pinned down in the freezing cold for a day, Oresko climbed out of his trench and yelled, "Okay, let's go!" None of his men moved. "Let's go!" he yelled again as he started forward. Still there was no movement behind him; by this time he was running alone through the heavy snow. He mumbled a prayer to himself: Lord, I know I'm going to die. Please just make it fast.

Automatic-weapons fire was crackling all around him. To his amazement, he covered the fifty feet to the first German gun position without getting hit. He tossed a grenade into the log bunker; after it exploded, he rushed in, shooting point-blank with his rifle and killing all the soldiers manning the position. Then the second German gun started firing on him, wounding him in the hip and knocking him down. While the gun continued to fire, he realized that because he was at the base of the bunker, below the gun slit, the gunners couldn't see him. As he crawled forward, his hand touched a wire hidden in the snow; he rolled into a shallow hole just as a booby trap went off close by.

By this time, Oresko was directly below the German machine gun, which continued firing over his head at his men. He reached inside his jacket for grenades, but there weren't any there—he had lost them in the snow. He crawled back to retrieve them, then headed back to the gun. He pulled the pin on one of the grenades, counted to four, and tossed it into the bunker. As it exploded, he followed it in, wiping out all the soldiers inside with his rifle. In all, he killed twelve Germans and cleared the way for his company to go back on the offensive.

The position secured, Oresko allowed medics to evacuate him to a field hospital. After weeks behind the lines in a French hospital, he returned to limited duty. In early August, he was told by his commanding officer that he was going home. "I don't have enough points," Oresko said, referring to the formula that determined who was eligible to return to the States. The officer explained that Oresko would be receiving the Medal of Honor, and that was all the points he needed. President Harry Truman presented the medal to him at the White House on October 12, 1945.

GUADALCANAL, WESTERN PACIFIC, 1942

Tripping Up the Enemy

MITCHELL PAIGE

PLATOON SERGEANT, U.S. MARINE CORPS 2nd Battalion, 7th Marines, 1st Marine Division

BIOGRAPHY

BORN
August 31, 1918
Charleroi, Pennsylvania

ENTERED SERVICE
Pennsylvania

BRANCH
U.S. Marine Corps

DUTY
World War II

DIED
November 15, 2003
Palm Desert, California

AS A BOY IN CHARLEROI, PENNSYLVANIA, MITCHELL Paige always looked forward to the annual Armistice Day parade, watching the veterans of World War I march down the town's main street. He particularly liked Marines in their snappy uniforms. On his eighteenth birthday, he walked two hundred miles to Baltimore to enlist in the Marine Corps.

He was sent to the Philippines in 1937 and transferred to China a year later; the Chinese-Japanese war was already under way. Assigned to the American embassy in Peking, he worked as an armed guard on the train bringing supplies from Shanghai. At stops throughout the war-torn countryside, he watched in horror as Japanese soldiers killed Chinese civilians.

Paige left China in 1940 to become a charter member of the 1st Marine Division, which was activated in Guantánamo, Cuba, in 1941. In the fall of 1942, his machine-gun platoon took part in the invasion of Guadalcanal. The Marines seized Henderson Field, a key landing strip for its planes, but the Japanese held the rest of the island. On October 24, Paige's battalion made a forced march to defend the field against an estimated 2,500 enemy troops about to attack. The battalion arrived in the dark, in a driving rainstorm, under heavy artillery fire. Sergeant Paige crawled to the perimeter of the American lines and set up his four water-cooled .30-caliber machine guns, establishing fields of fire to protect two rifle companies on his left and right. Then he crawled out to string a trip wire about ten feet in front of the guns, hooked empty C ration cans on it, and put an empty cartridge in each one.

In the darkness of the morning of October 26, he heard the cartridges rattling in the C ration cans and ordered his men to open fire. The blaze from the barrels of the machine guns illuminated scenes of close combat as the Japanese advanced into the Marines' guns. During the hand-to-hand struggle, a Japanese soldier thrust his bayonet at Paige's head. As Paige threw up his left hand to block it, the blade cut deeply, almost severing his fingers. He pulled his Marine-issue knife out of his belt and drove it into the soldier's neck.

In the chaos, the two Marine rifle companies behind Paige's platoon pulled back, leaving him and his thirty-three men to hold the line. Over the next few hours, the Japanese charged repeatedly. All of Paige's men became casualties, falling at their weapons. Paige continued to swivel his gun to shoot Japanese as they passed through his position in the dark.

By dawn, Paige was the only Marine from his platoon left alive. With the Japanese massing for a final attack, he yelled at the Marines in the rifle companies to his right rear, "Fix bayonets and follow me!" Then, unclamping the machine gun and cradling it in his left arm with two cartridge belts looped over his shoulder, he charged down the hill, firing from the hip. A Japanese officer and his guards stood up in the grass below. As Paige shot the guards, the officer emptied his pistol at him, then pulled out his samurai sword and prepared to charge. Paige cut him down. The Japanese retreated, and Paige sat down for the first time in ten hours.

After Guadalcanal was secured, Paige was sent to Australia and made a lieutenant. On May 21, 1943, he was presented with the Medal of Honor by Major General Alexander Vandergrift. Afterward, he walked through Melbourne until he found a shopkeeper who would help him pack his medal in a cigar box so he could mail it to his parents for safekeeping.

Hand-to-Hand Struggle

EVERETT P. POPE
CAPTAIN, U.S. MARINE CORPS Company C, 1st Battalion, 1st Marines, 1st Marine Division

EVERETT POPE ENLISTED IN THE MARINES RIGHT after graduating from Bowdoin College in 1941. He went through officer's training and fought as a lieutenant at Guadalcanal with the 1st Marines. By September 1944, he was a captain in command of a Marine company.

On September 15, his unit landed on Peleliu in the western Pacific. The Japanese had constructed an elaborate network of caves in the interior of the coral reef, and the fighting was costly—the Marines suffered casualty rates of up to 70 percent, among the highest in their history. On the afternoon of September 19, after four days of constant fighting, Pope's company was ordered to assault a steep, barren coral hill known as Hill 154. Though his men were disorganized by enemy cannon fire and suffered heavy casualties, Captain Pope rallied them and led them to the summit of the hill in the face of machine-gun, mortar, and sniper fire.

But once there, they were cut off from the rest of the battalion and outnumbered by the enemy. With his line of defense amounting to no more than a handful of able-bodied men, Pope had to hold the position through the night. First the enemy tried to infiltrate small bands of soldiers. When Pope and his men fought them off, the Japanese command sent groups of twenty to twenty-five. The Americans continued to fight them off. Running out of ammunition—they were so low on grenades that they alternated throwing rocks so the Japanese wouldn't know which was which—Pope and his men fought hand to hand. As the sun rose, they were defending themselves by hurling rocks and ammunition boxes, and by fighting with fists and throwing the enemy off the cliffs. When the

attacks intensified during the morning, Pope was finally ordered to withdraw.

Pope had brought 235 men ashore at Peleliu. After four days of fighting, only 90 of them were battle-ready and able to assault Hill 154. Of those, only 8 walked down the hill with him on September 20. It was another thirteen days before the Marines were able to return to bury their dead.

In the spring of 1945, Everett Pope was ordered to the White House to receive the Medal of Honor. His citation had been signed by President Franklin D. Roosevelt at Warm Springs the day before his death; President Harry Truman presented the medal to him at the White House on June 15, 1945.

Pope was later sent to Yale University for an intensive course in Japanese in preparation for the invasion of Japan. But the attacks on Hiroshima and Nagasaki made the invasion unnecessary.

BIOGRAPHY

BORN
July 16, 1919
Milton, Massachusetts

ENTERED SERVICE
Massachusetts

BRANCH
U.S. Marine Corps

DUTY
World War II

DIED
July 16, 2009
Bath, Maine

Out Front Under Fire

WILBURN K. ROSS

PRIVATE, U.S. ARMY Company G, 30th Infantry, 3rd Infantry Division

BIOGRAPHY

BORN
May 12, 1922
Strunk, Kentucky

ENTERED SERVICE
Strunk, Kentucky

BRANCH
U.S. Army

DUTY
World War II

CURRENT RESIDENCE
Washington State

GROWING UP IN THE SMALL KENTUCKY TOWN OF Strunk, Wilburn K. Ross decided that he didn't want to spend his life working in the local coal mines, so he studied welding. He was twenty years old and working in the naval shipyards in Norfolk, Virginia, in the fall of 1942 when his draft notice arrived. He opened it with the feeling that "destiny had come calling."

From the beginning, enemy fire had a way of finding Ross. He was hit by shrapnel in his arms and chest in his first action when the 30th Infantry landed in Sicily in July 1943. Following the invasion of Salerno two months later, Private Ross was firing on an enemy position when a large piece of shrapnel smashed into his helmet, leaving him unconscious for several hours. After the Anzio landing in January 1944, he became separated from his platoon during a nighttime maneuver and spent four days wandering alone in the snowy countryside behind enemy lines before finally limping into an American position on badly frozen feet. In mid-August 1944, after the 30th had landed at Marseille and started up through southwestern France, a piece of shrapnel hit Private Ross in the cheek, taking out two teeth.

He was back with his undermanned company on October 30, when it attacked an entrenched German position near the small French town of Saint-Jacques. Soon, more than half of the eighty-eight GIs were dead and the rest were pinned down. With enemy shells kicking dirt into his eyes, Private Ross manned a light machine gun at the head of the American position. Over the next five hours, he single-handedly halted repeated German attempts to overrun his unit.

With their ammunition exhausted and the enemy gathering for a final charge, Ross and the eight riflemen fighting with him fixed their bayonets and prepared to make a last stand. Just then, fresh ammunition arrived for the machine gun and Ross began firing again, forcing the Germans to withdraw for good. As he paused to catch his breath, he was told that he had just killed forty of the enemy and wounded many others.

Private Ross returned from a brief liberty in Belgium to find that he had been recommended for the Medal of Honor. It was awarded to him six months later, on April 23, 1945, by General Alexander Patch, commander of the U.S. Seventh Army, at a ceremony at Nuremberg's Zeppelinfeld stadium, once the site of huge Hitler Youth rallies. Afterward, Army engineers blew up the large swastika decorating the structure.

Wilburn K. Ross remained in the Army for the next twenty years. He was badly wounded in Korea and retired as a master sergeant in 1964.

"The Sight-Seeing Sixth"

DONALD E. RUDOLPH

TECHNICAL SERGEANT, U.S. ARMY Company E, 20th Infantry, 6th Infantry Division

BIOGRAPHY

BORN
February 21, 1921
South Haven, Minnesota

ENTERED SERVICE
Minneapolis, Minnesota

BRANCH
U.S. Army

DUTY
World War II

DIED
May 25, 2006
Bovey, Minnesota

IN FEBRUARY 1941, DONALD RUDOLPH VOLUNTEERED with the 6th Infantry Division—known as "the Sight-Seeing Sixth" because it had marched to several battles in World War I only to find the fighting over before it arrived. Rudolph thought he had enlisted for a year, but Pearl Harbor made it indefinite. The 6th trained in Yuma, Arizona, for desert fighting in North Africa. Then orders changed, and the division began training for jungle fighting in the Pacific.

Rudolph's unit saw action in New Guinea. Then came the Philippines. By this time a technical sergeant, Rudolph had seen so much combat on the island of Luzon in late 1944 that he was taken off the front lines. But while tending the wounded, he saw several GIs from his unit and returned to the front lines, without waiting for orders, to be with his men.

On February 3, 1945, he took over the unit after the platoon leader was evacuated. Two days later, the unit was raked by fire from enemy troops dug into well-fortified positions in an area that wasn't thought to be strongly defended. Kneeling down to administer first aid to one of his men, Technical Sergeant Rudolph noticed that some of the heaviest enemy fire was coming from a nearby culvert. He crawled to it and with his rifle and grenades killed three Japanese soldiers hidden there.

Then he began to work his way toward a line of enemy pillboxes that had another company pinned down. He ripped an opening in the tin roof of the first one and dropped in a grenade, killing the Japanese gunners inside. Advancing on the second pillbox, he knocked a hole in its roof with a discarded Japanese pickax, then tossed in a grenade and fired in several rifle rounds, killing the enemy inside.

In quick succession, Rudolph attacked and neutralized six more enemy pillboxes. His men, now able to advance, soon came under attack by a Japanese tank. Rudolph worked his way to the tank, climbed onto it, and dropped a white phosphorus grenade through the turret, killing the crew inside.

This action cleared the way for an advance that culminated in a decisive victory. A few weeks later, an enemy artillery shell hit the unit's position in Luzon. Rudolph was wounded in the back by shrapnel, and a piece struck him from the side, entering his nose and lodging under his eye. After being hospitalized for several weeks and released, he was informed that he had been recommended for a medal and was being taken out of hazardous duty. He served as a military policeman for a few weeks, then discovered that it was the Medal of Honor he was being given. President Harry Truman awarded it to him on August 23, 1945, in the East Room of the White House.

The Pillbox Defense

ALEJANDRO R. RUIZ

PRIVATE FIRST CLASS, U.S. ARMY 165th Infantry, 27th Infantry Division

BIOGRAPHY

BORN
June 26, 1924
Loving, New Mexico

ENTERED SERVICE
Carlsbad, New Mexico

BRANCH
U.S. Army

DUTY
World War II

DIED
November 20, 2009
Emeryville, California

ALEJANDRO RENTERIA RUIZ WAS BORN AND RAISED in New Mexico, the son of a Mexican immigrant who had been an officer in Pancho Villa's army. In 1944, twenty-year-old Ruiz was driving to Texas to see his girlfriend when he got into a legal scrape. He went before a judge, who gave him a choice between the Army and jail. Ruiz enlisted.

After training at Fort Bliss and Fort Ord, Private First Class Ruiz shipped out with the 165th Infantry. His unit landed on Okinawa in April 1945. On April 28, his company, exhausted from a series of engagements with Japanese troops in heavily fortified positions, was moving down into a deep ravine. The Japanese let his unit pass by a well-camouflaged pillbox before opening fire and lobbing grenades. As the Americans tried to find cover while Japanese grenades rained down on them, Ruiz saw his comrades falling all around him; after just a few minutes, only he and his squad leader had escaped injury.

Knowing that he needed more firepower than his rifle could offer, Ruiz grabbed a Browning automatic rifle and moved toward the pillbox. As he started to climb on top of it so he could open fire, the weapon jammed. At that moment, a Japanese soldier charged him; Ruiz clubbed him down, then tossed the rifle aside and ran back through the heavy fire to where his men were pinned down. Picking up another automatic rifle and grabbing some extra cans of ammunition, he headed back toward the pillbox while the Japanese machine gunners and riflemen were all concentrating their fire on him. Making it through the storm of bullets and grenades, he once again climbed on top of the emplacement and sent several bursts of fire

through the aperture, killing the twelve soldiers inside and destroying the position.

Unscathed except for a minor flesh wound in the leg, Ruiz found a place to sit down after the battle and tried to light a cigarette with shaking hands. The men he had saved told him they were going to recommend him for the Medal of Honor. Ruiz didn't think about it for the next several weeks as his unit continued the fight on Okinawa. It wasn't until May 1946, when he was back in the United States, living in the married soldiers' barracks, that he was told he was indeed to receive the medal. Ruiz's wife, mother, and sister accompanied him to the White House, where President Harry Truman made the presentation on June 12, 1946.

Ruiz remained in the service for the next eighteen years. He saw action again in Korea and retired as a sergeant in 1964.

Justice for a Japanese American

GEORGE T. SAKATO

PRIVATE, U.S. ARMY Company E, 442nd Regimental Combat Team

IN 1942, GEORGE SAKATO'S FAMILY MOVED FROM California to Arizona, to avoid being sent to an internment camp for Japanese Americans. The twenty-one-year-old Sakato tried to enlist in the Army Air Corps but was rejected because of his draft status—4-C, undesirable alien. Then in 1943, because of the exploits of Japanese Americans in the Hawaiian National Guard's 100th Infantry Battalion in battles at Salerno, Monte Cassino, and Anzio, the government allowed other Japanese Americans in the service. Sakato enlisted in the Army, joining his older brother, Henry, who had volunteered before Pearl Harbor. After finishing basic training in the summer of 1944, the brothers were sent to Naples as replacements for the "Go for Broke" Nisei 442nd Regimental Combat Team, which became the most decorated American unit in the war.

In August, the 442nd boarded ships for a landing at Marseille. For the next two months, Sakato's unit fought its way north through France. In late October, it attacked the Germans around the town of Biffontaine, an area near the German border that was too mountainous for armor. Its objective, Hill 617, overlooked an open valley cut in half by the railroad line running from Strasbourg to Paris. The Germans were entrenched at the top of the hill, firing down on the American troops trying to mount an assault.

Just before midnight on October 28, Private Sakato's company was ordered to flank the Germans and get behind their position. It was so dark that each GI had to hold on to the back strap of the man in front of him while moving forward. At dawn, the Americans attacked, Sakato leading the assault. With a Thompson submachine gun he had scavenged from a disabled tank, he killed five German soldiers.

Sakato's platoon secured the hill and sent prisoners back down to the Americans below. Then the Germans counterattacked; one of his close friends was hit and died in his arms. Seeking vengeance, Sakato took charge of the squad, fighting with an enemy rifle and pistol he picked up from the battlefield after his tommy gun ran out of ammunition. He killed another seven Germans and led his platoon in capturing thirty-four more. His unit held its position until it was relieved.

A few days later, the 442nd attempted to break through the Germans' encirclement of a battalion of the 141st Infantry Regiment, known as the Lost Battalion. The Japanese-American unit suffered more than 800 casualties in rescuing the 211 trapped GIs. During the battle, Sakato was knocked down by a mortar shell; the bulky winter overcoat he was carrying in his pack kept him from being killed by the shrapnel that struck his spine and lungs.

Sakato was hospitalized for eight months. He heard that he had been recommended for the Medal of Honor, but the decoration he received was the Distinguished Service Cross. He didn't think anything more about it until the morning fifty-five years later when he received a call from the Pentagon. His award was being upgraded to the Medal of Honor as the result of a review of the records of Asian-American soldiers who had received the DSC. He was presented with the medal by President Bill Clinton on June 21, 2000.

BIOGRAPHY

BORN
February 19, 1921
Colton, California

ENTERED SERVICE
Fort Douglas, Utah

BRANCH
U.S. Army

DUTY
World War II

CURRENT RESIDENCE
Colorado

Taking the Impact

RICHARD K. SORENSON

PRIVATE, U.S. MARINE CORPS 4th Marine Division

BIOGRAPHY

BORN
August 28, 1924
Anoka, Minnesota

ENTERED SERVICE
Minnesota

BRANCH
U.S. Marine Corps

DUTY
World War II

DIED
October 9, 2004
Reno, Nevada

ON DECEMBER 8, 1941, RICHARD SORENSON TRIED unsuccessfully to enlist in the Navy. He was only seventeen, and his parents refused to give permission. He finished his junior year in high school, but the next fall, the day after football season ended, he and some of his teammates joined the Marine Corps.

He trained at Camp Pendleton in 1943 with the 4th Marine Division. In January 1944, the unit sailed from San Diego and went directly into combat in the Marshall Islands. Sorenson was in a machine-gun squad in an assault battalion that landed on Namur, a small island in the Kwajalein atoll. It was defended by four thousand Japanese soldiers fighting from heavy concrete fortifications.

On February 1, the first day of the invasion, the Marines took over half of Namur, destroying enemy pillboxes by getting close enough to hurl satchel charges into their narrow gun slits. Sorenson's unit was in the forefront of the action. When night fell, he and thirty-five other men took cover behind the concrete foundation of a Japanese building the Marines had blown up that day. They didn't know that the rest of the American troops, who had no idea of the squad's whereabouts, had withdrawn to a more secure defensive line.

At dawn the next morning, the Japanese attacked Sorenson's position in what he later called a "full-fledged banzai charge." His squad had been fighting for its life for half an hour when a Japanese soldier got close enough to throw a grenade in their midst. Sorenson's first impulse was to jump to the other side of the concrete foundation, but he instantly realized that his buddies would take the impact and that the entire squad would be overrun, so he threw himself on the grenade and took the full force of the explosion.

He would have bled to death if a corpsman hadn't come up and quickly treated him, tying off a severed artery, spreading sulfa over his wounds, and giving him a shot of morphine. When he awoke an hour later, the rest of the Marine force had reached the squad and relieved it. As he was being carried back to a Higgins boat to be evacuated, one of the stretcher bearers was killed by a Japanese sniper.

Sorenson underwent six operations over the next nine months. He was convalescing in the Seattle Naval Hospital in mid-1944 when Captain Joel Boone, commanding officer of the hospital—himself a recipient of the Medal of Honor during World War I for crawling into the no-man's-land between the trenches to treat fallen Marines—told him he was to receive the medal. It was presented to him by General Joseph Fegan on July 19, 1944, in front of all the other applauding patients, doctors, and nurses.

Wildcat Defense

JAMES E. SWETT

FIRST LIEUTENANT, U.S. MARINE CORPS Marine Fighting Squadron 221,
Marine Aircraft Group 12, 1st Marine Aircraft Wing

BIOGRAPHY

BORN
June 15, 1920
Seattle, Washington

ENTERED SERVICE
California

BRANCH
U.S. Marine Corps

DUTY
World War II

DIED
January 20, 2009
Redding, California

JAMES SWETT LEARNED TO FLY IN JUNIOR COLLEGE in San Mateo, California, and graduated from the Civilian Pilot Training Program just before Pearl Harbor with 450 hours in the air. He enlisted in the Navy and became an aviation cadet, but when he was halfway through the program, one of his officers persuaded him to become a Marine Corps pilot.

Lieutenant Swett landed on Guadalcanal, in the Solomon Islands, in the spring of 1943 as part of Marine Fighting Squadron 221. He had not yet been in combat on the morning of April 7 when he led a squadron of Grumman Wildcats on routine dawn patrol. Upon landing to refuel, he learned that Japanese admiral Isoroku Yamamoto had ordered a major strike against Guadalcanal. In all, 76 American planes would have to defend against a wave of 150 Japanese bombers and fighter escorts.

Swett's Wildcats immediately got back in the air and engaged a formation of twenty Japanese dive-bombers that were readying an attack on American ships below. In the intense action of the next few minutes, always wondering if the Zeros above would pounce on him and the other Wildcats, Swett shot down seven of the dive-bombers. He was going for an eighth when the friendly fire of American antiaircraft guns below punched a hole in his wing. Low on ammunition, he drew close to the Japanese plane from behind. As the rear gunner in the dive-bomber fired on him, hitting his engine and shattering his windscreen, Swett fired his last few rounds, killing the gunner and setting the plane on fire. In this single combat mission lasting little more than fifteen minutes, he had become an ace. (He would go on to down eight more Japanese aircraft during his combat tour in the Solomons.)

Swett's Wildcat lost altitude rapidly. Too low to bail out, he crash-landed hard in the ocean and jumped out into the water as the plane began to sink. He was worried that the blood from his broken nose would attract sharks, but a Coast Guard picket boat soon spotted him and came alongside. "Are you an American?" one of the sailors yelled. "Damn right!" he yelled back.

For his actions on that memorable day of April 7, Lieutenant Swett received the Medal of Honor on October 10, 1943, from Major General Ralph Mitchell in a brief ceremony on an airstrip on Espíritu Santo Island, New Hebrides. In the spring of 1944, he was flown to Washington to meet President Franklin D. Roosevelt, who said to him, "Many hearty congratulations, son."

Swett spent the next several weeks training a new squadron of F4U Corsair fighter pilots, then returned to the Pacific and was stationed aboard the USS *Bunker Hill* as a carrier pilot. On May 11, 1945, as he was flying above the *Bunker Hill*, two kamikazes scored direct hits on the carrier, making it impossible for him to land. After putting down dye markers to aid in the rescue of the sailors who jumped overboard, he rallied the two dozen planes in the area and led them to the USS *Enterprise*, where they landed safely.

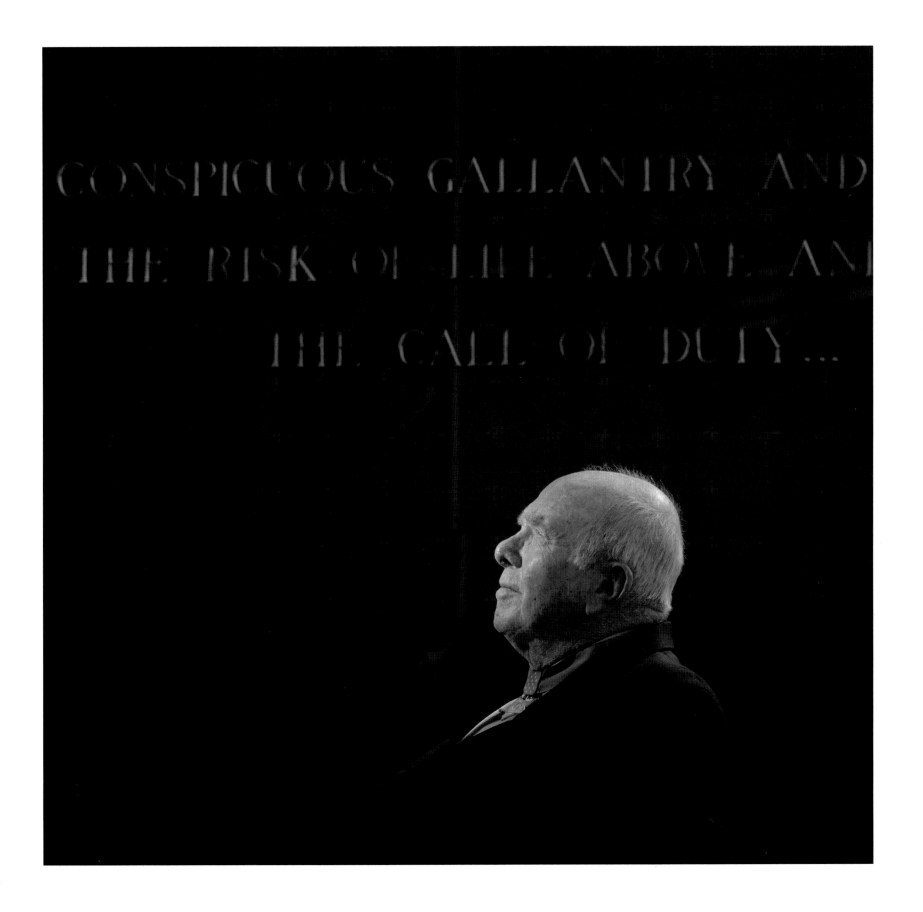

His Own Catch-22

GEORGE E. WAHLEN

PHARMACIST'S MATE SECOND CLASS, U.S. NAVY 2nd Battalion, 26th Marines, 5th Marine Division

BIOGRAPHY

BORN
August 8, 1924
Ogden, Utah

ENTERED SERVICE
Utah

BRANCH
U.S. Navy

DUTY
World War II

DIED
June 5, 2009
Roy, Utah

GEORGE WAHLEN STARTED HIS NAVY SERVICE WITH his own version of catch-22: Having volunteered in 1943 in hopes of becoming an aircraft mechanic, he was selected for medical corpsman training instead. When he protested, his commanding officer hinted that if he did well in his medical training, he might yet realize his ambition to work on planes. So he worked hard and finished near the top of his group—but when he again brought up the possibility of becoming a mechanic, he was told that the Navy couldn't afford to lose its best corpsman. He was attached to a Marine battalion as a pharmacist's mate second class.

In 1944, his unit boarded a ship for Guam. After the ship was under way, the top brass decided the unit wouldn't be needed in that battle, so it was shipped back to Hawaii, where Wahlen trained for another six months. In February 1945, his division headed for Iwo Jima.

As he was going ashore on February 19, Wahlen, not a religious man, found himself praying, "Please help me not let one of my buddies down; please help me do my job." Over the next few days, his unit was in constant action. On February 26, he was treating a wounded Marine when an enemy grenade exploded nearby and sent shrapnel into his face, temporarily blinding him in one eye. Refusing treatment, he continued to do his work in the midst of intense fighting. In one instance, he ran through fierce fire to carry a wounded Marine to safety on his back. In another, when an adjacent platoon lost its corpsman, he rushed through heavy mortar fire to take care of its wounded as well, treating fourteen casualties before returning to his own unit.

On March 2, Wahlen was wounded again, this time in the back. Again he refused evacuation. The next day, he moved out with his company in an assault that took him over more than six hundred yards of open terrain in the face of Japanese fire. He was hit in the leg; unable to walk, he crawled fifty yards to administer first aid to another fallen Marine.

Of the 240 men in Wahlen's company, only 5 came through the Battle of Iwo Jima without being wounded or killed. Counting replacements brought up during the fighting, the company suffered a 125 percent casualty rate.

Wahlen was taken back to Guam on a hospital ship, then to Hawaii, and finally to Camp Pendleton, where he was hospitalized until his release from the Navy in December 1945. While at Pendleton, he received two Navy Crosses and was ordered to go to Washington to receive the Medal of Honor. President Harry Truman made the presentation on October 5, 1945. "Well," he said to Wahlen with a smile, "I'm sure glad a pill pusher finally made it up here."

In 1948, Wahlen enlisted in the Army as a medical technician. He became an officer, served in the Korean and Vietnam wars, and retired as a major in 1968.

MEMORIAL STADIUM

ERECTED BY THE
CITY OF BALTIMORE
1954

DEDICATED BY

THE MAYOR AND THE CITY COUNCIL
AND THE PEOPLE OF BALTIMORE CITY
IN THE STATE OF MARYLAND

AS A MEMORIAL TO ALL
WHO SO VALIANTLY FOUGHT
AND SERVED IN THE WORLD
WARS WITH ETERNAL
GRATITUDE TO THOSE WHO
MADE THE SUPREME
SACRIFICE TO PRESERVE
EQUALITY AND FREEDOM
THROUGHOUT THE WORLD

TIME WILL NOT DIM THE GLORY OF THEIR DEEDS

At the Battle of the Bulge

PAUL J. WIEDORFER

PRIVATE, U.S. ARMY Company G, 318th Infantry, 80th Infantry Division

WORKING IN THE WAR INDUSTRIES GAVE PAUL Wiedorfer an automatic deferment until 1943, when he was drafted. The following year, he was in Europe with the 80th Infantry. After fighting through France and into Belgium, his battalion was taken out of combat and put on "corps reserve." But the rest wasn't for long—when the Battle of the Bulge began, his unit was loaded onto trucks and sent to the front. They were on the way to relieve the garrison at Bastogne when American troops, mistaking them for Germans, opened fire on them. Wiedorfer's commanding officer had to drape their vehicles with white sheets to convince the Americans to cease firing.

At around noon on Christmas Day 1944, Wiedorfer's company was near Chaumont, Belgium, clearing a wooded area of enemy snipers. The day was cloudless and very cold; the three-inch snowfall from the previous night had turned to ice. One of the platoons was crossing an open area when two German machine guns, flanked by riflemen, opened fire from dug-in positions. The Americans scrambled for cover behind a small ridge.

Afraid that his immobilized buddies would be cut to pieces, Private Wiedorfer stood up and charged the enemy. Slipping repeatedly on the frozen ground until he got to within a few yards of the first machine-gun nest, he tossed a grenade in, then shot the three enemy soldiers manning it. He continued to fight his way through the snow, crouching as he ran toward the second position, all the while sensing and hearing the shells from the small-arms fire the Germans were concentrating on him. He counted it a miracle that he wasn't hit. When the grenade he threw at the second enemy position killed one soldier, six others stood up

and surrendered to him. By this point, the pinned-down American platoon was able to get up and advance with the rest of the company.

Private Wiedorfer's platoon leader had been killed several days earlier; when his sergeant was also killed in this action, he took over and led the unit for the next several weeks. In early February 1945, fighting on German soil, he was hit during a mortar attack. Although the body of a GI, killed instantly near him, stopped some of the shrapnel, Wiedorfer was struck by fragments in the stomach and in both legs. His left leg was broken; his right hand was shot through. He was evacuated to England, where he was treated for two months, then sent home, where he was hospitalized at Walter Reed for the next two and a half years. One morning, a sergeant in the bed next to him, reading the GI newspaper *Stars and Stripes,* said, "Hey, Paul, what's your last name?" Wiedorfer spelled it for him. The sergeant looked up. "Hell, you got the Medal of Honor, man!"

Wiedorfer thought someone would just come by his hospital bed to hand the medal to him. But by the time Brigadier General E. F. Koening, the commanding officer of the hospital, arrived to make the presentation on May 29, 1945, he was surrounded by hundreds of people—officers, nurses, and a full military band.

BIOGRAPHY

BORN
January 17, 1921
Baltimore, Maryland

ENTERED SERVICE
Baltimore, Maryland

BRANCH
U.S. Army

DUTY
World War II

DIED
May 25, 2011
Baltimore, Maryland

Caretaker

HERSHEL W. WILLIAMS

CORPORAL, U.S. MARINE CORPS 21st Marines, 3rd Marine Division

BIOGRAPHY

BORN
October 2, 1923
Quiet Dell,
West Virginia

ENTERED SERVICE
West Virginia

BRANCH
U.S. Marine Corps

DUTY
World War II

CURRENT RESIDENCE
West Virginia

THE FIRST TIME THE FIVE-FOOT-SIX, NINETEEN- year-old Hershel "Woody" Williams tried to join the Marines, in the fall of 1942, he was too short. The second time he tried, a few months later, he wasn't: The Corps had relaxed its height requirements. He immediately enlisted. He was sent to the Pacific with the 3rd Marine Division and placed in a flamethrower/ demolition unit.

Williams took part in the invasion of Guam, which seemed horrific—until he was sent to Iwo Jima the following year. The beach area in Guam was clear and relatively undefended, and the Marines could advance into the jungle. At Iwo, all the jungle cover had been blown away, and the beach became a slaughterhouse.

His company was supposed to hit the beach on February 20, 1945, but there were so many Marines stuck on the beachhead that there was no place for them. They finally landed the next day, even though the Marines were still backed up, unable to advance. The island's volcanic ash was so porous that it was impossible to dig foxholes or create cover, and the Americans, exposed to enemy fire, were taking huge casualties. Williams's unit had landed with six flamethrower men and had lost them all in two days without advancing more than fifty yards. Morale was plummeting.

On February 23, Williams suddenly heard Marines shouting and firing their weapons in the air. Looking up, he saw that the American flag had been raised on Mount Suribachi. Spurred on by the sight, his company surged forward and finally advanced, crossing the first airfield and assaulting the enemy.

The Japanese defenses were organized around pillboxes of reinforced concrete arranged in pods of three, connected by a system of tunnels. Acting

Sergeant Williams saw the American tanks wallowing impotently in the soft volcanic sand. With covering fire from four riflemen, he strapped on a flamethrower and went after the pillboxes. Over the next four hours, he moved through intense enemy fire to assault one Japanese position after another. He climbed on top of one pillbox and stuck the nozzle of his flamethrower through the air vent, killing the soldiers inside and silencing the machine gun. When enemy soldiers from another pillbox fixed their bayonets and charged him, he killed them all with a burst of flame from his weapon. He repeatedly returned to his own lines to get new flamethrowers or pick up satchel charges, which he tossed into the pillboxes he had disabled. Finally, an opening in the Japanese lines was created, enabling the Marines to advance.

When Williams's company was taken off the line a week and a half later, only 17 of the 279 men who had hit the beach with the company had not been killed or wounded.

After the battle of Iwo Jima, Williams went back to Guam as part of the Marine force training for the invasion of Japan, which was unnecessary after the bombing of Hiroshima and Nagasaki. On October 5, 1945, he was ordered to Washington to receive the Medal of Honor. The moment President Harry Truman placed it around his neck, he resolved to consider himself the medal's caretaker for the Marines who didn't come home from Iwo Jima.

Hershel Williams later became active in his church as a lay minister. He served his fellow recipients and their loved ones as chaplain for many years. He is now chaplain emeritus of the Congressional Medal of Honor Society.

Top Marine

LOUIS H. WILSON

CAPTAIN, U.S. MARINE CORPS 2nd Battalion, 9th Marines, 3rd Marine Division

BIOGRAPHY

BORN
February 11, 1920
Brandon, Mississippi

ENTERED SERVICE
Mississippi

BRANCH
U.S. Marine Corps

DUTY
World War II

DIED
June 21, 2005
Birmingham, Alabama

LOUIS WILSON ENLISTED IN THE MARINE CORPS IN May 1941 after graduating from college. Commissioned as a second lieutenant after Officer Candidate School, he went to the South Pacific with the 9th Marines early in 1943 and first saw action on Bougainville as a captain in command of a rifle company.

After leading his men through the jungle fighting on Guadalcanal, Captain Wilson brought his company ashore on Guam, where they took heavy casualties in the first day of fighting. On July 25, 1944, Wilson was ordered to assault a large hill, the site of a Japanese command post. He led his Marines into heavy machine-gun and mortar fire, bringing down Japanese snipers himself. After pushing over rugged terrain and reaching the top of the hill, he took command of other units whose officers had been killed and set up a defensive position. Though he was wounded three times over the next five hours, he didn't seek treatment until he had organized his men for the night.

Soon after dark, the Japanese began a series of counterattacks. With flares lighting up the night sky, the enemy charged with fixed bayonets. Wilson left his command post and urged his men to repel them, exposing himself to fire from the enemy that at times was only a few feet away. At one point, he saw a wounded Marine who had been left outside the American lines and ran fifty yards to pick him up and carry him back.

Over the next ten hours, the Marines fought hand to hand, bayoneting the enemy and knocking them to the ground, where they stabbed them with knives. Wilson was beside his men all this time, firing his carbine and using it as a club. Though half the company was killed or wounded, the Marines were

still in control of the hill at dawn. Seeing that the remaining Japanese had congregated in an area down the hill, Wilson led seventeen of his men in an attack. He and four others survived the vicious machine-gun fire to finally take the position, killing all the Japanese soldiers there. In the two-day battle, the Marines killed 350 of the enemy.

Wilson was evacuated the next day and hospitalized for three months. On October 5, 1945, President Harry Truman presented him with the Medal of Honor.

Louis Wilson fought in Korea and Vietnam and held a series of prestigious positions during his distinguished career, including assistant chief of staff of the 1st Marine Division in Vietnam; commander of the Marine Amphibious Force on Okinawa; commander of the Fleet Marine Force, Pacific; and finally commandant of the Marine Corps from 1975 until his retirement in 1979. He was the fourth Marine commandant to have earned the Medal of Honor.

A Team of Heroes

JAY ZEAMER, JR.

CAPTAIN, U.S. ARMY AIR CORPS 65th Bombardment Squadron, 43rd Bomb Group (Heavy)

BIOGRAPHY

BORN
July 25, 1918
Carlisle, Pennsylvania

ENTERED SERVICE
Machias, Maine

BRANCH
U.S. Army

DUTY
World War II

DIED
March 22, 2007
Boothbay Harbor, Maine

JAY ZEAMER WAS ALREADY A SECOND LIEUTENANT IN the Army Reserve in 1939 when he took flight training as part of the Army Air Corps. After earning his wings early in 1941, he served as a pilot with the 19th Bomb Squadron at Langley Field, Virginia, and finished a degree in civil engineering at the Massachusetts Institute of Technology at the same time.

Zeamer was sent to the Pacific in October 1942, promoted to captain, and began flying reconnaissance bombers as part of the 43rd Bomb Group. He already had forty-seven missions under his belt when his B-17, called "Lucy," took off from Port Moresby, New Guinea, on June 16, 1943, and headed for Buka, a small island near Bougainville in the Solomon Islands. His orders were to photograph Japanese operations on Buka, then map the coastline of Bougainville in preparation for an American offensive planned for the fall. Zeamer had never encountered significant opposition in his other reconnaissance flights—although he had modified his plane to give it extra firepower by replacing all the .30-caliber guns with .50s. Army Air Force intelligence believed that there were no opposing aircraft in the area, which is why he had no fighter escort.

In fact, the Japanese had recently moved a large force of fighter planes into the Solomon Islands. The photoreconnaissance part of the mission over Buka went off smoothly, and Zeamer headed the B-17 for Bougainville. Then just before he completed his mapping run, the sky filled with about twenty Japanese Zeros. Zeamer proceded with the mission as several of them attacked his aircraft. The bombardier, Lieutenant Joseph Sarnoski, was wounded but still managed to shoot down two enemy planes with his nose gun.

Zeamer himself shot down another Japanese plane with a gun located in the fuselage of the plane.

Then a shell burst inside the cabin of the B-17, filling Zeamer's arms and legs with shrapnel and breaking one of his legs. Below him, Sarnoski was blown away from the nose of the plane by another shell; although mortally wounded, he crawled back to his gun and shot down two Japanese planes before dying.

Zeamer dived to around ten thousand feet. Fifteen Japanese fighters followed him down, continuing to attack in a fight that lasted forty minutes. During this time, his gunners shot down three more planes. Despite his wounds, Zeamer stayed at the controls until the Japanese planes became low on fuel and turned back to their base. Then he handed the controls over to his copilot. Drifting in and out of consciousness, he helped direct the battered B-17 to an emergency landing at a secondary airfield 580 miles away.

Zeamer returned home to receive medical treatment at Walter Reed Hospital in Washington, D.C. In July 1943, he was promoted to major, and he returned to duty the following March, when he was promoted to lieutenant colonel. But because of a physical disability resulting from wounds he suffered in the desperate air battle in the Pacific, he was forced to retire from the military in January 1945.

Both Jay Zeamer and his bombardier, Joseph Sarnoski, were awarded the Medal of Honor by General Hap Arnold on January 6, 1944, Sarnoski's posthumously. It was one of the few times in World War II that two members of the same aircraft were so honored.

Portraits of Valor

KOREAN WAR

VICTOR DAVIS HANSON

When Courage Is Second Nature

The Medal of Honor recipients in this volume are of all ages, ethnic backgrounds, and creeds—volunteers, draftees, officers, and enlisted men; pilots, foot soldiers (the vast majority), and sailors. But for all their diversity, the recipients share one thing: at a single, pivotal moment in battle, each pledged his own life well beyond the call of accustomed duty to advance the cause of his comrades and country.

As you read of their exploits, you can't help but wonder: What drives such men to do what seems to be beyond the capabilities of most of the rest of us? None of the recipients was drunk or drugged, much less crazed with promises of paradise and virgins to come. There were no gold bounties offered, in the manner that the Romans or Ottomans often incited their bravest.

Nor were these men carefully indoctrinated with a cult of militarism, what we might rightly call the fanaticism of an authoritarian state—such as the Bushido creed of the Japanese warrior in World War II or the Nazi zeal of an SS Totenkopf armored division heading into Russia in June 1941. We are not even talking of Spartan courage, a product of life in the barracks from the age of seven, or the centurions of Caesar's Tenth Legion, whose lives were pledged to the honor of, and rewards from, their magnetic leader.

All of these Medal of Honor heroes instead fought in a democratic military. The majority knew little of death and killing before volunteering or being drafted during wartime and would later return to quiet civilian lives after their service. But we can go beyond even civic militarism as the prompt for their audacity and perhaps turn to the wisdom of the ancients, who carefully explored what made some men truly brave and others less so.

At the battle of Plataea, the Spartan Aristodemus ranged out in front of the phalanx and, in superhuman fashion, cut down swathes of Persians. But the Spartans did not grant him their award for courage. And their reasons are very relevant to understanding America's own criteria for granting the Medal of Honor. Aristodemus, we are told by the historian Herodotus, fought as one who wished to die rather than to live, with a frenzy to make up for past laxity, while leaving his rank for personal glory and ignoring the line of men to his rear. In other words, Aristodemus was what's become known in military history as a berserker—a mad killer who either has nothing to lose or lapses into a state of temporary madness, as did the vengeful Achilles, oblivious of the larger cause and of all those around him.

The heroes in this book are different. Despite being in states of heightened anxiety, even exultation, they knew exactly what they were doing in risking their lives. Pericles, the great Athenian statesman, gives us further guidance about their valor, saying that true courage is the willingness to give up all that is dear when living is most precious. No one in this volume was ill or old or faced a bleak future. These were young men at the peak capacity for life and full of singular hope and optimism in a free America. They had the most to lose in offering up for others all they had and hoped to have.

Their heroism was also of a different sort from that of an Antigone, Socrates, or Sir Thomas More, who in peacetime made a thoughtful decision to lay down his or her life for a principle—a martyrdom whose example might advance the good cause for the benefit of others.

No, there is something carnal, physical, sudden about the battlefield heroics of those who have received the Medal of Honor, where there is no time for careful deliberation, and when thought and weighed language count little against a grenade or bullet. Speed, instant reflex, and physical strength in all these accounts make the difference between saving lives and failure. So these men were not just brave and principled, but both brave and principled as second nature in a moment's flash and equipped with the necessary poise, speed, and power to see their instant decision to fruition. They were athletes of a sort, the prize not being fame and money, but honor—with death, not defeat, the risk.

We can cite a final shared characteristic. In every story there appears a modesty of behavior or, as William Tecumseh Sherman noted, "The most courageous men are generally unconscious of possessing the quality." So, when on April 22, 1944, Second Lieutenant Ernest Childers was awarded the medal for his bravery at Oliveto, Italy, the perplexed lieutenant showed it to a nearby sergeant and asked, "What is this?" only to be told, "Why, that's the Congressional Medal of Honor, sir."

Braggadocio and ostentatiousness apparently mask uncertainty, while the true heroes in this book assume no need for such crutches. Apparently, they quietly understood all along what they might be capable of when their awful moment came, and found no need to be surprised when it passed.

There is much talk these days of American decline and decadence, the usual charges made against a democratic and free society that grows more wealthy and leisured as it ages. Yet the citations in this book, crossing generations from the world of the Depression before World War II to the confused 1960s of the Vietnam era through to our present conflicts, portray heroes who reflect the same bedrock constancy that we hear of at Valley Forge or that awful first day at Shiloh. And from what we know of Americans on patrol in the Hindu Kush and dying in the Sunni Triangle, there are still young men (now joined by young women) who have once more resolved to keep the rest of us safe and free.

Holding Fox Hill

WILLIAM E. BARBER

CAPTAIN, U.S. MARINE CORPS Company F, 2nd Battalion, 7th Marines, 1st Marine Division

BIOGRAPHY

BORN
November 30, 1919
Dehart, Kentucky

ENTERED SERVICE
West Liberty, Kentucky

BRANCH
U.S. Marine Corps

DUTY
Korean War

DIED
April 19, 2002
Irvine, California

WILLIAM BARBER WAS ABOUT TO BEGIN HIS third year at Morehead State Teachers College on September 1, 1939, when Hitler's armies invaded Poland. Convinced that the United States would inevitably be drawn into the European war, he enlisted in the Marines instead of registering for his classes. He fought in the Pacific and won the Silver Star on Iwo Jima. But none of the action he saw in World War II equaled what he and his men would endure in the Korean conflict five years later.

On the afternoon of November 28, 1950, Captain Barber's F Company was trying to dig foxholes into Fox Hill, a frozen, snow-covered spot in the North Korean wilderness overlooking the Tokong Pass near the Chosin Reservoir. The pass was the only escape route for two Marine regiments in the north in danger of being surrounded and cut off by Chinese Communist divisions that had recently poured across the Yalu River. F Company's orders were to keep the pass open until the Marine regiments arrived. Most of Barber's men were nineteen- and twenty-year-old reservists who until then had been involved only in limited engagements with North Korean troops. Now the 240 men of F Company found themselves facing a Chinese force that outnumbered them about five to one.

The first attack came after midnight. The Chinese overwhelmed Barber's two forward squads and seized the crest of the hill, but small groups of the Marines made a stand, preventing a breakthrough. By dawn, F Company had regained control of the high ground. It had also lost twenty men and counted fifty-four wounded. Early in the fighting, Barber took a bullet in the hip; supported by his men or carried on a stretcher, he rallied his troops through the rest of the battle.

The next morning was bitterly cold; blood and plasma supplies were freezing, and corpsmen had to thaw morphine syrettes by putting them in their mouths before they could inject the wounded. Ammunition was so low that Barber ordered shells to be stripped out of the machine-gun belts and distributed to the riflemen. When he finally made radio contact with his regimental commander, he was ordered to evacuate the area and march his men to the 1st Division's forward base at the abandoned town of Hagaru-ri. But Barber knew that this would allow the enemy to close the Tokong Pass and place the eight thousand Marines marching toward it squarely in a death trap, so he told his commanding officer that if his men were air-dropped supplies, they would hold Fox Hill.

American planes immediately began to resupply F Company. A huge Chinese force attacked over the next three days, but the Marines held off the assault. More than half of Barber's men were killed or wounded—six of his seven officers were injured—and Barber estimated that more than one thousand Chinese soldiers were killed.

A relief battalion headed by Lieutenant Colonel Raymond Davis reached F Company on December 3. A day later, after the two Marine regiments arrived from the north, the entire American force marched to Hagaru-ri. Captain Barber followed in a jeep until they neared the city, then got out and limped into town at the head of his battered command. He was sent to a military hospital in Japan for treatment of his hip, which was badly infected as a result of the gunshot wound. After surgery and two months of recuperation, he had recovered well enough to return to the United States. On August 20, 1952, he was awarded the Medal of Honor by President Harry Truman.

Modern-Day Hercules

DAVID B. BLEAK

SERGEANT, U.S. ARMY Medical Company, 2nd Battalion, 223rd Infantry Regiment, 40th Infantry Division

EARLY IN 1950, DAVID BLEAK WAS EIGHTEEN, LIVING in Wyoming, and "shaking the trees" to make something happen in his life. Dissatisfied with his other options, he decided to volunteer for the Army. He was surprised when the recruiting sergeant told him that there was not much need for soldiers right then. But a few months later, after war broke out in Korea, the sergeant called him back and told him that things had changed: The Army needed him now. Bleak joined up.

In basic training, he was slated to be a tanker until one day his sergeant gave him an appraising look and said, "You look like a medical aide man to me." Bleak understood that he had just been volunteered. After transferring to a medical company, he was sent to Japan as part of the 40th Infantry Division in the spring of 1951.

Bleak was sent on to Korea and promoted to sergeant during 1952's brutal winter of constant fighting. By June, his infantry unit was in the vicinity of Minari-gol, North Korea, facing a large force of Chinese dug into a mountain. While the bulk of the U.S. forces prepared for a frontal assault, Bleak volunteered to join a reconnaissance patrol assigned to circle around to the rear of the Chinese position in order to capture prisoners for interrogation.

The patrol stealthily advanced up a hill, captured three isolated enemy soldiers in a trench line, and was starting to withdraw when it was discovered. Large numbers of Chinese opened fire. Several Americans went down almost immediately, and Bleak went to help them. Jumping into a trench to tend to one wounded soldier, he was charged by three enemy soldiers. He killed two of them with his bare hands by smashing their heads against rocks. He killed the third with his

trench knife. Having returned to treating his comrade, Bleak saw a Chinese concussion grenade hit the ground and he used his body to shield the man from the impact of the blast. He continued to treat the wounded and was shot in the leg during the heavy fighting.

As the patrol withdrew with its prisoners, Bleak grabbed another injured American and began carrying him to safety. While he was limping down the hill, two more Chinese soldiers came at him with fixed bayonets. Bleak dropped his comrade and managed to evade the bayonet thrusts. He got ahold of both men, smashing their heads together and killing one of them. Then he picked up the wounded American and made it back to safety.

After recuperating from his wounds in the United States, Sergeant Bleak was back in Japan in 1953, working at a military hospital, when his commanding officer informed him that he was to receive the Medal of Honor. On November 2, 1953, at the White House, as President Dwight Eisenhower struggled to fasten the ribbon around Bleak's neck, he whispered, "You have a damned big neck."

Bleak went on to raise four children with his wife on their small farm. Later, he went to work in the nuclear industry for Argonne National Laboratory, developing electricity from nuclear energy.

BIOGRAPHY

BORN
February 27, 1932
Idaho Falls, Idaho

ENTERED SERVICE
Shelley, Idaho

BRANCH
U.S. Army

DUTY
Korean War

DIED
March 23, 2006
Arco, Idaho

One-Man Fighting Force

HECTOR A. CAFFERATA

PRIVATE, U.S. MARINE CORPS Company F, 2nd Battalion, 7th Marines, 1st Marine Division

HECTOR CAFFERATA WAS A MARINE RESERVIST ON inactive status when the Korean War broke out. At six feet two inches, 220 pounds, and a former semipro football player, Cafferata was a big, strong Marine. He also was an excellent marksman, having been a hunter since he was twelve years old.

On November 28, 1950, Cafferata's company was on a barren Korean mountainside overlooking a narrow road near the Chosin Reservoir. Under the command of Captain William Barber, its orders were to hold the Tokong Pass, the escape route for two Marine regiments in the area in danger of being cut off. Cafferata was unaware that a massive Chinese unit was very close by.

As darkness fell and the temperature plummeted below zero, the company commander sent Cafferata and three other Marines out to a listening post just beyond the American perimeter. They decided that Cafferata and his friend Kenny Benson would sleep while the other Marines took the first watch. Unable to dig a foxhole in the frozen ground, the two men cut down pine trees to serve as a windbreak, then took off their parkas and boots and climbed into their sleeping bags.

Around 1:30 A.M., the Chinese began a sudden massive assault; Cafferata and Benson awoke to a cacophony of enemy screams, bugles, and gunfire. Cafferata struggled out of his sleeping bag and grabbed his rifle. With Benson firing beside him, he emptied a clip into the troops closing in on them. Eight Chinese soldiers fell.

Cafferata and Benson moved back to take cover in a dry wash in which several Marines lay dead and wounded. They decided to stay to protect their fallen comrades. As they began shooting, a Chinese soldier heaved a satchel charge. It hit about thirty yards away, blowing several of the Marines into the air. When a grenade landed a few feet away, Benson picked it up to fling it back, but it exploded near his face, blinding him. Cafferata grabbed several weapons from the fallen Marines and shouted at Benson to load for him by feel.

Over the next seven hours, Cafferata never stopped shooting. The wooden front hand guard on one of his rifles started to smolder from the heat generated by his rapid fire. He moved along the wash, shooting the Chinese as they came up over its lip and batting away enemy grenades with his entrenching tool. During the battle, a grenade fell near Benson and him; Cafferata tried to throw it away, but it exploded as soon as it left his hand and blew the flesh off his frozen fingers. Isolated and alone except for his blind comrade, he fought until dawn, when some Marines finally made their way to the ditch.

Only after the Chinese force finally withdrew did Cafferata realize that he had fought through the freezing night in his socks and shirt. As he tried to retrieve his boots and parka from his sleeping bag, he was hit in the arm and chest. He was evacuated and hospitalized for eighteen months. Later, he learned that American officers had counted approximately one hundred Chinese dead around the ditch where he had fought that night but had decided not to put the figure into their report because they thought that no one would believe it.

In 1952, back home in New Jersey, Cafferata was informed by telegram that he had been awarded the Medal of Honor and was to go to Washington to receive it. When he replied that he'd prefer to have it mailed to him, he was contacted by a Marine officer who barked at him, "You will get down here so that President Truman can personally give this Medal of Honor to you!" It was presented on November 24, 1952.

BIOGRAPHY

BORN
November 4, 1929
New York, New York

ENTERED SERVICE
Dover, New Jersey

BRANCH
U.S. Marine Corps

DUTY
Korean War

CURRENT RESIDENCE
Florida

Sole Surviving Corpsman

WILLIAM R. CHARETTE

HOSPITAL CORPSMAN THIRD CLASS, U.S. NAVY Attached to Company F, 2nd Battalion, 7th Marines, 1st Marine Division

BIOGRAPHY

BORN
March 29, 1932
Ludington, Michigan

ENTERED SERVICE
Ludington, Michigan

BRANCH
U.S. Navy

DUTY
Korean War

CURRENT RESIDENCE
Florida

WILLIAM CHARETTE'S PARENTS DIED WHEN HE WAS four, and he was raised by an uncle. After high school, he took a job on a Lake Michigan ferryboat, which led him to join the Navy. There was a shortage of medical corpsmen, so he volunteered. He worked in a Navy hospital for a year, then volunteered again, this time as a medic with the Marine Corps. He was assigned to a rifle company in the 7th Marines in Korea.

In the spring of 1953, Navy Corpsman Charette's Marine unit was in an area near Panmunjom between North and South Korea, guarding the route to the South Korean capital of Seoul. In the early-morning hours of March 27, Chinese troops overran three outposts on a hill the Americans called Vegas; the Marines counterattacked to retake the position several hours later. It was the beginning of a solid twenty-four hours of combat.

The well-entrenched enemy hit the Americans with small-arms and mortar fire. As the Marines tried to ascend Vegas Hill, the Chinese rolled grenades down on them. There were so many explosions that Charette couldn't keep count. At one point, he was working on a badly wounded rifleman when a Chinese grenade hit nearby. Figuring that the man couldn't survive another wound, Charette threw himself over his body. The explosion tore off Charette's helmet, destroyed his medical pack, and knocked him out. When he came to and couldn't see because of the blood in his eyes caused by shrapnel wounds to his face, he thought he was blind. But his vision eventually cleared, and he returned to his duties.

Charette's medical supplies were destroyed by enemy fire, but he improvised by tearing off pieces of his uniform to make bandages for the men in his unit as well as for those in nearby platoons. He put his own battle vest on a wounded Marine whose vest had been destroyed by an explosion. When a trench was completely blown out, he swiftly went to the aid of five soldiers wounded in the explosion. One of them was severely injured, his leg nearly severed. When the order came at dawn to pull back and Marines started carrying the wounded out, they had to bend down to avoid enemy fire and were unable to get the man out without injuring him further. Charette picked the Marine up in his arms and, standing up despite enemy guns, carried him to safety.

Following this engagement, Charette was pulled back in reserve. He was recommended for the Navy Cross, but as the citation was forwarded up through the ranks, it was upgraded to the Medal of Honor. In all, five Navy corpsmen were recommended for the medal during the Korean War. Charette was the only one who survived to receive it.

On January 12, 1954, William Charette received the medal from President Dwight Eisenhower. The man who explained the protocol for the ceremony to him, submarine commander Captain Edward L. Beach, Jr., the president's naval aide, went on to write the best-selling *Run Silent, Run Deep*. Years later, Charette served under Beach on the USS *Triton*.

Defining Moment

RAYMOND G. DAVIS

LIEUTENANT COLONEL, U.S. MARINE CORPS 1st Battalion, 7th Marines, 1st Marine Division

BIOGRAPHY

BORN
January 13, 1915
Fitzgerald, Georgia

ENTERED SERVICE
Atlanta, Georgia

BRANCH
U.S. Marine Corps

DUTY
Korean War

DIED
September 3, 2003
Stockbridge, Georgia

RAYMOND DAVIS FIRST SAW COMBAT AS A YOUNG Marine second lieutenant in World War II, on Guadalcanal and later at Peleliu, where he earned the Navy Cross. He last saw combat as a two-star general commanding the 3rd Marine Division in Vietnam. In between, he experienced the defining moment of his thirty-four-year military career in 1950 on a frozen mountaintop in Korea.

On November 30, 1950, Davis, a lieutenant colonel and battalion commander with the 7th Marines, was informed by his commanding officer that Chinese troops were about to overrun a Marine rifle company trying to defend a mountain pass about eight miles from the American lines near the Chosin Reservoir. If the company was wiped out, a division-size Chinese force could then cut off two Marine regiments that had to go through that pass on their way back to American-held territory. Davis's job was to mount a rescue operation.

Setting out on a forced march over a primitive mountain trail, Davis's battalion fought its way toward the embattled Marine company through heavy snow and subzero temperatures. Their water froze, as did their radios, cutting them off from the American command. Along the way, they were involved in constant skirmishes; Davis surmised that some of the enemy forces had just arrived from South China when he saw them frozen to death in their foxholes wearing shoes without socks and thin uniforms that offered no protection against the forbidding Korean winter.

On the morning of December 2, Lieutenant Colonel Davis's battalion engaged the troops that had been assaulting the Marine rifle company. The Chinese occupied the high ground, so Davis immediately led an attack up steep, ice-covered slopes, fighting hand to hand alongside his men as they forced their way through troops occupying three successive ridges in the deep snow. Two bullets pierced his flak jacket without injuring him, and a shell fragment struck his helmet and knocked him down, but he got up and pushed through the last Chinese soldiers to reach the surrounded Marines.

What he saw was shocking. The badly outnumbered rifle company commanded by Captain William Barber had taken terrible casualties: More than one hundred men had been killed or wounded fighting off an enemy willing to take huge losses in the effort to overrun the Americans. Hundreds of frozen Chinese bodies were strewn around the American position. The Marines, desperately low on ammunition and supplies, probably wouldn't have been able to hold out another day.

Calling in air support on the rifle company's radios, Davis secured the pass and continued to repel Chinese counterattacks for another twenty-four hours until the two threatened Marine regiments made it through. He put these troops in charge of the rifle company's survivors—which included twenty-two litter cases— and ordered his battalion to spearhead the march back to the Chosin Reservoir.

Not long after this engagement, the reassembled 1st Marine Division fought its way to the port of Hungnam to await evacuation by U.S. ships. At division headquarters several days after they arrived, Davis's regimental commander handed him a piece of paper: a recommendation for the Medal of Honor for the action at the Chosin Reservoir. But a fire destroyed the document; it took two years for it to be reissued. Davis received his medal on November 24, 1952, from President Harry Truman at the White House.

Raymond Davis retired from the Marine Corps in 1972 with the rank of general.

Body of Steel

DUANE E. DEWEY

CORPORAL, U.S. MARINE CORPS Company E, 2nd Battalion, 5th Marines, 1st Marine Division

WHEN NINETEEN-YEAR-OLD DUANE DEWEY JOINED the Marines soon after North Korean forces rolled into the South, it was an "indefinite" enlistment—the duration of the war plus six months. Dewey was part of the 1st Marine Division, which was near Panmunjom in the spring of 1952. The command had established a series of outposts beyond the main American force. Corporal Dewey was the leader of a machine-gun squad in a reinforced platoon dug in at one of these positions when it was attacked by a battalion-size Chinese force around midnight on April 16.

The American outpost was quickly overrun. Carrying their machine guns, Dewey and his men fell back; now out of their foxholes and fighting on exposed ground, they tried to stabilize their position. Dewey worked his gun—firing so regularly that he feared the barrel might melt—and the bodies of Chinese soldiers piled up on one another in front of him. Seeing that he had only three cans of ammunition left, he ran to another machine gun for more. As he was returning, a grenade exploded at his feet, knocking him down. Bleeding heavily from the thigh and groin, he lay on the ground a moment, trying to reorient himself. A medic appeared, and as he knelt over Dewey to remove his blood-soaked pants, another grenade hit the ground beside them. Dewey grabbed it and for a second considered throwing it back. But he decided he didn't have the time or the strength, so he tucked it underneath him, pulling the medic down with his other hand and yelling, "Hit the dirt, Doc." The grenade detonated, lifting Dewey several inches off the ground and tearing up his hip. The medic was unharmed.

Dewey was taken back to the aid station. For an hour he lay outside waiting for treatment, not sure that he would make it. Then he was given a shot of morphine and taken to a trench filled with other wounded Americans. He spent the rest of the night wondering which side would win the battle raging outside. Shortly after dawn, when American troops relieved his company, he was evacuated. Doctors treating him in the field hospital found that in addition to the gaping shrapnel wounds throughout the lower part of his body, he had also taken a bullet in the stomach. He was hospitalized in Japan for a month, then flown to the States, where he would spend three more months convalescing. On the way home, the plane stopped over briefly in Hawaii, where an officer visited him in the hospital and presented him with the Purple Heart. When Dewey casually mentioned that he had heard his captain was going to recommend him for the Medal of Honor, the officer shot him a look that made him resolve never to mention it again.

Dewey was back home in South Haven, Michigan, when he received a telegram informing him that he had indeed been awarded the Medal of Honor. On March 12, 1953, President Dwight Eisenhower presented it to him at the White House. "You must have a body of steel," the President said to him after reviewing his citation.

Dewey and his wife returned home after a week in Washington to a great surprise: To honor him, the townspeople had built a three-bedroom prefabricated house for them, completely furnished and with fully stocked cupboards and refrigerator.

BIOGRAPHY

BORN
November 16, 1931
Grand Rapids, Michigan

ENTERED SERVICE
Muskegon, Michigan

BRANCH
U.S. Marine Corps

DUTY
Korean War

CURRENT RESIDENCE
Michigan

Giving Veterans Hope

RODOLFO P. HERNANDEZ

CORPORAL, U.S. ARMY Company G, 187th Airborne Regimental Combat Team

BIOGRAPHY

BORN
April 14, 1931
Colton, California

ENTERED SERVICE
Fowler, California

BRANCH
U.S. Army

DUTY
Korean War

CURRENT RESIDENCE
North Carolina

RODOLFO "RUDY" HERNANDEZ'S PLATOON, PART OF the 187th Airborne, was holding a hill near the Korean town of Wontong-ni on May 31, 1951, when it heard the weird symphony of bugles, whistles, and human shrieks that typically preceded a North Korean attack. It was 2:00 A.M., pitch black and raining. Soon the night erupted with enemy artillery, mortar, and machine-gun fire. Seeing the enemy advancing in overwhelming numbers, twenty-year-old Corporal Hernandez and the other soldier in his foxhole opened up with their rifles; almost immediately, both men were wounded.

Though the rest of the platoon retreated, Hernandez and his foxhole mate held their position and kept firing. When a shell ruptured in the chamber of his weapon, Hernandez climbed out of the foxhole and charged the North Koreans, armed only with grenades and a rifle with a fixed bayonet. His actions stopped the enemy advance and gave his comrades time to reload their weapons, regroup, and counterattack. But by then, his men had lost sight of him.

Hernandez was found the next morning near death, lying among the bodies of the six North Koreans he had killed before falling to bayonet wounds and fragments from artillery shells. He was initially pronounced dead, but then someone saw a slight movement of his hand, and medics frantically began to work on him. He finally drifted up to semiconsciousness in a South Korean hospital a month later, but he still couldn't fully comprehend where he was, and he was unable to move his arms or legs, talk, or swallow. Doctors explained that shrapnel from an artillery shell had torn away a portion of his brain. After eight weeks, he was brought home to Letterman Hospital in San Francisco, where doctors replaced the damaged part of his skull with a

plastic plate and covered it with hairless skin. It was months more before he uttered his first word. After several compliments on the cheerful look he had worn during his darkest days, he realized that his frozen "smile" was the result of operations on the bayonet wounds to his face.

When he eventually learned to walk again several months later, he was told he was to receive the Medal of Honor. His brother accompanied him to Washington—he was still so disoriented that when he heard the things he had done recited in the citation, he thought someone else's actions were being described. President Harry Truman presented the medal to him on April 12, 1952.

It took Hernandez several more years of treatment and therapy before he could use his body, though he never regained use of his right arm. Twelve years after he returned from Korea, he became a counselor to wounded veterans of Korea and Vietnam at the Veterans Administration. By letting them know how he had worked his way back to a happy and productive life, Hernandez believed he could give them hope that they, too, could overcome their own problems.

Korea's First Honoree

THOMAS J. HUDNER, JR.

LIEUTENANT JUNIOR GRADE, U.S. NAVY Fighter Squadron 32, USS *Leyte*

THOMAS HUDNER HAD NO PARTICULAR INTEREST IN airplanes when he graduated from the Naval Academy in 1946. He wanted only to serve aboard a ship. But in 1948, after he had been at sea for several months and had worked as a communications officer at Pearl Harbor for a year, he was ready for a new challenge and volunteered for flight training. He was briefly stationed in Lebanon before being assigned to the carrier USS *Leyte* as an F4U Corsair pilot.

By the fall of 1950, Lieutenant Hudner was flying combat missions in Korea. On December 4, he was one of a flight of six fighters sent out on an armed reconnaissance mission over North Korea. Hudner was wingman for a Navy flier named Jesse Brown, the son of a Mississippi sharecropper who had attracted a good deal of attention—and some discrimination—as the Navy's first black pilot.

While strafing enemy positions at a low altitude, Brown's plane was hit by antiaircraft fire. Smoking badly and without power, the aircraft was too low for Brown to bail out or clear the snow-covered mountains. Hudner followed Brown down, calling off a checklist to help prepare him for the crash landing.

Brown put his plane down in a wheels-up landing in a clearing below. The impact buckled the fuselage at the cockpit, and Hudner was certain that Brown was dead. To his amazement, Brown opened the canopy and waved weakly, but he appeared to be unable to free himself. Knowing that rescue helicopters had a long distance to travel, Hudner decided to help Brown get out of the plane himself. He didn't ask permission from the flight leader because he knew it would be denied.

Hudner radioed, "I'm going in," then dumped his ordnance, dropped his flaps, and landed wheels up,

hitting the hilly area hard. He got out and struggled through the snow to get to the downed plane. Hudner saw that Brown's right leg was crushed by the damaged instrument panel, and he was unable to pull him out of the wreckage.

Hudner kept packing snow into the smoking engine and talking to Brown as he drifted in and out of consciousness. When a U.S. helicopter arrived, the pilot worked with Hudner for forty-five minutes trying to get Brown out. They hacked at the plane with an ax, and even considered amputating Brown's trapped leg with a knife. The snow packed on the bottom of their boots prevented them from getting any firm footing on the plane's wing. As nightfall approached, bringing temperatures as low as thirty degrees below zero, it was clear that Brown was dead. Hudner hated to leave the body behind, but the helicopter pilot couldn't fly in the mountainous terrain after dark. Reluctantly, the two men returned to base camp.

The next morning, reconnaissance showed that Brown's body, still in the cockpit, had been stripped of clothing during the night by enemy soldiers. Because of the hostile forces in the area, it was impossible to retrieve it. The following day, the commander of the *Leyte* ordered four Corsairs to napalm the downed plane so that Brown could have a warrior's funeral.

By February 1951, the *Leyte* was back in port in the United States. In mid-March, Hudner found out that he was to be the first American serviceman in the Korean War to receive the Medal of Honor. Daisy Brown, the widow of Jesse Brown (who had been posthumously awarded the Distinguished Flying Cross), was present when President Harry Truman put the medal around Thomas Hudner's neck on April 13, 1951.

BIOGRAPHY

BORN
August 31, 1924
Fall River, Massachusetts

ENTERED SERVICE
Fall River, Massachusetts

BRANCH
U.S. Navy

DUTY
Korean War

CURRENT RESIDENCE
Massachusetts

A Grand Feast

EINAR H. INGMAN

CORPORAL, U.S. ARMY Company E, 17th Infantry Regiment, 7th Infantry Division

BIOGRAPHY

BORN
October 6, 1929
Milwaukee, Wisconsin

ENTERED SERVICE
Tomahawk, Wisconsin

BRANCH
U.S. Army

DUTY
Korean War

CURRENT RESIDENCE
Wisconsin

GROWING UP ON A FARM IN WISCONSIN, EINAR Ingman was always fascinated with heavy machines. When a military recruiter told him he could learn a trade involving this equipment in the Army, Ingman signed up, but after the Korean War broke out, his unit, the 17th Infantry, was rushed into battle, and he found himself carrying a rifle instead of driving a truck.

On February 26, 1951, Corporal Ingman was in the assault platoon of his company, patrolling the mountainous terrain near the town of Malta-ri and clearing the way for the rest of the U.S. forces to advance. Suddenly, the patrol ran into a Chinese force dug in at the top of a ridge above them. When the squad leaders and several men were hit by enemy fire, Ingman assumed command. He first radioed for artillery and tank support, then raced up the hill, his men following.

Ingman charged an enemy machine-gun nest, threw a grenade into it, and shot the gunners. As he approached a second machine-gun emplacement, an enemy grenade exploded near his head, knocking him down and tearing off a piece of his left ear. As he struggled to his feet, a Chinese soldier jumped up from a trench and shot him in the face. The bullet hit next to his nose, tearing out his upper teeth and exiting behind his ear.

He immediately lost all memory—even of getting shot. Acting by reflex, he got up and moved forward toward the machine gun, emptying his clip and attacking the gunners with his bayonet. Then he passed out.

As a result of Ingman's action, the enemy defenses were broken, his unit secured its objective, and one hundred enemy soldiers abandoned their weapons and fled in disorganized retreat.

Seven days later, Ingman regained consciousness in a Tokyo hospital. He had lost the hearing in his left ear, was blind in his left eye, and had no recall, even of his own name. After he underwent emergency brain surgery, his memory slowly began coming back.

He was sent to a hospital in Battle Creek, Michigan, where he underwent twenty-three more operations in the next two years. Although he recovered physically, his memory would come and go.

In the summer of 1951, he was flown from the hospital to Washington, where he was met by a stretcher and an ambulance, and where he got a renewed sense of how serious his injuries were when one of the waiting medics was surprised to see that he could actually walk. He was fitted for a new dress uniform, and President Harry Truman presented the Medal of Honor to him on July 5, 1951.

After the ceremony, Ingman flew back home to Tomahawk, Wisconsin, where the townspeople staged a party for him and gave him a new car, boat, and trailer to go along with it. In the boat was a huge northern muskie that had just been caught. They cooked the fish and everyone in the town joined Ingman in a grand feast.

Court-Martialed Hero

LEWIS L. MILLETT

CAPTAIN, U.S. ARMY Company E, 27th Infantry Regiment

BIOGRAPHY

BORN
December 15, 1920
Mechanic Falls, Maine

ENTERED SERVICE
Mechanic Falls, Maine

BRANCH
U.S. Army

DUTY
Korean War

DIED
November 14, 2009
Idyllwild, California

IN 1940, LEWIS MILLETT LEFT HIGH SCHOOL AFTER his junior year to enlist in the Army so he could fight fascism. Assigned to an Air Corps gunnery school, he became increasingly upset with Europe's weak resistance against German aggression, with the Nazis' treatment of the Jews, and especially with the way the United States was paralyzed by isolationism. To get into combat, he deserted, crossed the Canadian border, and enlisted in the Canadian army. He was sent to London shortly afterward and manned an antiaircraft gun during the Blitz.

When American troops began arriving in England in 1942, Millett took advantage of a provision that allowed American citizens serving with an allied country to transfer into the U.S. military. He served with the American Army in North Africa, where he was awarded the Silver Star and promoted from private to sergeant, then fought at Salerno and Anzio. It was at Anzio that his old records finally caught up with him. He was told he had been court-martialed and found guilty of desertion. His sentence was a fifty-two-dollar fine. The same day, he received a battlefield promotion to lieutenant for his fearlessness in combat.

Millett went to college when the war ended, then joined the Maine National Guard. Soon after the outbreak of the Korean War, he joined the 8th Field Artillery of the 25th Division and was sent to Korea. Not long after his arrival, the commanding officer of an infantry company in the 27th Infantry (the "Wolfhounds") was killed, and Millett took over. On February 7, 1951, he was in command of an under-strength company of about one hundred soldiers near the Korean village of Soam-ni. They were proceeding up a road in subzero temperatures when they ran into a superior force of Chinese Communist soldiers dug

into the hills above. One of Millett's platoons was pinned down by automatic-weapons fire; he brought up another platoon for support. A few weeks earlier, he had heard that the Chinese army was circulating handbills among their troops accusing the Americans of being "afraid of cold steel"—the bayonet—so he had trained his men hard in the use of that weapon. Now, with the Communists raking his position with small-arms fire and his men running low on ammunition, he ordered them to fix bayonets and led a charge up the hill.

A conspicuous figure at the head of his company with his large red handlebar mustache, Millett reached the enemy trench line and bayoneted two enemy soldiers. Then, using his rifle as a club against the others, he forced the Chinese to break and run. He was wounded by grenade fragments but refused evacuation until the position was secured. Later, he explained that he engaged in this action as an homage to his grandfathers, both of whom had fought in the Civil War and had participated in bayonet charges.

Millett was pulled off the line a few weeks later. When he asked why, he was told that he had been recommended for the Medal of Honor and his commanders didn't want him to get killed before the ceremony. President Harry Truman presented the medal to him on July 5, 1951.

After Korea, Millett attended Infantry Officers Advanced Course and Ranger school as a major. He was assigned to the 101st Airborne Division and became involved in the special operations community. During the war in Vietnam, he helped establish the Vietnamese Ranger school and the Commando training program in Laos. At the time of his retirement in 1973, he was the only colonel in American military history to have been found guilty of desertion.

Prisoner of War

HIROSHI H. MIYAMURA

CORPORAL, U.S. ARMY Company H, 7th Infantry Regiment, 3rd Infantry Division

HIROSHI MIYAMURA GREW UP IN GALLUP, NEW Mexico, one of only a handful of Japanese Americans in the town. A teacher, unable to pronounce his first name, called him Hershey, and his friends adopted this nickname.

Early in 1944, eighteen-year-old Miyamura was drafted and assigned to the Nisei 442nd Regimental Combat Team, which would gain fame as the most decorated American unit of World War II. When the 442nd shipped out, Miyamura had to stay behind because he hadn't reached the minimum age for overseas duty. He finally got to Europe just after the war ended and did occupation duty in Italy, then came home to pick up his life as an auto mechanic and joined the Army Reserve.

In 1950, at the start of the Korean War, Miyamura was called to active duty. In command of a machine-gun squad in Company H of the 7th Infantry Regiment, he was part of the American retreat from the Chosin Reservoir after Chinese Communist forces surprised General Douglas MacArthur by crossing over the Yalu River into North Korea. His unit, evacuated from the port of Hungnam, immediately headed back to the front lines to guard Seoul against a Chinese assault. Then it moved farther north.

On the morning of April 24, 1951, Miyamura was ordered to set up his machine-gun squad on a pockmarked hill near the Imjin River and hold it as long as possible. He had fifteen men, five of them riflemen and the rest machine gunners; some of them were South Korean conscripts who disappeared after darkness fell.

That night, the men in Miyamura's diminished unit crouched in their foxholes listening to Chinese troops banging on pots and pans and blowing on whistles. The racket was followed by a brief silence during which the enemy sent up flares. Then came the attack. The Americans opened fire with their two .30-caliber machine guns. As the enemy threatened to overwhelm his position, Miyamura rose from his machine gun and charged them, killing ten with his bayonet and rifle. He returned to his gun; when it jammed, he bayoneted his way to the second one and resumed firing, telling his men he would cover their retreat.

Not realizing that Miyamura was still fighting, American forces began lobbing phosphorus bombs at his position. As he started to make his way down the hill to the U.S. fallback position, he ran into a Chinese soldier and bayoneted him. The dying soldier dropped a grenade, and the explosion filled Miyamura's legs with shrapnel. He stumbled toward what he thought were the American lines until he was too weak to go any farther. He crawled into a ditch, where he lost consciousness. When he came to the next morning, a Chinese officer standing over him was saying, "Don't worry, we have a lenient policy." He was taken on a forced march to a Communist prison camp.

In the late summer of 1953, emaciated from two years of captivity, Miyamura was finally repatriated. After being turned over to U.S. authorities at "Freedom Village" in Panmunjom, he was informed that he had been awarded the Medal of Honor shortly after his capture, when he was still listed as missing in action; the award had been kept secret to keep his Chinese captors from killing him. President Harry Truman had signed his citation, but it was President Dwight Eisenhower who presented the medal to him on October 27, 1953.

BIOGRAPHY

BORN
October 6, 1925
Gallup, New Mexico

ENTERED SERVICE
Gallup, New Mexico

BRANCH
U.S. Army

DUTY
Korean War

CURRENT RESIDENCE
New Mexico

The Fight for Outpost Harry

OLA L. MIZE

SERGEANT, U.S. ARMY Company K, 15th Infantry Regiment, 3rd Infantry Division

BIOGRAPHY

BORN
August 28, 1931
Albertville, Alabama

ENTERED SERVICE
Gadsden, Alabama

BRANCH
U.S. Army

DUTY
Korean War

CURRENT RESIDENCE
Alabama

OLA MIZE, SON OF AN ALABAMA SHARECROPPER, dropped out of school in 1946 after the ninth grade to help take care of his mother, brothers, and sisters. A few years later, earning just fifteen dollars a week, he decided he could do better in the Army but was rejected because he weighed only 120 pounds. He kept pestering recruiters until they finally let him enlist.

Mize was finishing his tour of duty with the 82nd Airborne when the Korean War broke out. He had planned to go back to school, but he didn't want to miss the experience of combat, so he extended his enlistment and volunteered for a front-line unit.

On the evening of June 10, 1953, Sergeant Mize's unit and another platoon were defending a position called Outpost Harry near Surang-ni, Korea, when Chinese troops attacked. First came a shattering artillery barrage, followed by an assault by a battalion-size force that overran the Americans.

Some weeks earlier, knowing that his M-1 rifle with its eight-round clip would be ineffective in close fighting, Mize had found a carbine and "traded" his rifle for it. Now he picked up the weapon, which could hold two taped-together clips of thirty rounds each, and attacked the Chinese clogging the American trench line. Firing constantly, he killed about forty of them.

With all the company's officers dead or wounded, Mize worked frantically to establish a defensive position, dragging wounded into shelters made of timbers pulled from American bunkers destroyed by enemy fire. Over the next several hours of hand-to-hand fighting, he assembled an impromptu patrol that went from bunker to bunker, firing out of the apertures in an effort to make the Chinese believe that they were still opposed by a vigorous force. At one point, seeing a Chinese soldier level his weapon at one of his men, Mize killed

the soldier with a single shot. At another point, as Communist troops swarmed over an American machine gun, he charged the position, killing ten enemy soldiers and dispersing the rest. He was knocked down several times by grenades, and his uniform was shredded by shrapnel, but he escaped serious injury.

When the situation seemed lost, Mize got his men to crawl into bunkers and called in American artillery. He decided that it was better to get killed by your own fire than the enemy's. Around midnight, Mize dug himself out and made his way through enemy fire to his company command post, which had been overrun by Chinese forces. Then he worked his way back to his men.

They continued to repel the enemy in hand-to-hand fighting. American counterattack forces reached Mize's position at about noon on June 11. After helping to resecure the outpost, Mize got permission to take his wounded men back to the American lines. When he reached friendly territory, the regimental commander and the division commander were standing together. The two men did not recognize Mize; his uniform was in tatters, his flak jacket smoking, and his face badly swollen from burns. "Who are you?" demanded the regimental commander. "Sergeant Mize," he answered. "You're not Mize," the commander responded. "He's dead."

Several months later, informed that he would receive the Medal of Honor, Mize told his commanding officer that he didn't want it because it really should go to his entire platoon. He was reluctantly flown back to the United States so he could attend the ceremony in Denver. He was decorated by President Dwight Eisenhower on September 7, 1954.

In the early 1960s, Ola Mize joined the Special Forces and did three tours of duty in Vietnam. He retired as a colonel in 1981.

Going to Bat with Ted Williams

RAYMOND G. MURPHY

SECOND LIEUTENANT, U.S. MARINE CORPS Company A, 1st Battalion, 5th Marines, 1st Marine Division

RAYMOND MURPHY WAS ATTENDING ADAMS STATE College on a football scholarship when he heard that the Marines were trying to quickly rebuild their officer corps through a special program within Officer Candidate School. When he graduated from college in May 1951, he signed up and was sent to Quantico, Virginia, for training. One of the highlights of that experience was spending a leave in Washington and seeing his idol, Ted Williams, when the Boston Red Sox were playing the Washington Senators. As he left the stadium, he thought that whatever happened in Korea, he had at least gotten a chance to see Williams at bat.

Murphy went to Seoul in June 1952, in command of an infantry platoon in the 5th Marines. His unit was trucked immediately to the front lines, where it saw heavy action, and he was awarded the Silver Star four months later.

At the beginning of February 1953, Murphy's unit was above the Imjin River facing Chinese Communist troops that had been dug into high ground there for more than a year. The area was a moonscape of barren land, having been pounded repeatedly by artillery from both sides. An American assault on the well-entrenched Chinese position took place at dawn on February 3, led by two of the company's platoons, with Murphy's held back in reserve. After an hour, sensing that the operation wasn't going as planned, Murphy led his reserve platoon up the hill to check things out; he found all the officers and noncoms of the two assault platoons dead or wounded, and mass confusion among the troops.

In the face of horrific machine-gun fire, he ordered his men to find their fallen comrades and evacuate them. Murphy himself made several trips into the

heaviest fighting to rescue casualties. As he was helping lift a stretcher, he was hit in the back by fragments of an enemy grenade, but he refused medical attention and continued to rally his men to protect the wounded. At one point, he came face-to-face with two Chinese soldiers and killed them both with his pistol.

As the last of the American wounded were being evacuated, Chinese troops entered the trenches. Murphy grabbed an automatic rifle and held them off. When all the Marines were safe, he went back up the hill with a search party to look for the handful of missing. He located the bodies of a machine-gun crew; as they were being brought back down, he was wounded a second time. Again he refused treatment until all his men had preceded him to the main lines.

About midnight, Murphy finally arrived at a MASH unit. He was treated aboard a hospital ship and in Japan before being sent to the U.S. Naval Hospital in San Francisco. (It was not until many years later that he discovered that Ted Williams, who had left baseball to go back into the Marine Corps, had been flying support over Murphy's unit that day. Williams had repeatedly strafed the Chinese position until his plane was riddled by Chinese fire. He had barely made it back to his base, where he crash-landed and surprised onlookers by walking away without a scratch.)

Murphy was enrolled in graduate school in Massachusetts in October 1953 when he received a call telling him that he was to be awarded the Medal of Honor—the third recipient from the small town of Pueblo, Colorado. When President Dwight Eisenhower presented the medal to him on October 27, he gave Murphy a quizzical look and said, "What is it about Pueblo, anyway?"

BIOGRAPHY

BORN
January 14, 1930
Pueblo, Colorado

ENTERED SERVICE
Pueblo, Colorado

BRANCH
U.S. Marine Corps

DUTY
Korean War

DIED
April 6, 2007
Albuquerque, New Mexico

Holding East Hill

REGINALD R. MYERS

MAJOR, U.S. MARINE CORPS 3rd Battalion, 1st Marines, 1st Marine Division

BIOGRAPHY

BORN
November 26, 1919
Boise, Idaho

ENTERED SERVICE
Boise, Idaho

BRANCH
U.S. Marine Corps

DUTY
Korean War

DIED
October 23, 2005
Jupiter, Florida

DURING WORLD WAR II, REGINALD MYERS SAW action in the Marine Corps' invasions of Guadalcanal, the Marshall Islands, and Okinawa. After the war, he served with the occupation forces in northern China. In the fall of 1950, Major Myers was the executive officer of the 3rd Battalion, 1st Marines in Korea, a veteran of the Inchon landing in 1950 and of fighting around Seoul.

By November 29, 1950, an outnumbered combined Army and Marine force had been battered by two days of Chinese attacks at the Chosin Reservoir. The small force of men from the Army Signal Corps and other noncombatants who had been assigned to defend East Hill, the high ground overlooking the U.S. base at Hagaru-ri, had been routed shortly after midnight. A few hours later, some four thousand Chinese Communist troops were on East Hill poised to rain artillery fire down on the weakened Americans below. Myers's commanding officer ordered him to assemble a force made up of any personnel he could find and take them up the hill.

As a steady snowfall accumulated in temperatures reaching twenty degrees below zero, Myers reorganized the demoralized remnant troops who had just been driven off East Hill and added reinforcements from several Army and Marine units, putting together a ragtag force of about 250 men in all. Slipping on the ice, they started the steep ascent in the dark while the enemy shot down at them from above.

Without a command structure to help him organize his makeshift unit, Myers struggled to get the men to the top of East Hill before daybreak. By 10:00 A.M., he had gotten the eighty soldiers still capable of fighting near the crest of the hill, but because of the fierce

enemy machine-gun fire, he couldn't advance farther. He called in artillery fire and warplanes, which strafed and bombed the enemy, but though the Chinese took heavy casualties, they were still able to keep Myers's depleted force from taking full control of the hill. After a grueling daylong battle, Myers fell back to a defensive position as night approached. Eventually, he was relieved by Marine Captain Carl Sitter, who would also receive the Medal of Honor for his actions in finally securing the position. Myers's leadership of a group of men who had never trained or fought together resulted in six hundred enemy killed and five hundred wounded and kept the Chinese troops from focusing their firepower on Hagaru-ri.

Although he wasn't hurt in the assault on East Hill, Myers was badly injured several months later, in the spring of 1951. (It was not so much the pain that he remembered later on, but the sensation of doctors cutting off his clothing to treat him for shrapnel wounds.) He returned to the United States shortly afterward and was awarded the Medal of Honor by President Harry Truman on October 29 of that year.

Following the Korean War, Myers continued to serve in many positions with the Corps before he retired as a colonel in 1967.

Retaking the Hook

GEORGE H. O'BRIEN

SECOND LIEUTENANT, U.S. MARINE CORPS RESERVE Company H, 3rd Battalion, 7th Marines, 1st Marine Division

GEORGE H. O'BRIEN WAS A TEENAGER WHEN HE joined the Merchant Marines near the end of World War II, serving aboard a gasoline tanker in the Pacific. After the war, he enrolled in college, majored in geology, and joined the Marine Corps Reserve. When the Korean War broke out, he was ordered to active duty and sent to Quantico for officer training. He shipped out in the summer of 1952 as a second lieutenant in charge of a rifle platoon in the 7th Marines.

On October 27, 1952, a Marine force holding a vitally important hill position in an area near the 38th Parallel known as the Hook had been overrun by a numerically superior Chinese Communist force. Lieutenant O'Brien's company, which had been held in reserve, was ordered to retake the position the next day—about one hundred men against several hundred enemy soldiers. When the signal to attack was given at daybreak, O'Brien leaped out of the trench and shouted for his men to follow. He raced across an exposed saddle of ground and up the enemy-held hill as the Chinese unleashed ferocious mortar and automatic-weapons fire. He said later he could see the mortar shells as they fell and had the peculiar thought that they looked like teardrops.

As he approached the Chinese line, he was shot through the arm and knocked to the ground. Managing to get to his feet, he immediately went to the aid of another wounded Marine. Then he rallied his men to follow and continued the assault. As they entered the Chinese entrenchments, he threw a grenade into a bunker, then jumped in after it exploded and killed three enemy gunners with his carbine.

During the next four hours of fighting, much of it hand to hand, O'Brien was knocked down three times by the concussion of enemy grenades. Though bleeding from shrapnel wounds, he refused evacuation and continued to direct the attack. When it finally halted, he set up a defense, preparing for a counterattack. He tended to his wounded, and even after his unit was relieved by other Marines, he remained behind to make sure that none of his men was left there.

O'Brien was evacuated to the hospital ship USS *Hope* for treatment. When he returned to the line later in the year, he received a second Purple Heart after being wounded again. He was on a troopship home late in the summer of 1953, serving as a liaison officer for the first group of American POWs released from Communist camps, when the ship picked up a broadcast from a commercial station in San Francisco reporting that he was to be awarded the Medal of Honor. The news was rebroadcast over the ship's radio. George O'Brien was awarded the medal by President Dwight Eisenhower on October 27, 1953, exactly one year after the action at the Hook.

BIOGRAPHY

BORN
September 10, 1926
Fort Worth, Texas

ENTERED SERVICE
Big Spring, Texas

BRANCH
U.S. Marine Corps

DUTY
Korean War

DIED
March 11, 2005
Midland, Texas

Breaking the Enemy Defense

JOSEPH C. RODRIGUEZ

PRIVATE FIRST CLASS, U.S. ARMY Company F, 17th Infantry Regiment, 7th Infantry Division

JOSEPH RODRIGUEZ HAD FINISHED TWO YEARS of college and was working for an architect in San Bernardino, California, when he was drafted in the fall of 1950. By the middle of May 1951, he was in Korea, a private first class with the 17th Infantry Regiment, part of the Eighth Army, when it was attacked by twenty-one Chinese and nine North Korean divisions. In the weeklong battle, American forces, fighting alongside the South Koreans, inflicted a staggering ninety thousand casualties on the enemy and began a counterattack to regain lost ground once the Communist offensive was blunted.

On May 21, as part of the assault, Company F was trying to take the high ground north of the village of Munye-ri. Its third platoon was ordered to attack a small peak dominating the ridgeline. The enemy, well entrenched, waited until the Americans were within a hundred yards of the top before opening fire. The platoon made three efforts to storm the position but was driven back each time. Rodriguez's second platoon was then ordered to take the hill. It got to within sixty yards of the top before being stopped by automatic-weapons fire from five Communist positions.

As the enemy began to roll grenades down the hill, Rodriguez suddenly leaped to his feet and ran sixty yards over open terrain toward the enemy. Though bullets kicked up dirt all around him, he wasn't hit. He made it to the first Chinese foxhole and destroyed it with grenades. Then he wiped out an enemy machine gun with rifle fire. At the top of the peak, he dropped grenades into two more foxholes. Then, approaching the last enemy position from the rear, he destroyed the machine gun and killed its crew with his rifle and remaining grenades.

In all, Rodriguez was responsible for fifteen Chinese dead in the space of a few minutes, single-handedly breaking the enemy defense and allowing U.S. forces to secure the strategic strongpoint.

A week later, he was badly wounded in the continuing operation and required a long hospitalization in Japan. When he asked to be sent back to his unit, he was told he could train with his men but not fight with them; the explanation he was given for this order was that he had been recommended for some award. It wasn't until after he returned to his old outfit in the fall of 1951 and spent several frustrating weeks restricted from combat that he was officially notified that the award he had been chosen to receive was the Medal of Honor. General Matthew Ridgway's personal plane had to return to the States for maintenance, and Rodriguez was given a ride home on it. He was presented with the medal by President Harry Truman on January 29, 1952.

Joseph Rodriguez, commissioned as an officer, made a career in the Army. He retired as a colonel in 1980.

BIOGRAPHY

BORN
November 14, 1928
San Bernardino, California

ENTERED SERVICE
California

BRANCH
U.S. Army

DUTY
Korean War

DIED
November 1, 2005
El Paso, Texas

Revenge for a Brother

RONALD E. ROSSER

CORPORAL, U.S. ARMY Heavy Mortar Company, 38th Infantry Regiment, 2nd Infantry Division

AS THE OLDEST OF SEVENTEEN CHILDREN, RONALD Rosser always looked out for his brothers and sisters. He joined the Army right after turning seventeen in 1946 and served for three years. In 1951, he reenlisted because his kid brother was killed early in the Korean conflict and he was bent on revenge. When he was sent to Japan instead of the combat zone, he complained to his commanding officer and was reassigned to a heavy mortar company in the 38th Infantry in Korea.

On January 12, 1952, Corporal Rosser was a forward observer directing U.S. mortar fire while his infantry company assaulted a snow-covered hill held by a Chinese battalion near the town of Ponggilli. Seeing hundreds of enemy troops swarming over the area, he called in mortar fire, but the Americans continued to take heavy casualties—by the time they reached a point about a hundred yards below the crest of the hill, only 35 of the 170 who had begun the battle were still able-bodied. When the commanding officer, badly wounded, used Rosser's radio to call headquarters for instructions, he was ordered to try once again to take the hill. Seeing that the officer was in no condition to carry out the order, Rosser volunteered to organize the remaining men and lead the charge.

As he made his way up the hill, some of the soldiers who had started with him had already been driven back down; others never followed him at all. Halfway to the Chinese position, he realized that he was alone, but he was determined to make the enemy pay for his brother's death. Armed only with a carbine and a grenade and screaming like a wild man, he plowed on through the snow, oblivious to the heavy fire all around him. Reaching a bunker in which nine Communist soldiers were crouching, he shot one of them in the

face, then whirled and killed another one who had a machine gun trained on him. He then jumped into the trench and killed five more of the enemy. When two escaped to another bunker, Rosser followed them and threw his grenade inside; he shot both as they emerged from the explosion.

Rosser moved on to another trench line and killed five more Chinese soldiers. His ammunition finally exhausted, he went back down the hill to resupply himself by stripping rifle magazines and grenades off dead GIs, then climbed the hill again. He threw a grenade into the first trench he came to, killing seven more of the enemy, then moved over open ground, firing at every Chinese soldier in sight. When his ammunition was gone again, he repeated his resupply trip down the hill, then returned a third time to continue his one-man battle.

After more than an hour of fighting, Rosser organized a withdrawal of his decimated company, ordering those who could walk to take a dead or wounded comrade with them. He calculated that he personally had killed more than twenty Chinese with grenades and another twenty-eight with rifle fire.

Rosser returned to the States in May 1952 and announced to his mother that he had avenged his brother's death. After being awarded the Medal of Honor by President Harry Truman on June 27, 1952, he decided to stay in the Army.

In 1968, he lost another brother, this time in Vietnam. When he requested assignment to the combat zone to even his personal score once again, he was refused. "If something happened to you, even by accident, it would be hard to explain," his commanding officer told him. Rosser retired from the Army soon after.

BIOGRAPHY

BORN
October 24, 1929
Columbus, Ohio

ENTERED SERVICE
Crooksville, Ohio

BRANCH
U.S. Army

DUTY
Korean War

CURRENT RESIDENCE
Ohio

Fulfilling a Solemn Promise

TIBOR RUBIN

CORPORAL, U.S. ARMY Company I, 8th Cavalry Regiment, 1st Cavalry Division

BIOGRAPHY

BORN
June 18, 1929
Hungary

ENTERED SERVICE
Oakland, California

BRANCH
U.S. Army

DUTY
Korean War

CURRENT RESIDENCE
California

TIBOR "TED" RUBIN WAS THIRTEEN IN 1943 WHEN THE Nazis began to round up the Jews of his native Hungary. Rubin was sent to the Mauthausen concentration camp in Austria; the rest of his family, he learned later, was sent to Auschwitz. His father was eventually transferred to Buchenwald and was never heard from again. His older sister survived Auschwitz, but his mother and younger sister did not.

Rubin was barely clinging to life when the U.S. Army liberated Mauthausen in May 1945. It was then that he made a solemn promise that if he was ever allowed to immigrate to the United States, he would join the Army and become a "GI Joe" like the men who freed him from the Nazis. Nursed back to health, he became a "displaced person" until 1948, when he finally came to the United States. He found work as a butcher, but he still wanted to be a GI Joe. Rubin learned just enough English to join the Army in February 1950. He was assigned to the 8th Cavalry Regiment. By early summer, his unit was in Korea.

At Chirye, in one of his unit's first engagements, the company commander decided to redeploy the men under the cover of darkness. Corporal Rubin was ordered by his first sergeant to stay behind to cover the movement. Rubin stocked each empty foxhole with grenades, and when the North Koreans attacked the following morning, he ran from one foxhole to another, firing his rifle and lobbing grenades at the enemy. He single-handedly held the hill throughout the next day, inflicting a large number of casualties on the North Koreans.

Following the breakout from the Pusan Perimeter, the 8th Regiment advanced into North Korea. During this advance, Rubin helped capture several hundred North Korean soldiers. On October 30, Chinese forces that had just entered the war attacked his unit at Unsan in a massive night assault. Rubin took over a .30-caliber machine gun after three other gunners were hit. He continued to man it for several hours while his unit retreated. With his ammunition exhausted, Rubin was seriously wounded and then captured.

He was taken to the infamous Death Valley camp for several weeks before being moved to Camp Number 5 at Pyoktong. When the Communists discovered he was from Hungary, they offered to return him to that "People's Republic." Rubin refused. For the next two and a half years, he employed everything he had learned in surviving the Holocaust to keep himself and other prisoners at Pyoktong alive. Many nights, he crawled out into the prison compound to steal food from supply houses, returning to distribute it to his fellow captives. Rubin also provided desperately needed medical care and moral support for the sick and wounded of the POW camp. Later, the Army would credit him with saving more than forty lives during his captivity.

After the cease-fire, Rubin was repatriated to the United States and finally received his U.S. citizenship. He knew that on at least four separate occasions he had been recommended for the Medal of Honor; he had also been recommended for the Distinguished Service Cross and Silver Star (twice)—but as he returned to civilian life, he forgot about medals and moved on with raising a family.

In 1996, Congress passed legislation requiring the military to review the records of certain Jewish-American war veterans to determine if any of them should be awarded the Medal of Honor. Rubin's case was one of those reopened; the evidence of his bravery astonished the reviewers. On September 23, 2005, he was awarded the medal in a White House ceremony presided over by President George W. Bush.

Career Army, Career Hero

EDWARD R. SCHOWALTER

FIRST LIEUTENANT, U.S. ARMY Company A, 31st Infantry Regiment, 7th Infantry Division

BIOGRAPHY

BORN
December 24, 1927
New Orleans, Louisiana

ENTERED SERVICE
Metairie, Louisiana

BRANCH
U.S. Army

DUTY
Korean War

DIED
November 21, 2003
Auburn, Alabama

AFTER GRADUATING FROM HIGH SCHOOL IN JUNE 1945, Edward Schowalter begged his parents to let him enlist in the military, although he was just seventeen. They compromised by allowing him to go into the Merchant Marines. He went through boot camp, fearing that the war in the Pacific would end before he got to sea. Just after V-E Day, he went out on a Liberty ship that brought American soldiers home from combat, so he got to taste the war vicariously through them.

Schowalter decided to make a career of the military and wanted to be an officer. After graduation from Virginia Military Institute, he entered the Army as a second lieutenant. He arrived in Korea on April Fools' Day 1952 and was assigned to the 31st Infantry, 7th Division. Now a lieutenant and company commander, he was told by his battalion commander that his company would lead the attack against a hill nicknamed Jane Russell (for the actress's famous curves) near Kumwha. On October 14, when the first platoon attacked a key approach to the objective, it came under vicious small-arms, grenade, and mortar fire and was stopped within fifty yards of the enemy strongpoint. Schowalter led the second platoon to support it. As they neared the objective, he was severely wounded in the side by a grenade fragment, but he refused medical aid. He then led his men into the trenches and began routing the enemy from its bunkers with grenades. A sudden burst of fire from a hidden cave off the trench wounded him again. Refusing to relinquish command, he continued to encourage his men until the position was secured. Then he was finally evacuated.

An account of Schowalter's action recommending him for the Medal of Honor was written up by the company radio operator and signed by the men in the company. A year later, while recovering from his wounds at Brook Army Medical Center in San Antonio, Texas, he was notified of the award. The medal was presented to him by President Dwight Eisenhower on January 12, 1954.

Schowalter went on to command a battalion in the 82nd Airborne Division and did two combat tours of duty in Vietnam. While serving as senior province adviser in the Mekong Delta, he was shot three times during the Tet Offensive of 1968. On his return home, he was awarded the Silver Star. He continued to serve in the Army until his retirement as a colonel in 1977.

At Observation Post Irene

ROBERT E. SIMANEK

PRIVATE FIRST CLASS, U.S. MARINE CORPS Company F, 2nd Battalion, 5th Marines, 1st Marine Division

LIKE OTHER YOUNG MEN WHO GREW UP IN THE Detroit area, Robert Simanek went to work in the auto industry after high school. He was employed by General Motors when war broke out in Korea. Having two uncles who had served in the Marines during World War II helped him decide to become a Marine himself.

Private First Class Simanek became a radio operator. He had been in Korea for about six months when his unit encountered Chinese troops in mid-August 1952, at a place called the Hook, near Panmunjom. The Marines had been occupying a forward observation post called Irene on high ground during the day, when they had air support, and relinquishing it to the enemy during the night. On the morning of August 17, a sixteen-man patrol was sent to reclaim the post for the daylight hours, with Simanek as their radioman. The platoon sergeant happened to take a new route to the position, and that kept them from walking right into the company of Chinese troops waiting in ambush. As they reached the post, however, the enemy opened fire with mortars and machine guns.

Simanek jumped into the trench line with six comrades as the rest of the patrol headed back down the hill. Though wounded by an exploding grenade, he continued to operate the patrol's radio and fire at the enemy with a .45-caliber pistol. Then his weapon jammed; he yelled to a Marine to toss him another one, but at that moment a second Chinese grenade landed in the middle of the trench. Realizing that it could kill or injure all the Marines in the bunker, he rolled over on top of it and absorbed the force of the explosion with his legs.

Simanek tried to make his legs move but couldn't—he was also badly wounded in the hip and knee. With

the enemy becoming bolder, he asked for air support, and a P-51 swooped down to drop napalm. For the next two hours, he maintained radio communications with the command post and directed tank and artillery fire against enemy positions, while at the same time shooting at the Chinese with his pistol. The Chinese finally retreated.

Two members of the patrol who were still able-bodied carried down one badly injured Marine. Two other severely wounded Marines managed to get down the hill on their own. Simanek crawled down from the outpost on his hands and knees.

He was treated on board a hospital ship and then in Japan before returning to the States. It took him six months to recuperate from his wounds and to learn to walk again. He found out he was to receive the Medal of Honor almost exactly a year after the action near the Hook. It was presented to him on October 27, 1953, by President Dwight Eisenhower. When the press asked him after the award ceremony what the President had said to him, Simanek replied, "Congratulations on a fine award." What the President had actually said was, "Turn around, son, and face the crowd."

BIOGRAPHY

BORN
April 26, 1930
Detroit, Michigan

ENTERED SERVICE
Detroit, Michigan

BRANCH
U.S. Marine Corps

DUTY
Korean War

CURRENT RESIDENCE
Michigan

Rediscovering a Lost Faith

CARL L. SITTER

CAPTAIN, U.S. MARINE CORPS Company G, 3rd Battalion, 1st Marines, 1st Marine Division

BIOGRAPHY

BORN
December 2, 1922
Syracuse, Missouri

ENTERED SERVICE
Pueblo, Colorado

BRANCH
U.S. Marine Corps

DUTY
Korean War

DIED
April 4, 2000
Richmond, Virginia

CARL SITTER'S GRANDFATHER, A PRESBYTERIAN minister, exerted a powerful influence over him in his youth, although Sitter fell away from religion as he reached adulthood in Pueblo, Colorado. He joined the Marines in 1941 and fought several engagements in the Pacific. In 1944, a twenty-two-year-old lieutenant, he was on Eniwetok, where he was first wounded. A few months later he was on Guam, where several Marine rifle companies had suffered casualties as high as 50 percent. He was pushing his platoon to attack a Japanese position when he was knocked down by a powerful blow to the chest. Bleeding profusely, he thought he had been hit in the heart, until he felt his chest and realized that the shattered .45-caliber pistol holstered under his left shoulder had absorbed a machine-gun round, saving his life. He later said that he had begun to rediscover his lost faith at that moment.

In 1950, Sitter, now a captain, was commanding officer of a company in the 1st Marines in Korea. It was the coldest winter there in one hundred years. He was still wearing his World War II pistol, which was a good luck charm as much as a weapon, under his left arm, and he was also carrying his grandfather's Bible.

Surrounded by a numerically superior Chinese Communist force near Hagaru-ri and the Chosin Reservoir, Sitter's unit was ordered to break through the enemy encirclement and reinforce his battalion on November 29. His company fought a vicious daylong battle with Chinese troops. By the time Sitter's unit had reached Hagaru-ri, only 150 of his 265 men were still able to fight. The next morning, Sitter was informed that a hostile force of regimental strength was entrenched on East Hill, a snow-covered vantage point commanding the entire valley, which allowed the Chinese to fire down on the town. A battered unit under the command of Major Reginald Myers (who would win a Medal of Honor for his part in this battle) had tried to drive the Chinese off the hill but had been stopped short. Sitter reorganized his depleted Marines and led them up the steep, frozen hillside to relieve Myers's outpost. After managing to advance almost to the peak of the hill, Sitter's men dug in for the night.

Just before midnight, the Chinese counterattacked with mortars and machine guns. Low on ammunition, Sitter sent men down the hill for supplies. They returned just before the next attack. Sitter moved from foxhole to foxhole, encouraging his outnumbered men as the enemy penetrated his lines; at one point, when the Chinese got close enough to the command post to throw grenades inside, Sitter grabbed a rifle and rushed forward to join the hand-to-hand combat. Although badly wounded in the arms, face, and chest by shrapnel, he fought on for another two days until Myers was relieved and the area was secured. More than half of that Chinese force was killed, wounded, or captured.

Carl Sitter was awarded the Medal of Honor by President Harry Truman on October 29, 1951. After leaving the military in 1970 with the rank of colonel, he served as a lay minister in his church. In 1998, at the age of seventy-seven, he decided to follow in his grandfather's footsteps and became a student at a theological seminary.

Holding Fast

JAMES L. STONE

FIRST LIEUTENANT, U.S. ARMY Company E, 8th Cavalry Regiment, 1st Cavalry Division

BIOGRAPHY

BORN
December 27, 1922
Pine Bluff, Arkansas

ENTERED SERVICE
Houston, Texas

BRANCH
U.S. Army

DUTY
Korean War

CURRENT RESIDENCE
Texas

ON NOVEMBER 21, 1951, LIEUTENANT JAMES STONE, a month away from his twenty-ninth birthday, was trying to keep warm in a desolate hilltop outpost above the Imjin River near Sokkogae. That morning his platoon, part of the 1st Cavalry, had relieved another American unit at an outpost facing the Chinese Communist forces on an opposing hill. During the day, the enemy fired white phosphorus shells at the Americans. Stone knew that this meant they were marking his position for an artillery barrage and probable assault later on.

Around 9:00 P.M., the Chinese unleashed a ferocious artillery and mortar attack. After the barrage ended, Stone radioed U.S. gunners to send up flares. When they burst high in the sky and illuminated the nightscape, he could see hundreds of enemy troops—roughly a battalion—scrambling up the hill to attack. Within minutes, the Chinese were nearly on top of Stone's platoon. The Americans repelled this assault and five others over the next three hours.

Shortly after midnight, the Chinese added another battalion to the assault. The forty-eight U.S. troops now faced perhaps eight hundred of the enemy. During the fighting, Stone continued to call in artillery support; moving calmly among his men, he encouraged them to hold fast and make every shot count. He climbed up on the sandbagged trenches to direct the defense, exposing himself to enemy fire. When a flamethrower crucial to the U.S. defense malfunctioned and its operator was killed, Stone ran to the position, pulled the gas tanks off the dead man, repaired the flamethrower by flare light, and handed the weapon off to another operator.

The Chinese used bangalore torpedoes to destroy the wires and fortifications marking the American platoon's perimeter, then entered the U.S. trench lines.

Stone joined his men in a hand-to-hand fight, at times using his rifle as a club or knifing the enemy with his bayonet. At one point, he picked up the platoon's one functioning machine gun and carried it from place to place to train fire on the Chinese. Already wounded twice, he was then hit in the neck. One of his men—Stone didn't see who it was—saved his life by immediately wrapping a bandage around his neck to stop the flow of blood.

Realizing that his dwindling force (twenty-four of his men had been killed, he later learned) would be annihilated, Stone gathered his remaining men together and told those who were still mobile to try to make it back to the company. He said he would stay behind with the badly wounded to cover their retreat. Those who escaped could hear him continuing the fight as they left. Just before dawn, Stone and six other survivors were overwhelmed. The next day, when U.S. forces retook the hill, they counted the bodies of 545 enemy dead.

Stone, unconscious when he was taken prisoner by the Chinese, was carried on a stretcher to a command post behind enemy lines and interrogated. He was then taken to a prison camp on the Yalu River, where he spent the next twenty-two months. On September 3, 1953, he was repatriated in a prisoner exchange. Immediately mobbed by reporters and cameramen asking him how it felt to have won the Medal of Honor, Stone, who had no knowledge of his award, was speechless.

A month later, on October 27, 1953, he was at the White House. President Dwight Eisenhower presented the medal to Stone and to six others. Then, looking around at the servicemen whose extraordinary exploits he had just discussed, Ike quipped to the audience, "I feel perfectly safe up here."

Reacting on the Point

ERNEST E. WEST

PRIVATE FIRST CLASS, U.S. ARMY 2nd Squad, 3rd Platoon, Company L, 3rd Battalion, 14th Infantry Regiment, 25th Infantry Division

BIOGRAPHY

BORN
September 2, 1931
Russell, Kentucky

ENTERED SERVICE
Wurtland, Kentucky

BRANCH
U.S. Army

DUTY
Korean War

CURRENT RESIDENCE
Kentucky

PRIVATE FIRST CLASS ERNEST WEST DID HIS BASIC training as part of the 25th Infantry in Hawaii—a "paradise" in comparison to what he would experience in Korea, which he regarded as a frozen hell in the winter and a suffocating hell in the summertime. For a Kentucky boy who had dropped out of high school to take a job on the railroad before being drafted in 1950, Korea was simply the most unfriendly environment he could imagine.

In the fall of 1952, West's unit was near Sataeri. It was a hilly area, and after dark the U.S. soldiers were monitoring Chinese troops with primitive night vision equipment. The Americans were struck by how tall the enemy troops were—six-footers from northern China and Mongolia, who were dug into bunkers along a high ridgeline.

On October 12, West was one of sixteen Americans who volunteered for a mission to try to capture some of the enemy for interrogation. Moving as silently as possible through a valley separating the U.S. and Chinese positions, they came to a rise leading up to the enemy bunkers. Half of the group stayed behind with machine guns. The others began to climb up toward the enemy, with West walking ahead as the point man. Suddenly, the Chinese began to roll grenades down onto them. One passed between West's legs and exploded near his lieutenant, who was just behind him. Two other Americans also went down. Realizing that his contingent had walked into an ambush, West ordered those who were not hurt to retreat. Then he ran through heavy small-arms fire and exploding grenades to his lieutenant, who was badly hurt. Using his body to shield the helpless officer from flying shrapnel, West picked him up and started down the hill. Four enemy soldiers

came at him, but he killed them with his rifle. West made it back to the U.S. position with the lieutenant, then returned for another wounded American, killing eight more of the enemy along the way. As he dragged the second man to safety, a grenade exploded near him, deadening his left arm and sending shrapnel into his eye. Bleeding heavily, West returned for another wounded comrade and got him down the hill.

West spent the next ten months in the hospital, most of it at Walter Reed. Doctors tried to save his eye by positioning a large powerful magnet over it to draw out the shrapnel, but the procedure didn't work and the eye had to be removed. Finally released from the service, West returned to Kentucky. It was hard for him not to feel that he was still at war. On his first day back at his old job on the railroad, a coworker came up behind him and clapped him on the shoulder. West instinctively turned and wrestled the man down. He quickly apologized: "Sorry, but you'll have to give me a month or so. Just talk to me, don't touch me."

Early in 1954, West got a telegram informing him that he was to receive the Medal of Honor. His railroad arranged to make a special stop in his hometown of Russell, where he boarded a private car that carried him to Washington, D.C. After putting the medal around his neck on January 12, 1954, President Dwight D. Eisenhower said to West, "In addition to this decoration, you have an old soldier's admiration."

Ernest West returned home and continued to work on the railroad until his retirement in 1993.

Portraits of Valor

VIETNAM WAR

Ennobled by Example

I owe not only respect and gratitude but my life to a Medal of Honor recipient. After I was shot down and captured during the Vietnam War and had spent some time in a hospital, where my condition did not particularly improve, I asked to be transferred to a prison camp where other Americans were being held. My North Vietnamese captors moved me to a camp called "the Plantation." To my great relief, I was placed in a cell in a building with two other prisoners, both Air Force majors, George "Bud" Day, who is profiled in this book, and Norris Overly. I could have asked for no better companions. There has never been a doubt in my mind that Bud Day and Norris Overly saved my life.

Bud and Norris later told me that their first impression of me, emaciated, bug-eyed, and bright with fever, was of a man at the threshold of death. They thought the Vietnamese expected me to die and had placed me in their care to escape the blame when I failed to recover.

Despite my condition, I was overjoyed to be in the company of Americans. I wouldn't stop talking all through that first day with Bud and Norris. They were the souls of kindness as they eased my way to what they believed was my imminent death.

Bud himself had been seriously injured when he ejected from his aircraft. Like me, he had broken his right arm in three places and had torn the ligaments in his knee. After his capture, he had attempted an escape to the south, and had nearly reached an American airfield when he was recaptured. He was brutally tortured for his efforts, and for subsequently resisting his captors' every entreaty for information.

First held in prison in Vinh before making the 150-mile trip north to Hanoi, Bud had experienced early the full measure of the mistreatment that would be his fate for nearly six years as a prisoner of war in Vietnam. His captors had looped rope around his shoulders, tightened it until his shoulders were nearly touching, and then hung him by the arms from the rafter of the torture room, tearing his shoulders apart. Left in this condition for hours, Bud never acceded to the Vietnamese demands for military information. They had to refracture his broken right arm and threaten to break the other before Bud gave them anything at all.

Bud was a tough man, a fierce resister, whose example was an inspiration to every man who served with him. For his heroic escape attempt, he received the Medal of Honor.

Bud and I were roommates for about three months in prison. When the Vietnamese observed that I could get around on crutches, they moved Bud to another cell. I cannot adequately describe how sorry I was to part company with my friend and inspiration. I don't believe I had ever relied on any other person for emotional and physical support to the extent I had relied on Bud.

You will read about Bud in this book, and about Rear Admiral James Stockdale, our legendary senior ranking officer in North Vietnam's prison camps. As a resistance leader, Jim had few peers. He was a constant inspiration. Many of his Vietnamese captors hated him for his fierce and unyielding spirit. One, whom we had nicknamed the Rabbit, hated him the most.

One day, the Rabbit ordered Jim cleaned up so that he could be filmed for a propaganda movie in which he would play a visiting American businessman. He was given a razor to shave. Jim used it to hack off his hair, severely cutting his scalp in the process and spoiling his appearance, in the hope that this would render him unsuitable for his enemies' purpose.

But the Rabbit was not so easily dissuaded. He left to find a hat to place on Jim's bleeding head. In the intervening moments, Jim picked up a wooden stool and repeatedly bashed his face with it. Disfigured, Jim succeeded in frustrating the Rabbit's plans for him that evening.

On a later occasion, after being whipped and tied in ropes at the hands of a demented Vietnamese interrogator we called Bug, Jim was forced to confess that he had defied camp regulations restricting communication with fellow prisoners. But Bug was not through with him. He informed Jim that he would be back tomorrow to torture him for more information. Jim feared that he would be forced to give up the names of the men he had been communicating with. In an effort to impress his enemies with his determination not to betray his comrades, he broke a window and slashed his wrist with a shard of glass.

As his Medal of Honor citation reads,

> Rear Admiral Stockdale resolved to make himself a symbol of resistance regardless of personal sacrifice. He deliberately inflicted a near-mortal wound to his person in order to convince his captors of his willingness to give up his life rather than capitulate. He was subsequently discovered and revived by the North Vietnamese who, convinced of his indomitable spirit, abated in their employment of excessive harassment and torture toward all of the Prisoners of War. By his heroic action, at great peril to himself, he earned the everlasting gratitude of his fellow prisoners and of his country.

As you read in these pages about Bud and Jim, and Leo Thorsness and Jon Cavaiani, who were in prison with us, and about my friends Bob Kerrey and Dan Inouye, and all the other heroes whose extraordinary service to America is memorialized in this book, you will be awed, as I am, not only by their courage and character, but by the country that produced such men and that was ennobled by the example they set for the rest of us.

Night Ambush

JOHN P. BACA

SPECIALIST FOURTH CLASS, U.S. ARMY Company D, 1st Battalion, 12th Cavalry, 1st Cavalry Division

BY HIS OWN ACCOUNT, JOHN BACA WAS A PROBLEM kid. Growing up in the San Diego area, he was in and out of juvenile hall for a variety of petty crimes. At seventeen, after serving a brief sentence in a California Youth Authority correctional facility, he wanted to join the military but couldn't because he was still on parole. Two years later, in 1969, he was drafted.

Early in 1970, Baca was a specialist fourth class in a heavy-weapons platoon with the 12th Cavalry, 1st Cavalry Division in Phuoc Long Province, Vietnam. Engagements with the enemy had become more intense as his unit moved closer to the Cambodian border. In one of them, the unit was pinned down by the enemy for hours. Ankle-deep in red clay, Baca had just bent over to set up his recoilless rifle when he heard the snapping sound of a sniper's bullet pass right over his back.

On the morning of February 10, after being in the bush for almost a month, Baca's company returned to its base. The men were to have a few days of rest before going out again, but late that afternoon they and a rifle platoon were ordered to set up a night ambush and were helicoptered to the target area at dusk.

The Americans established a position near a trail and placed warning devices—trip wires connected to claymore mines—on either end of it that would alert them to the presence of the enemy. When an eight-man patrol from the rifle platoon went out to investigate a mine explosion, it soon came under attack from enemy soldiers concealed along the trail. Baca, sprinting through heavy fire with his recoilless rifle to aid the patrol, had just set up a firing position for his weapon and fired one round when a grenade landed close by. He would later remember thinking, Do I pick it up?

Do I run? Then he ripped off his helmet, put it over the grenade, and covered it with his body.

The grenade exploded, and several GIs picked Baca up and carried him to the shelter of a tree. Leaning against the trunk, he felt no pain, although when he looked down at his stomach he could see his intestines poking out of his uniform. He remembers wondering if his mother, whom he had called that morning and told that he would remain in the rear for a few days, would be angry with him. The noises of the battle raging all around him seemed distant, and the movement of his comrades seemed to be in slow motion. With death very near, Baca felt he was held in the arms of an angel—peaceful and gentle moments.

It was close to two hours before Baca was carried to a landing zone and helicoptered out. On the flight back to the base, he gripped the hand of another wounded soldier, then began to hemorrhage and lost consciousness. After being treated in Long Binh for a week, he was sent to a hospital in Japan. His mother, told that he might not survive, flew to his bedside and stayed with him for a few weeks, then accompanied him back to the States in late April. Over the next several months, he continued to improve, although he wound up in intensive care on two occasions.

John Baca was out of the Army and starting college when he was informed that he would receive the Medal of Honor. President Richard Nixon presented it to him at the White House on June 15, 1971. Baca returned to Vietnam in 1990 and worked for two months alongside former enemy soldiers to build a United States–Vietnam friendship clinic.

BIOGRAPHY

BORN
January 10, 1949
Providence, Rhode Island

ENTERED SERVICE
Fort Ord, California

BRANCH
U.S. Army

DUTY
Vietnam War

CURRENT RESIDENCE
California

Saving the Cavalry

NICKY D. BACON

STAFF SERGEANT, U.S. ARMY Company B, 4th Battalion, 21st Infantry, 11th Infantry Brigade, Americal Division

THE SON OF AN ARKANSAS SHARECROPPER, NICKY Bacon grew up working on farms. After serving in the Arizona National Guard, he volunteered for active duty in Vietnam in 1964. He ended his first tour in 1967, after having fought mainly in small-unit engagements against the Vietcong.

Early the next year, he was sent to Hawaii to help train the 21st Infantry—the "jungle warriors"—of the Americal Division. That fall, Bacon, now a staff sergeant, returned with the 21st to Vietnam for his second tour. But the war had changed. Well-supplied and disciplined units of the North Vietnamese Army, filtering into the Republic of Vietnam down the Ho Chi Minh Trail, had begun to take over the brunt of the fighting from the Vietcong. The engagements were larger and far bloodier, particularly during and after the Tet Offensive early in 1968.

On August 26, 1968, Bacon's company was returning to base for a respite after a month of fighting. The men expected steak and beer and long showers. Instead, they were hustled onto helicopters and sent to help a unit of the 1st Cavalry under heavy attack near Tam Ky.

The stalled tanks and armored personnel carriers of the 1st Cavalry were ready to move forward by the time Staff Sergeant Bacon's unit arrived. As they were deploying, a reinforced and well-camouflaged North Vietnamese regiment dug into the hillside opened fire.

Bacon organized his men and began an assault. He assaulted one enemy bunker and destroyed it with grenades. Seconds later, several GIs, including the lieutenant leading his platoon, were hit by machine-gun fire. Bacon took command: He got the badly wounded officer back to a personnel carrier, then returned to destroy the machine gun. Another platoon moved up to support his position; when its lieutenant went down, Bacon assumed command of that unit as well.

Armored personnel carriers were needed to evacuate the wounded, but they were unable to reach the American position because of heavy fire from rocket-propelled grenades. Bacon killed four more of the enemy and destroyed an antitank weapon with a grenade. Now that the American armor could move again, Bacon climbed onto the deck of a tank and directed fire into the enemy position while the wounded were evacuated. The company commander then called in air strikes, which took the pressure off Bacon's unit and allowed it to advance.

Several weeks after this engagement, Staff Sergeant Bacon was awarded the Distinguished Service Cross. He didn't know that because of reports about his conduct from his company commander, the cavalry troop commander, and others both in the air and on the ground who had watched the action, an upgrade in his medal was being considered. The following year, he was back at Fort Hood when General William Westmoreland phoned to tell him that he was to receive the Medal of Honor. Bacon was out on a date and missed the call; his buddies went looking for him to make sure he'd be there when the general called again.

Bacon received the medal from President Richard Nixon on November 24, 1969. Afterward, he tried to get back into the war one last time, even though Medal of Honor recipients weren't supposed to return to combat. His request for a volunteer reassignment had almost passed through the chain of command when he got a call from General John K. Bowles berating him for trying to sneak back into action.

BIOGRAPHY

BORN
November 25, 1945
Caraway, Arkansas

ENTERED SERVICE
Phoenix, Arizona

BRANCH
U.S. Army

DUTY
Vietnam War

DIED
July 17, 2010
Rosebud, Arkansas

Jungle Assault

JOHN F. BAKER, JR.

PRIVATE FIRST CLASS, U.S. ARMY Company A, 2nd Battalion, 27th Infantry, 25th Infantry Division

BIOGRAPHY

BORN
October 30, 1945
Davenport, Iowa

ENTERED SERVICE
Moline, Illinois

BRANCH
U.S. Army

DUTY
Vietnam War

CURRENT RESIDENCE
South Carolina

PRIVATE FIRST CLASS JOHN BAKER HAD BEEN IN several small actions in Vietnam, but they were nothing like what he saw on November 5, 1966, in Tay Ninh Province near the Cambodian border. Part of the 27th Infantry, his Company A had been ordered to assist another company that was pinned down by the Vietcong, whose numbers had been growing throughout the battle. By the time Company A arrived late on November 4, and set up for the night, there were three thousand enemy soldiers in the area.

Baker's unit moved out at dawn to relieve its embattled sister company. As he entered the dense jungle, Baker couldn't see the enemy but knew they were near. Then machine-gun and mortar fire broke out from Vietcong soldiers who had tied themselves onto the limbs of trees and hidden in a concrete bunker complex in the thick undergrowth. When Baker saw the lead man in his column go down, he immediately moved up and with another soldier charged two of the bunkers where the heaviest fire was coming from. The man with him was shot, his arm hanging by a shred of flesh. In an effort to protect him, Baker killed four enemy snipers, then dragged his mortally wounded comrade to safety.

After grabbing more ammunition, Baker returned to the thick of the fighting. He was knocked down by a grenade explosion, but he got back up and with one of his men assaulted another bunker. When the GI was hit and dropped his machine gun, Baker picked it up and attacked a fourth bunker, killing several more Vietcong. As he was trying to evacuate the fallen soldier, they both came under fire from more snipers. Baker shot four of them; then, finally out of ammunition, he dragged two more GIs off the battlefield. At the end of the two-hour-long battle, he had killed ten Vietcong, destroyed six machine-gun bunkers, and saved eight of his comrades.

The day John Baker left Vietnam in August 1967, he heard that he was to receive the Medal of Honor, but he refused to believe it. However, the enlisted men he had fought alongside that day in Tay Ninh had indeed written a recommendation and pushed it up through the ranks. On May 1, 1968, President Lyndon Johnson awarded the medal to him and to Captain Robert Foley, who had commanded the American action that day.

CONGRESSIONAL
MEDAL OF HONOR
RECIPIENT
JOHN F. BAKER

"Corpsman Up!"

DONALD E. BALLARD

HOSPITAL CORPSMAN SECOND CLASS, U.S. NAVY (FMF) Company M, 3rd Battalion, 4th Marines, 3rd Marine Division

DONALD BALLARD WAS TWENTY YEARS OLD, married, and working in a dental lab with the hope of someday becoming a dentist when he decided to join the Navy in 1965. Midway through basic training, informed that dental assistants were plentiful but corpsmen were in short supply, he was sent to surgical assistant school. He assisted in orthopedic and general operations, then was "volunteered" to serve as a medic with the Marine Corps. His unit soon sailed for the Mediterranean, where it made a simulated amphibious landing on Corsica. While there, Ballard and the other American servicemen got to know some French Legionnaires, who told them daunting stories about Vietnam. In 1967, he was sent into the war zone on a transport plane, which had a strange smell; he later found out that it served as a "morgue plane" on its outbound trips.

On the day he arrived, he was issued a .45-caliber pistol, but there was no magazine. "Don't worry, Doc," the supply sergeant told him when he asked about it. "If you need a weapon, there'll be plenty on the ground when the fighting starts." He would learn from personal observation that corpsmen were more likely to be wounded than riflemen because they had to be the first men standing after everyone else had hit the dirt. "Corpsman up!" was part of the Marine battle cry.

Ballard was shot in one of his Marine unit's first actions and received the first of his three Purple Hearts. (He should have had eight by the time he left Vietnam, but he tended to his own wounds on five occasions.)

On May 16, 1968, having just treated two Marines for heat exhaustion during a patrol, Ballard was returning from the evacuation landing zone when his company was ambushed by a North Vietnamese unit firing automatic weapons and mortars. He rushed to a group of wounded Marines, one of whom had had both legs shredded by a grenade. As he kneeled to care for him, another Marine who had been shot in the face yelled, "Grenade!" Ballard's first thought as he saw it hit nearby was that it would kill the men he was treating if it exploded, so he threw himself on the grenade and cradled it to his body. After what seemed like an eternity with no explosion, he threw the grenade away and turned his attention back to the wounded men. He was told later that the grenade, which apparently had a defective fuse, had exploded in the air.

After being wounded again in the fall of 1968, Ballard returned to the United States and was assigned to work in a Navy surgical clinic. One day an Army recruiter came to the hospital and offered him a commission to make a "lateral transfer" from the Navy. He had already decided to make a career of the military, so he joined the Army. While waiting to attend Officer Candidate School, he was informed that he was to receive the Medal of Honor. It was presented to him on May 14, 1970, by President Richard Nixon, who told him, "The country has a lot to be thankful for having men of your caliber. I am very proud of you."

After serving a total of thirty-five years, active and reserve, Donald Ballard retired from the Kansas National Guard in 2000 as a colonel.

BIOGRAPHY

BORN
December 5, 1945
Kansas City, Missouri

ENTERED SERVICE
Kansas City, Missouri

BRANCH
U.S. Navy

DUTY
Vietnam War

CURRENT RESIDENCE
Missouri

FRANCIS A
KEITH D
JAMES G
SYLVESTER
CLARK A MILLER
BUCHANAN
D O GRIFFIN · PAUL C HUNTER
ARLES W LANTZ · JAMES D LAW
D TUCKER · RICHARD
BROWER · LAWRENCE
HAEL N JOHNSON
EORGE MORGAN · DAVID W MORRILL
S W SANDERS · HARRY W BRANHAM
OMAS M WHITMAN

"Thanks for Saving My Life"

HARVEY C. "BARNEY" BARNUM, JR.

FIRST LIEUTENANT, U.S. MARINE CORPS Company H, 2nd Battalion, 9th Marines, 3rd Marine Division

AT THE CHESHIRE, CONNECTICUT, HIGH SCHOOL military assembly in 1958, representatives of all branches of the military made presentations to the student body. After the Navy, Army, and Air Force speakers were all interrupted by hoots and catcalls, the Marine recruiter stood up and gave a tongue-lashing to the rude students, as well as to the faculty members who had made no effort to correct their behavior. As he began to stalk out of the auditorium, he was surrounded by students eager to sign up. Among them was senior class president Harvey C. "Barney" Barnum, Jr.

In late 1965, Barnum, a first lieutenant, arrived in Vietnam with the 9th Marines. On the morning of December 18, as the battalion was moving through heavy overgrowth in Quang Tin Province south of Da Nang, the area suddenly exploded with fire from enemy rockets, mortars, and machine guns. Barnum's company of about 110 men was cut off from the rest of the American force; the company commander was down, his radioman alongside him. Barnum ran to help them, but the radio operator was already dead, and the captain died in Barnum's arms. It was clear that the enemy had targeted the two men to destroy the company's command and control and overwhelm the survivors of the initial attack. Barnum took the radio off the dead operator, strapped it on his back, and assumed command.

Estimating that the Marines were outnumbered about ten to one, Barnum quickly organized defenses, called in artillery fire, and led a counterattack on the enemy trench lines to destroy the machine guns that had his men pinned down. He saw that they weren't facing Vietcong but North Vietnamese regulars, troops disciplined enough to have let the bulk of the Marine battalion pass through before triggering the ambush.

At close to 6:00 P.M., after nearly eight hours of continuous fighting, the battalion commander radioed Barnum that it would be impossible to mount a rescue for his cut-off Marines. Barnum knew that if he tried to hold out through the night, his dwindling force would be wiped out by morning, so he ordered the company engineers to blow a space in the heavy tree cover to allow two H-34 helicopters to land for the evacuation of the dead and wounded. Then he ordered the rest of his men to move out in fire-team rushes. Perhaps because the maneuver was so unexpected, they were able to break through North Vietnamese lines, crossing five hundred yards of fire-swept ground to rejoin the forward elements of his battalion before darkness.

Barnum was told two days later that the commanding general was recommending him for the Medal of Honor.

He was presented the medal on February 27, 1967, by Secretary of the Navy Paul Nitze. But it would take months, even years, for the fragments of this day to come together in his memory. When they did, it was often only with the help of messages he occasionally received from the men he had commanded. "Somebody gave me your name," one Marine e-mailed him decades later. "I think you're the lieutenant who fought beside me with a .45-caliber pistol and a 3.5 rocket launcher for a while back in '65. If so, thanks for saving my life." Until this communication, Barnum hadn't remembered the incident.

First Lieutenant Barnum left Vietnam in February 1966. He worked as a military aide in Washington on the condition that he be allowed to pick his next assignment. When it came time to make the move, he chose Vietnam. He was the first man who received the Medal of Honor in Vietnam to return to action there.

BIOGRAPHY

BORN
July 21, 1940
Cheshire, Connecticut

ENTERED SERVICE
Cheshire, Connecticut

BRANCH
U.S. Marine Corps

DUTY
Vietnam War

CURRENT RESIDENCE
Virginia

Saving Lives at All Costs

GARY B. BEIKIRCH

SERGEANT, U.S. ARMY Company B, 5th Special Forces Group, 1st Special Forces

BIOGRAPHY

BORN
August 29, 1947
Rochester, New York

ENTERED SERVICE
Buffalo, New York

BRANCH
U.S. Army

DUTY
Vietnam War

CURRENT RESIDENCE
New York

GARY BEIKIRCH FOLLOWED HIS HIGH SCHOOL sweetheart to college in 1965. Within two months, she broke up with him, and he dropped out, figuring he'd get even with her by enlisting in the Green Berets. During his advanced training, Beikirch decided to become a medic.

By the summer of 1967, he was in Kontum Province, Vietnam, as part of the 5th Special Forces Group. His twelve-man team was assigned to Camp Dak Seang, a village of Montagnard tribesmen in the Central Highlands—a beautiful jungle environment of triple-canopy forests, where tigers and enemy soldiers hid in the lush vegetation. The Montagnards were fiercely independent fighters who wore loincloths and had aligned themselves with the U.S. war effort. Accompanied by the Special Forces team, they conducted raids into Laos to disrupt North Vietnamese supply routes down the Ho Chi Minh Trail.

Early on April 1, 1970, a huge force of North Vietnamese attacked Camp Dak Seang. The Special Forces team called in gunships, whose constant fire over the next few hours was the only thing that kept the camp from being overrun.

In the early part of the assault, Sergeant Beikirch manned a 4.2-inch mortar. When it was destroyed by an enemy mortar round, he took over a machine gun, covering his Montagnard assistants as they treated wounded villagers. Then, seeing a fellow Green Beret go down, Beikirch ran through heavy fire to help the man, until he himself was hit by mortar shrapnel, which struck near his spine and paralyzed him. Beikirch got his Montagnard "bodyguards" to carry him through withering enemy fire so that he could treat the fallen villagers. He was hit in the side as he gave mouth-to-

mouth resuscitation to a Montagnard fighter, and then he was shot in the stomach. Bleeding heavily and barely conscious, he continued to fire on the enemy from his litter as his "bodyguards" dragged him from one position to another.

Some time later, Sergeant Beikirch passed out; he came to in a bomb crater awaiting evacuation by helicopter. He was taken to Pleiku and from there to Japan, and finally to the Valley Forge Medical Center, where he stayed for six months, slowly relearning to walk.

Released from the Army in August 1971, Beikirch spent a year wandering around the country before experiencing a spiritual rebirth that led him to the White Mountain Seminary in New Hampshire. There, he went to school and lived as a recluse in a cave he discovered while hiking in the rugged country nearby. In the early fall of 1973, while he was still at the seminary, a letter arrived in his post office box in town, asking him to be at a pay phone on a certain date and time for an important call. When the call came in, the voice on the other end of the line told Beikirch that he was being awarded the Medal of Honor. President Richard M. Nixon presented the medal to him on October 15, 1973.

Beikirch finished seminary in 1975 and had a job lined up to work in a missionary hospital back in Kontum Province, where he had served in the Army five years earlier. But Vietnam fell to the Communists before he could get there. Instead, he became a pastor in a New Hampshire church for a while, then decided to earn a master's degree in counseling. For more than twenty years, he has worked at a middle school in Rochester, New York.

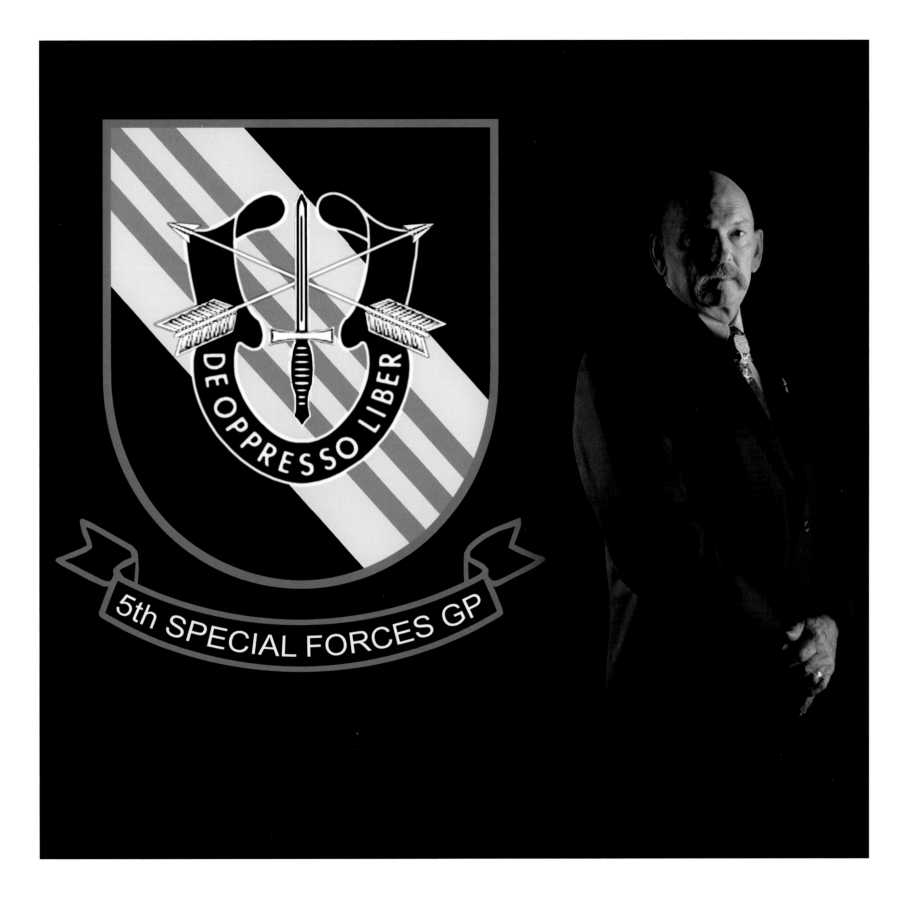

Chopper Rescues

PATRICK H. BRADY

MAJOR, U.S. ARMY Medical Service Corps, 54th Medical Detachment, 67th Medical Group, 44th Medical Brigade

RESERVE OFFICERS TRAINING WAS MANDATORY AT Patrick Brady's college in the late 1950s. He hated it and eventually got booted out. He later got back into ROTC and was commissioned in the Medical Service Corps after graduation.

Brady's first posting was to Berlin as a medical platoon leader at the time the Berlin Wall was constructed in 1961. Soon he was eager for new challenges, so he applied to flight school and became a helicopter pilot. In 1963, he went to Vietnam.

Flying a UH-1 medevac helicopter, Major Brady was on his second tour of duty as part of the 54th Medical Detachment in Chu Lai when he volunteered to rescue two badly wounded South Vietnamese soldiers in enemy territory on January 6, 1968. Several attempts had been made to get the men out; all had been aborted because of bad weather. When Brady arrived, thick fog shrouded the evacuation site. He descended slowly until he could make out the shape of trees beyond his rotor blades, then used them to orient the craft and moved sideways toward the extraction point. Despite the close-range enemy fire, he was able to locate the South Vietnamese soldiers and evacuate them.

Not long after this rescue mission, Brady was called to another fogged-in area where American casualties lay close to enemy lines. Earlier in the day, two other U.S. helicopters had been shot down trying to reach the site. Brady lowered his chopper through a space in the fog, orienting himself by a streambed to get to the wounded. In total, he made four flights over the next hour to rescue all thirty-nine GIs.

On his third mission of the day to rescue more American soldiers, Brady once again put down at a landing zone in enemy territory. During his descent, the controls of his helicopter were hit, but he was able to evacuate the injured.

Back at base, he got a replacement helicopter and returned to the action. On his fourth mission, he was watching another medevac trying to extract members of a trapped American platoon when a mine exploded nearby, causing the helicopter to leave without the casualties. Brady touched down as close to the marks left by the other craft's skids as he could to avoid mines. The soldiers were reluctant to cross the minefield, so his crewmen had to go get them. All were brought aboard, except for one who was being carried back on a stretcher by two of Brady's crew members. They had almost reached the plane when one of the stretcher bearers stepped on a mine. The explosion blew a hole in the helicopter and caused every warning light on the control panel to go on, but Brady managed to get the damaged craft off the ground and deliver the six severely injured soldiers to medical aid. Then he picked up a new helicopter and kept flying. In all, he evacuated fifty-one men that day. Four hundred bullet holes were counted in the helicopters he flew.

Back in the United States, Brady was awarded his second Distinguished Service Cross. The award was later upgraded to a Medal of Honor, which was presented to him by President Richard Nixon on October 9, 1969.

Patrick Brady retired as a major general in 1993. His daughter, Meghan, followed in his military footsteps, entering the Medical Service Corps. She served as a medic in the 1991 war against Iraq. Since retirement, Brady has supported many service organizations. He serves as the chairman of the Citizens Flag Alliance—a coalition of organizations determined to protect the American flag from physical desecration.

BIOGRAPHY

BORN
October 1, 1936
Philip, South Dakota

ENTERED SERVICE
Seattle, Washington

BRANCH
U.S. Army

DUTY
Vietnam War

CURRENT RESIDENCE
Texas

Outwitting the Enemy

PAUL W. BUCHA

CAPTAIN, U.S. ARMY Company D, 3rd Battalion, 187th Infantry, 3rd Brigade, 101st Airborne Division

A HIGH SCHOOL ALL-AMERICAN SWIMMER IN THE early 1960s, Paul Bucha was offered athletic scholarships from schools such as Yale and Indiana University, but he chose West Point instead. After graduation, he got an MBA from Stanford University, then reported to Fort Campbell. In 1967, he arrived in Vietnam with the 187th Infantry as a captain in charge of an infantry company.

On March 16, 1968, as part of the U.S. forces' effort to push the enemy away from Saigon after the Tet Offensive, Bucha's eighty-nine-man company was inserted by helicopter into a suspected North Vietnamese stronghold southwest of Phuoc Vinh. For the next two days, the unit destroyed enemy fortifications and base camps and eliminated scattered resistance. Late in the afternoon of March 18, the lead element of the company, about twelve men, exchanged fire with enemy soldiers. Then suddenly the entire area exploded with heavy machine guns, rocket-propelled grenades, and claymore mines, and the twelve men were immediately pinned down.

Realizing that his company had stumbled upon an entire North Vietnamese Army battalion bivouacked for the night, Bucha began to organize a defense to protect the men who were cut off. Crawling toward them through heavy fire, he spotted an enemy soldier whose machine gun was perched in the Y of a tree. He killed the soldier with his rifle and destroyed the bunker behind him with a grenade. As the North Vietnamese attacked repeatedly, he ordered a withdrawal and called for a platoon to evacuate the wounded. But the platoon was cut off as it was heading to a medevac landing zone.

As darkness fell, a grim thought passed through Bucha's mind: I don't even know the name of this place.

What a godforsaken place to die. Just then one of his men ran by, calling out enthusiastically, "We're really kicking some tail, aren't we, Captain?" The comment was so out of sync with what he had been thinking that Bucha laughed out loud and refocused on the struggle ahead.

Over the next few hours, everything unfolded in slow motion. Bucha was constantly on the move, encouraging his men, and shoring up the line of defense while directing artillery and helicopter gunship fire on the North Vietnamese. He did everything he could think of to make the enemy believe that his vastly outnumbered force was larger than it was—lobbing grenades at set times from different positions, spreading the firing patterns along the edges of his perimeter. At one point, with sniper fire whizzing around him and North Vietnamese soldiers so close that he could hear their conversation, he used flashlights to direct the evacuation of three air-ambulance loads of wounded, despite the fact that this illuminated him in the dark. At daybreak, he was able to lead a rescue party to the men who had been cut off from the company all night.

By then, the North Vietnamese had melted away. They took most of their dead with them, but more than 150 bodies remained behind on the battlefield. After Bucha's dead and wounded had been medevaced out, he loaded the rest of his company, about forty men, onto helicopters and returned to Phuoc Vinh.

In April 1970, at the end of his Vietnam tour, Bucha returned to West Point to teach an accounting course he had designed. After one of his classes, he found a telephone message from Washington. Returning the phone call, he was informed that he had been awarded the Medal of Honor. He received it on May 14 from President Richard Nixon.

BIOGRAPHY

BORN
August 1, 1943
Washington, D.C.

ENTERED SERVICE
United States Military
Academy, West Point,
New York

BRANCH
U.S. Army

DUTY
Vietnam War

CURRENT RESIDENCE
Connecticut

TO ALL THE MEN AND WOMEN
WHO SERVED DURING THE VIET-NAM WAR
1961-1975
WELCOME HOME

Clandestine Operations

JON R. CAVAIANI
STAFF SERGEANT, U.S. ARMY Vietnam Training Advisory Group, Republic of Vietnam

BORN IN ENGLAND, JON CAVAIANI CAME TO America with his parents in 1947 at the age of four. Although he was classified 4-F because of an allergy to bee stings, and although he was married with two children, Cavaiani enlisted in the Army shortly after being naturalized in 1968. He qualified for Special Forces and arrived in Vietnam in the summer of 1970; later he joined the Studies and Observation Group (SOG), an unconventional-warfare task force, and was soon leading clandestine operations against the North Vietnamese.

In the spring of 1971, Staff Sergeant Cavaiani was in charge of the security platoon for an isolated radio relay site deep in the northwesternmost outpost of South Vietnam near Khe Sanh. The mission of his unit, which comprised seventy indigenous troops and thirteen Americans, was to provide security for this intelligence-gathering operation.

On the morning of June 4, the camp came under attack by an overwhelming enemy force. Cavaiani moved through the exploding mortars, rocket-propelled grenades, and automatic-weapons fire to organize a defensive perimeter and direct the U.S. force's fight for survival. When a grenade knocked him down and wounded him as he was firing a .50-caliber machine gun, he picked himself up and continued to organize the fight.

By midday, it was clear that the small American contingent wouldn't be able to fight off the North Vietnamese. Cavaiani called in help and directed the evacuation, but the helicopters broke off the mission before the last seventeen of his men could be taken out. While they remained in the camp overnight trying to fend off enemy attacks, Cavaiani again established a defensive position and concentrated his efforts on strengthening the morale of his men.

The next morning, obscured by heavy ground fog, the North Vietnamese massed. Ordering his remaining men to try to escape, Cavaiani attempted to keep the enemy at bay with small arms and hand grenades. The survivors, who last saw him standing with a machine gun spraying the two columns of advancing soldiers, reported his heroic death when they got back to the American lines.

Although he had been shot in the back, Cavaiani was able to crawl into a bunker with another American, Sergeant James Jones. When two NVA soldiers entered, Cavaiani killed one with a dagger, and Jones shot the other. Then an enemy grenade exploded in the bunker. Badly wounded, Jones stepped out to surrender and was killed by rifle shots; Cavaiani played dead. When the North Vietnamese set the bunker on fire, he was severely burned but managed to escape into the jungle. He evaded capture for eleven days and had almost made it back to an American camp when he was caught by a seventy-year-old peasant with an antique bolt-action rifle.

Cavaiani was taken to North Vietnam by his captors and spent time in "Plantation Gardens," a prisoner-of-war camp, and in the interrogation center known as the Zoo before winding up in the "Hanoi Hilton." When he was released in 1973, he heard that he had been recommended for the Medal of Honor. It was awarded to him on December 12, 1974, by President Gerald Ford, who spent an hour with the Cavaiani family after the ceremony.

BIOGRAPHY

BORN
August 2, 1943
Royston, England

ENTERED SERVICE
Fresno, California

BRANCH
U.S. Army

DUTY
Vietnam War

CURRENT RESIDENCE
California

"Well Done, Marine"

RAYMOND M. CLAUSEN, JR.

PRIVATE FIRST CLASS, U.S. MARINE CORPS Marine Medium Helicopter Squadron 263, Marine Aircraft Group 16, 1st Marine Aircraft Wing

BIOGRAPHY

BORN
October 14, 1947
New Orleans, Louisiana

ENTERED SERVICE
New Orleans, Louisiana

BRANCH
U.S. Marine Corps

DUTY
Vietnam War

DIED
May 30, 2004
Ponchatoula, Louisiana

RAYMOND CLAUSEN WAS ENROLLED IN SOUTHEASTERN Louisiana University when he picked up the newspaper one morning in 1966, read depressing news about the lack of progress in the war in Vietnam, and decided to enlist in the Marine Corps. Trained as a helicopter mechanic, he did an eighteen-month tour of duty in Vietnam, then returned for a second combat tour with Marine Aircraft Group 16 in 1969.

Because of problems with authority, Clausen was repeatedly broken in rank each time he was promoted. He was a private first class and crew chief on January 31, 1970, when he volunteered to participate in the rescue of a Marine platoon that had become trapped in a minefield outside of Da Nang while pursuing a small group of enemy soldiers. One Marine was already dead and eleven others were wounded.

It had been Clausen's helicopter that had inserted the Marines into the area earlier, and the crew felt responsible for getting them out. As the Marine CH-46 chopper hovered above the Marines, Clausen leaned out of the open side door to determine where mines had already exploded in the waist-high grass and to help the chopper touch down safely. Ignoring the pilot's orders to stay put, he jumped out immediately after the chopper touched down and moved toward one of the wounded men. As enemy fire bracketed him, he picked the man up, carried him back to the helicopter, and returned to the minefield for a second soldier. When a mine detonated, killing another Marine and wounding three others, Clausen guided the helicopter to the site of the explosion and loaded the casualties. In all, he made six trips into the minefield, saving eighteen Marines. Only when he was sure that all of them were safely aboard did he signal to the helicopter pilot to lift off and leave the combat zone.

Back at base, Clausen's pilot—also his commanding officer—chewed him out for leaving the craft against orders, then gave him orders to have a drink at the enlisted men's club on him.

Not long after this event, Clausen became involved in another disciplinary situation and was broken to private—the only one to win the Medal of Honor in Vietnam. President Richard Nixon presented the medal to him on June 15, 1971. Of the six soldiers who received the medal that day, Clausen was the only member of the Corps. The president shook his hand and said, "Well done, Marine."

Snake to the Rescue

BRUCE P. CRANDALL

MAJOR, U.S. ARMY Company A, 229th Assault Helicopter Battalion, 1st Cavalry Division (Airmobile)

GROWING UP IN OLYMPIA, WASHINGTON, BRUCE Crandall, a high school baseball All-American, hoped to become a professional ballplayer. But he was drafted into the Army in 1953 before he could be signed to a contract. He went through Officer Candidate School and went into aviation after graduation, learning to fly fixed-wing aircraft and helicopters. During much of the next decade he served in Combat Engineer units or flew topographic missions all over the world.

In 1964, Crandall, known as Snake, was assigned to the 11th Air Assault Division and helped develop tactics that would later be used in Vietnam. The next year, Crandall, now a major, became commanding officer of Company A, 229th Assault Helicopter Battalion at An Khe, Vietnam.

On November 14, 1965, Major Crandall's flight of sixteen helicopters was lifting troops of the 1st Battalion, 7th Cavalry into an isolated area near the Cambodian border known as Landing Zone (LZ) X-Ray in the Ia Drang Valley. It was supposed to be a routine search-and-destroy mission but became the first major battle between a U.S. unit and a large combat force of North Vietnamese Army regulars. The battle was later dramatized in the film *We Were Soldiers*.

After Crandall's helicopters had made four lifts into the LZ, they came under intense enemy fire. The enemy, firing from within the landing zone, wounded or killed a number of those on the assaulting aircraft, some before they could exit. Crandall's aircraft exited the battlefield with three dead and three wounded. Due to the intense fire, the infantry commander closed the LZ to further helicopter operations. Crandall, recognizing that the American force urgently needed ammunition and was taking heavy casualties, asked for another volunteer crew to fly with his to the aid of the besieged battalion. Captain Ed Freeman (himself a recipient of the Medal of Honor for this action) stepped forward and the two helicopters returned to the fray.

In the first fourteen hours of the three-day battle, Crandall made twenty-two flights into the LZ in his unarmed helicopter. On some of his passes, he could see North Vietnamese soldiers just beyond his rotor blades. He kept coming back into the heavy enemy fire because he knew there was only a "magic minute" to get badly wounded soldiers off the battlefield and into medical treatment. That day, Crandall and his wingman evacuated more than seventy wounded and delivered the ammunition and supplies that kept the Americans from being overrun.

In early 1966, Major Crandall flew two more voluntary missions after others had refused, evacuating twelve badly wounded troopers at night under intense enemy fire. He received the 1966 Aviation and Space Writers Association Helicopter Heroism Award given for the outstanding act of heroism during that year.

Major Crandall served two tours of duty in Vietnam. In January 1968, he was badly wounded during another rescue attempt. He returned home after more than nine hundred combat missions in Vietnam. Following his convalescence, he continued to serve in the Army until his retirement in 1977 as a lieutenant colonel. On February 26, 2007, Crandall, who had been to the White House to see Ed Freeman receive his Medal of Honor and came back a second time for a screening of *We Were Soldiers*, returned for his own ceremony. Before placing the medal around his neck, President George W. Bush said, "Welcome back to the White House again, Bruce," adding, "It's about time."

BIOGRAPHY

BORN
February 17, 1933
Olympia, Washington

ENTERED SERVICE
Olympia, Washington

BRANCH
U.S. Army

DUTY
Vietnam War

CURRENT RESIDENCE
Washington State

The "Real" Forrest Gump

SAMMY L. DAVIS

PRIVATE FIRST CLASS, U.S. ARMY Battery C, 2nd Battalion, 4th Artillery, 9th Infantry Division

SAMMY DAVIS TOOK SOME RIBBING IN THE ARMY because he shared a name with the famous entertainer. Much later, long after his military days were over, he would again gain some acclaim among his old comrades, this time as the "real" Forrest Gump.

Davis enlisted in the Army directly out of high school in 1966. Volunteering for the artillery because his father had been an artilleryman in World War II, he was assigned to the 4th Artillery. Soon after completing training, he asked to be sent to Vietnam.

Early on November 18, 1967, his unit of four guns and forty-two men was helicoptered into an area west of Cai Lay to set up a forward fire-support base—Firebase Cudgel—for the American 9th Infantry Division operating in the area. Shortly after midnight the next morning, Private First Class Davis's Battery C came under heavy mortar attack. Simultaneously, an estimated fifteen hundred Vietcong soldiers launched an intense ground assault, failing to overrun the Americans only because a river separated the two forces.

Davis's squad was operating a 105 mm howitzer that fired eighteen thousand beehive darts in each shell. When he saw how close the enemy had come, Davis took over a machine gun and provided covering fire for his gun crew. But an enemy recoilless rifle round scored a direct hit on the howitzer, knocking the crew from the weapon and blowing Davis sideways into a foxhole. Sometime before dawn, as he lay unconscious, he was seriously wounded in the back and buttocks by a beehive round fired from an American weapon. When Davis regained consciousness, he was convinced that the heavily outnumbered Americans couldn't survive the attack, so he decided to fire off at least one round from the damaged artillery piece before being overrun. He struggled to his feet, rammed a shell into

the gun, and fired point-blank at the Vietcong who were advancing five deep directly in front of the weapon; the beehive round cut them down. An enemy mortar round exploded nearby, knocking Davis to the ground, but he got up and kept firing the howitzer. When there were no more rounds left, he fired a white phosphorus shell, and then the last round he had—a "propaganda shell" filled with leaflets.

At this point, he heard yelling from the other side of the river and realized that GIs had been cut off there. Despite the fact that he could not swim due to his injuries, he got in the water and paddled across on an air mattress from the American camp. Scrambling up the bank, he found three wounded soldiers, one of them suffering from a head wound that looked fatal. He gave them all morphine and got the gravely wounded soldier back across the river, where others pulled him to safety. Davis then went back for the other two wounded soldiers and pulled them onto the air mattress across the river to the firebase. He eventually made his way to an American howitzer crew and resumed the fight.

While he was recovering in the hospital, Davis learned that he was going home. He petitioned General William Westmoreland to be allowed to stay with his unit. Permission was granted, although Davis was so hobbled by his wounds that he was made a cook.

On November 19, 1968, exactly one year and one day after the nightlong firefight at Cai Lay, Davis received the Medal of Honor from President Lyndon Johnson. Years later, footage of LBJ putting the medal around Davis's neck appeared in the movie *Forrest Gump* (with Tom Hanks's head substituted for Davis's), and Gump's fictional Medal of Honor citation was loosely based on Davis's real one.

BIOGRAPHY

BORN
November 1, 1946
Dayton, Ohio

ENTERED SERVICE
Indianapolis, Indiana

BRANCH
U.S. Army

DUTY
Vietnam War

CURRENT RESIDENCE
Indiana

Maximum Resistance

GEORGE E. "BUD" DAY

MAJOR, U.S. AIR FORCE Misty Forward Air Controller Squadron

BIOGRAPHY

BORN
February 24, 1925
Sioux City, Iowa

ENTERED SERVICE
Sioux City, Iowa

BRANCH
U.S. Air Force

DUTY
Vietnam War

CURRENT RESIDENCE
Florida

GEORGE "BUD" DAY WAS SEVENTEEN IN LATE 1942 when he badgered his parents into allowing him to volunteer for the Marine Corps. He spent nearly three years in the South Pacific during World War II, then returned home, went to college, and got a law degree. In 1950, he joined the Air National Guard. When he was called up for active duty a year later, he applied for pilot training and flew fighter jets during the Korean War. After being promoted to captain in 1955, he decided to become a "lifer" in the Air Force.

In 1967, Day, now a major, was put in command of a squadron of F-100s in Vietnam involved in a top secret program. Nicknamed the Misty Super Facs, their mission was to fly over North Vietnam and Laos as "forward air controllers," selecting military targets and calling in air strikes on them. On August 26, ground fire hit Day's plane, destroying its hydraulic controls and forcing it into a steep dive. When he ejected, he smashed against the fuselage and broke his arm in three places. North Vietnamese militiamen below, seeing his parachute open, were waiting for him when he landed. They marched Day to a camouflaged underground shelter. When he refused to answer his captors' questions, they staged a mock execution, then hung him from a rafter by his feet for several hours. Certain that he was so badly hurt that he wouldn't try to get away, they tied him up with loosely knotted rope. On his fifth day in the camp, while a pair of distracted teenage soldiers stood guard, he untied himself and escaped.

On his second night on the run, Day was sleeping in thick undergrowth when either a bomb or a rocket landed nearby. The concussion left him bleeding from his ears and sinuses and sent shrapnel into his leg. Even

so, he continued to hobble south for the next several days, eating berries and frogs and successfully evading enemy patrols.

Sometime between the twelfth and fifteenth day after his escape—he had lost track of time—Day heard helicopters and stumbled toward the sound. It was U.S. choppers evacuating a Marine unit, but they left just as he got to the landing zone. The next morning, still heading south, he ran into a North Vietnamese Army patrol. As he limped toward the jungle, he was shot in the leg and hand and captured soon afterward. He was taken back to the camp from which he had escaped and subjected to more torture.

A few days later he was moved to the "Hanoi Hilton." His untreated wounds were infected, and he was suffering from malnutrition and unable to perform even the simplest task for himself. The fingers on both hands were curled into fists as a result of his torture; he regained some motion by peeling them back, flattening them against the wall of his cell, and leaning into them with his full weight.

For more than five years, Day resisted the North Vietnamese guards who tortured him. On one occasion in 1971, when guards burst in with rifles as some of the American prisoners gathered for a forbidden religious service, Major Day stood up, looked down the muzzles of the guns, and began to sing "The Star-Spangled Banner." The other men, including James Stockdale, the ranking U.S. officer in the prison, joined him.

George Day was released on March 14, 1973. Three years later, on March 6, 1976, both he and Admiral Stockdale were presented with the Medal of Honor by President Gerald Ford.

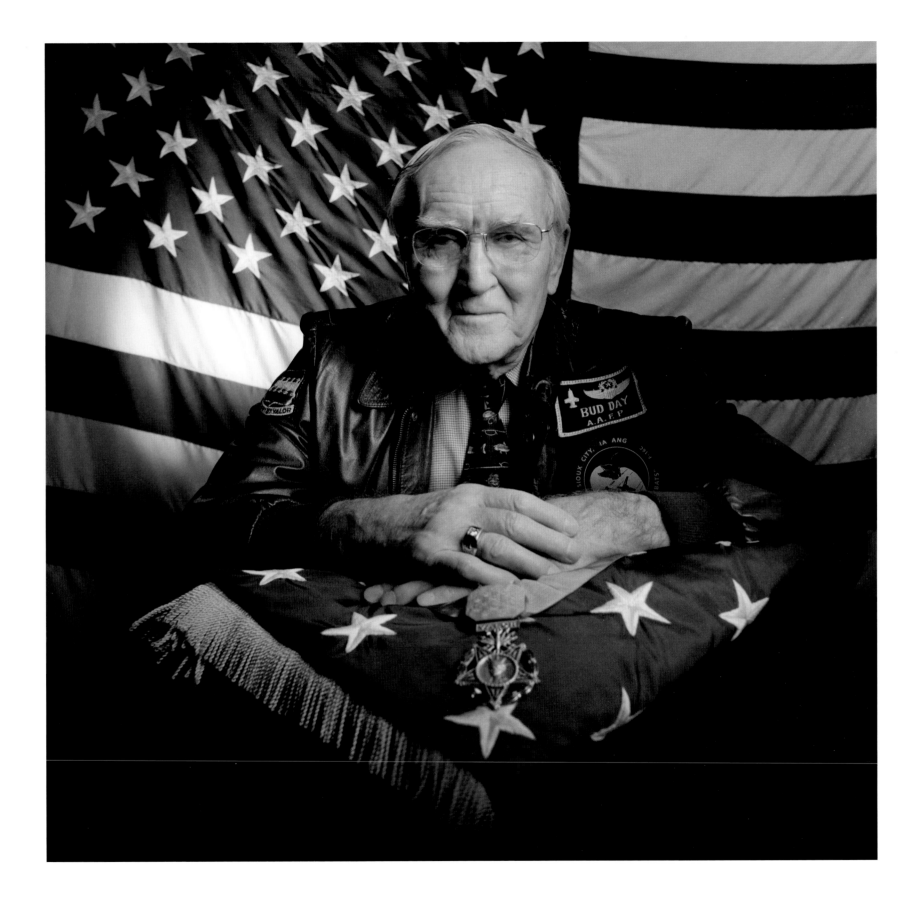

The Liberation of Chau Phu

DREW D. DIX

STAFF SERGEANT, U.S. ARMY U.S. Senior Adviser Group, IV Corps, Military Assistance Command

DREW DIX VOLUNTEERED FOR THE ARMY IN 1962.
He wanted to be in Special Forces, but at eighteen he was too young, so he spent the next three years with the 82nd Airborne and participated in the peacekeeping operation in the Dominican Republic in 1965.

By 1968, Dix had become a Special Forces adviser and was in Vietnam working on a CIA project in the provincial capital of Chau Phu near the Cambodian border. His mission was to coordinate intelligence gathering with a company-size unit made up mainly of indigenous Vietnamese, Cambodians, and Chinese Nungs, primarily by capturing Vietcong soldiers for interrogation.

In late January, Staff Sergeant Dix and several of his men were operating in and around Cambodia with part of a Navy SEAL platoon to try to acquire definitive intelligence about a rumored Vietcong offensive. Just after dawn on January 31, Dix's unit returned to Chau Phu in the SEAL riverboats to find that the Tet Offensive had already begun and the city had been overrun by two heavily armed Vietcong battalions. (South Vietnamese units hadn't resisted because they thought a cease-fire had been arranged for the New Year holiday.) When they tried to land, they encountered such heavy fire that one of them later said, "It was like a little Normandy."

Dix began to move methodically through the city, picking up isolated pockets of friendly soldiers as he went. One of his first objectives was to rescue an American nurse who had been working in the local hospital. Then he reached several U.S. civilians whose building was being mortared and brought them to safety. One SEAL was killed; the rest pulled out, leaving Dix with only a handful of indigenous soldiers. For the next several hours, he and his men moved from house to house in an effort to liberate Chau Phu. At one point he alone assaulted a building in the face of heavy machine-gun fire to rescue two Filipinos who had been working there; he killed six Vietcong and brought out the two trapped men.

Dix fought through the night. By the next morning, he had assembled a force of twenty men and supplied them with new machine guns and a recoilless rifle. Using classic urban-warfare techniques, his force cleared the Vietcong out of the city's hotel, theater, and other buildings. At each step, Dix left wounded soldiers to hold each of the buildings and ensure that he and his men wouldn't be attacked from behind. Then he moved on to the residence of the deputy province chief and rescued the official's wife and children.

By February 2, after a running battle of fifty-six hours, the city was liberated. Dix's small band had killed an estimated two hundred enemy troops, with Dix himself accounting for some two dozen. One of the prisoners he took was the head of the enemy force that was supposed to take over and administer Chau Phu.

A year later, Dix was back in the United States. He had been told he was to receive the Medal of Honor, but he had been involved in so many dangerous actions that he wasn't sure exactly which one he was being singled out for. He was presented with the medal by President Lyndon Johnson on January 16, 1969, in one of the last official acts of his presidency.

Dix is the author of *Rescue at River City*, which was published in 2000.

BIOGRAPHY

BORN
December 14, 1944
West Point, New York

ENTERED SERVICE
Denver, Colorado

BRANCH
U.S. Army

DUTY
Vietnam War

CURRENT RESIDENCE
New Mexico

A Bounty on His Head

ROGER H. C. DONLON

CAPTAIN, U.S. ARMY Detachment A-726, 7th Special Forces Group (Airborne), 1st Special Forces

BIOGRAPHY

BORN
January 30, 1934
Saugerties, New York

ENTERED SERVICE
Albany, New York

BRANCH
U.S. Army

DUTY
Vietnam War

CURRENT RESIDENCE
Kansas

ROGER DONLON ALWAYS FELT THAT THE MILITARY was his destiny in life. His father had served in World War I; all four of his brothers served in the Army or Air Force. He had wanted to go to the newly established Air Force Academy and learn to fly, but an eye examination detected the beginning of a cataract. Instead, Donlon graduated from the U.S. Military Academy Preparatory School and qualified for West Point in 1955. After two years he resigned to join the Army. He graduated from Officer Candidate School and was eventually assigned to the 7th Special Forces Group in 1963.

In the spring of 1964, Donlon, now a captain, was sent to Vietnam as commander of the 12-man Special Forces Team A-726. Their mission was to train, advise, and assist a civil-defense force that provided physical security and improved the living conditions for approximately five thousand peasants in several villages in the Nam Dong Valley, a few miles from the Laotian border. Camp Nam Dong, as the Americans' base was called, also included 311 South Vietnamese irregulars and 60 Nungs, ethnic Chinese fighters who fiercely opposed the Communists.

At around 2:00 A.M. on the morning of July 6, 1964, Captain Donlon, having just finished walking guard, entered the camp mess hall as a mortar round exploded on the roof, knocking him down. He got up and sprinted toward the camp's main gate. He saw three Vietcong sappers, each with dynamite strapped to their backs, and killed them. Another mortar round hit, knocking him down again and tearing off one of his boots. Hearing one of his men yell that the enemy was near the ammunition bunker, he ran there. A third mortar round exploded, tearing off his other boot and all his equipment and wounding him badly in his arm

and stomach. He tore off a piece of his shirt and stuffed it into his stomach wound to stop the bleeding. He later learned that approximately nine hundred Vietcong were threatening to overrun the camp.

Over the next several hours, Donlon scampered from one position to another, providing his men with encouragement and ammunition. As he moved the wounded team sergeant to safety, another mortar round hit, injuring him in the shoulder and killing the sergeant. Donlon then treated four wounded Nungs so they could stay in the fight. Withdrawing his force to the few remaining secure areas in the camp, he was hit repeatedly by shrapnel in his face and over the rest of his body.

Finally, a U.S. aircraft dropped flares. The sky was suddenly illuminated and Donlon saw how deeply into the camp the enemy had penetrated. Directing his force's firepower, he and his men were able to keep the Vietcong at bay until daylight. The next day supplies were air-dropped to the camp, and Marine reinforcements arrived, allowing Donlon and his wounded team members to be evacuated by helicopter.

Roger Donlon left Vietnam on November 20, 1964. On December 5, President Lyndon Johnson awarded Donlon the Medal of Honor, the first of the Vietnam War, as Secretary of Defense Robert McNamara read the citation. All nine survivors of Team A-726 were present. Introducing them to the President, Donlon said, "The medal belongs to them, too."

Donlon later asked to go back into combat in Vietnam, but the Pentagon had learned that the Vietcong had put a bounty on his head and refused until 1972, when Donlon returned for a second tour. He retired in 1988 as a colonel with thirty-two years' service in the Army.

Along the Perfume River

FREDERICK E. FERGUSON

CHIEF WARRANT OFFICER, U.S. ARMY Company C, 227th Aviation Battalion, 1st Cavalry Division (Airmobile)

BIOGRAPHY

BORN
August 18, 1939
Pilot Point, Texas

ENTERED SERVICE
Phoenix, Arizona

BRANCH
U.S. Army

DUTY
Vietnam War

CURRENT RESIDENCE
Arizona

FREDERICK FERGUSON GOT A PART-TIME JOB driving a gas truck to pay for flying lessons while serving out his enlistment in the Navy, earning his pilot's license before his discharge in 1962. Over the next two years, he hung out at airports and got his commercial license. Then he took his first helicopter ride and knew instantly that he wanted to be a helicopter pilot. He joined the Army's Warrant Officer program and graduated from the nine-month program in May 1967 certified in rotary-winged aircraft. Two weeks later, he was in Vietnam, a copilot with the 227th Aviation Battalion of the 1st Cavalry (Airmobile). By August, he was in command of his own helicopter, a UH-1D slick.

On January 31, 1968, at the beginning of the Tet Offensive, Chief Warrant Officer Ferguson was flying back to base, having just dropped off engineers to repair a damaged truck. As he was monitoring the radio traffic, he heard that a helicopter carrying members of the 1st Cavalry had gone down in the enemy-controlled city of Hue and that another helicopter had been badly shot up in a failed attempt to rescue them. "The Air Cav doesn't leave its men behind," Ferguson said to his three-man crew. They all agreed that they should go get the downed Americans.

Waiting to refuel at his base, Ferguson asked the crews of three Huey gunships if they wanted to accompany him on a rescue mission. "Why not?" was the reply, and the four helicopters took off.

On the ground, the beleaguered GIs had taken refuge in a tiny, isolated South Vietnamese Army compound, reporting by radio that they were under heavy fire. Ferguson circled until the fire abated; he knew he would have to get in and out quickly because enemy mortars had already targeted the site.

Then, despite warnings to stay clear of the area, Ferguson and his gunship escort began a low-level flight at maximum airspeed along the Perfume River. The North Vietnamese were everywhere, and the gunships were firing at them constantly. Ferguson located the compound, stood his helicopter on its tail, and began to descend blindly in the dust storm created by his rotors. When he touched down, he saw that there was a one-foot clearance between a flagpole and a rotor blade on one side of the craft and one foot between the blade and a wall on the other.

As the GIs quickly got on board, the enemy mortar fire began. One shell hit near the helicopter's tail. When the last man was pulled aboard and Ferguson was powering the helicopter straight up, another mortar hit beneath him, spinning the craft 180 degrees. He regained control, put his nose down, and headed out.

One of the Hueys was shot down as it was heading back to base, but its crew was rescued. The other two that did manage to land were so badly damaged that they were no longer able to fly.

Ferguson went home in June. He was serving as an instructor at Fort Walters in Texas a year later when he received a call from the Pentagon ordering him to go to Washington. President Richard Nixon presented him with the Medal of Honor on May 17, 1969.

Daring Skyraider Rescue

BERNARD F. FISHER

MAJOR, U.S. AIR FORCE 1st Air Commandos

BIOGRAPHY

BORN
January 11, 1927
San Bernardino, California

ENTERED SERVICE
Kuna, Idaho

BRANCH
U.S. Air Force

DUTY
Vietnam War

CURRENT RESIDENCE
Idaho

AFTER SERVING BRIEFLY IN THE NAVY AT THE END of World War II, Bernard Fisher spent 1947 to 1950 in the Air National Guard, then joined the ROTC while he was a college student in Utah. Commissioned a second lieutenant in the Air Force in 1951, he served as a jet fighter pilot in the Air Defense Command until 1965, when he volunteered to serve in Vietnam.

During his first year there, Fisher, now a major, was assigned to the 1st Air Commandos and flew two hundred combat missions in a propeller-driven A-1E/H Skyraider, which was suited for close support missions because it could carry large bomb loads, absorb heavy ground fire, and fly for long periods at low altitude.

On March 10, 1966, Fisher and his wingman were headed to a U.S. Special Forces camp near the Cambodian border where North Vietnamese troops were on the verge of overrunning an outnumbered contingent of Green Berets. Near their target, the two Skyraiders were joined by four other planes. They all had to run a gauntlet of enemy antiaircraft guns as they flew straight down the A Shau Valley and delivered their bombs. The cloud cover was so thick that they were forced to fly as low as three hundred feet, allowing enemy guns on either side of the valley to fire down on them.

Once the six planes completed a strafing run, they made the 180-degree turn and lined up for another. The plane that Major D. W. "Jump" Myers was flying was hit and burst into flames. Too low to bail out, Myers crash-landed on the Special Forces camp's airstrip and hid from the enemy in the underbrush near an embankment. While the other aircraft began to strafe the area around Myers to keep the North Vietnamese away, Fisher called for a helicopter rescue. When he heard the nearest choppers were at least half an hour away, and seeing that the North Vietnamese were closing in on Myers, Fisher decided to land and pick up the airman himself. "I'm going in," he radioed the other planes.

The short, 2,500-foot airstrip was littered with signs of battle—unexploded ordnance and debris from nearby buildings. Fisher touched down, but he was going too fast to stop and had to climb out and make another approach. The second time, he managed to skid to a stop before reaching the end of the runway. Then he turned and taxied to where Myers was hiding as the other aircraft continued to provide cover from above. Myers rushed out and climbed onto the wing of the plane; Fisher opened the canopy and pulled him in. Then, dodging the shell holes and parts of exploded bombs on the steel-planked runway, Fisher pushed forward on the A-1's throttle and headed down the strip. With the enemy concentrating fire on him from both sides, he managed to get enough ground speed to lift off at the end of the runway. When he returned to base at Pleiku, the ground crew counted nineteen bullet holes in his plane.

Bernard Fisher was presented with the Medal of Honor by President Lyndon Johnson on January 19, 1967, the first airman in Vietnam to receive this distinction. He returned to the Air Defense Command and flew jet fighters until 1974, when he retired as a colonel. In 1999, the Navy honored Fisher by naming a newly commissioned container ship the *Bernard F. Fisher*.

Fighting Blind

MICHAEL J. FITZMAURICE

SPECIALIST FOURTH CLASS, U.S. ARMY Troop D, 2nd Squadron, 17th Cavalry, 101st Airborne Division

IN THE SPRING OF 1971, THE 2ND SQUADRON OF THE 17th Cavalry was guarding the airstrip at Khe Sanh in South Vietnam for American planes flying missions into Laos. At about 2:00 A.M. on March 23, Michael Fitzmaurice—at twenty-one one of the older men in his unit—had just returned from guard duty to his bunker living quarters. The North Vietnamese had been intermittently mortaring American positions during the day, but the night seemed calm. Suddenly, the shells started coming in again. Specialist Fourth Class Fitzmaurice realized it was more than a mortar attack when he looked out of the bunker and saw that a large number of North Vietnamese sappers had charged through the perimeter wire and were inside the U.S. position on a suicide mission.

Fitzmaurice and a buddy got out to the trench that connected the Americans' sandbagged fighting positions. Enemy sappers were everywhere; they tossed two explosive charges at Fitzmaurice, who managed to throw them back. A third one thudded to the ground near him; figuring that it was about to go off, he threw his flak jacket and body over it. The explosion blew the door shut on the bunker, trapping the sleeping GIs inside, but it saved their lives.

Fitzmaurice suffered multiple wounds and was blinded in his left eye. As the enemy spread out through the area, he figured that the end was coming and that he might as well go out fighting, so he got to his feet. Barely able to see because of the blood on his face, he climbed out of the trench, and as his buddy yelled directions to him, he began firing at the sappers. When a North Vietnamese grenade destroyed his rifle, he knelt down and felt around on the ground for another. Suddenly, an enemy soldier was on top of him; he engaged the North Vietnamese in hand-to-hand combat and killed him. Then he found another weapon, returned to the trench, and began to fire on the enemy again. He refused to be evacuated until the fight was over.

Besides the loss of sight, Fitzmaurice's eardrums were shattered and he had shrapnel throughout his body. He was hospitalized for the next thirteen months. In 1973, out of the service for about two years, he was working in a meatpacking plant when Washington called to inform him that he was to receive the Medal of Honor. He traveled to the White House, where President Richard Nixon awarded him the medal on October 15.

BIOGRAPHY

BORN
March 9, 1950
Jamestown, North Dakota

ENTERED SERVICE
Sioux Falls, South Dakota

BRANCH
U.S. Army

DUTY
Vietnam War

CURRENT RESIDENCE
South Dakota

Green Hornets

JAMES P. FLEMING

FIRST LIEUTENANT, U.S. AIR FORCE 20th Special Operations Squadron

BIOGRAPHY

BORN
March 12, 1943
Sedalia, Missouri

ENTERED SERVICE
Pullman, Washington

BRANCH
U.S. Air Force

DUTY
Vietnam War

CURRENT RESIDENCE
Texas

JAMES FLEMING NEVER HAD ANY DOUBT THAT HE would follow in the footsteps of his father, a career Air Force pilot. After graduating from Washington State University, he was commissioned as a lieutenant in the Air Force. Following flight school, he became a UH-1F (Huey) helicopter pilot with the Air Force 20th Special Operations Squadron. In 1968, he was living in the jungle of Vietnam and flying Special Forces teams on long-range reconnaissance patrols deep into enemy territory. On November 26, his five-ship Green Hornet flight—two Huey gunships and three lightly armed Huey slicks—heard over the radio that one of the Special Forces patrols it had inserted earlier was being overrun by a large group of North Vietnamese. The Green Hornets went to get them.

They found the patrol in a clearing, surrounded by the enemy on three sides and being forced to retreat to a river. The gunships immediately took out two enemy machine guns. Then one of them was hit and went down. One of the slicks rescued the crew and returned to base, accompanied by a second slick that was running short on fuel. This left one Huey gunship and Fleming's lone slick to rescue the encircled American patrol.

Fleming descended into the clearing, facing the jungle area where the enemy was concentrated; he positioned the tail of his chopper over the riverbank, so low that his blades cut the foliage of the trees. The North Vietnamese gunners in the bushes below immediately zeroed in and began to rake Fleming's ship with heavy machine-gun fire. The trapped patrol couldn't make it to the helicopter. It was forced to return to the river.

Though he was running low on fuel, Fleming knew he was the only hope the patrol had. He rose above the battleground to take stock of the situation, then descended again. He turned the chopper so his side gunners could lay down suppressing fire, then positioned it again over the riverbank so the U.S. soldiers could board it. The patrol set off a series of claymore mines, allowing six of the men to board as enemy shells smashed into Fleming's windscreen. The last, the team leader of the patrol who had been separated earlier from the others, dove into the river and swam toward the helicopter. When he finally grabbed onto the rope ladder held by a crew member, Fleming took off with him dangling in the air and managed to make it back to base.

Fleming was recommended for the Medal of Honor by his commanding officer, who was killed in action in April 1969, about the time that Fleming heard that the recommendation had been accepted. The medal was presented at a White House ceremony by President Richard Nixon on May 14, 1970.

After returning from combat, Fleming served four years at the Air Force Academy. Later, he was vice commander of the Air Force Officer Training School in Texas and the operations officer of the Squadron Officers School in Alabama. He retired as a colonel after more than thirty years of military service.

An Athlete's Instincts

ROBERT F. FOLEY

CAPTAIN, U.S. ARMY Company A, 2nd Battalion, 27th Infantry, 25th Infantry Division

BIOGRAPHY

BORN
May 30, 1941
Newton, Massachusetts

ENTERED SERVICE
Newton, Massachusetts

BRANCH
U.S. Army

DUTY
Vietnam War

CURRENT RESIDENCE
Virginia

ROBERT FOLEY WAS A BASKETBALL STAR IN HIGH school. At six foot seven, he had received fifteen college scholarship offers by the end of his senior year. He was still considering his options when the hockey coach from West Point happened to pass through Massachusetts on a weekend Foley scored forty-four points in a game. He told the West Point basketball coach about Foley. The coach invited him for a visit and asked him to play Army basketball. Foley knew that going to West Point would eliminate the possibility of his playing professional basketball, but he was impressed with the history and the sense of purpose he saw at the academy and decided to enroll.

He graduated in 1963 (having been captain of the 1962–1963 basketball team and a member of the East All-Stars), then joined the infantry and went through Airborne and Ranger schools. By 1966, he was a twenty-five-year-old captain and company commander in the 27th Infantry in Vietnam.

On November 3, his company returned to base from a ten-day search-and-destroy mission, hoping for some rest. The next morning, however, Foley received new orders. Another company in his brigade had come upon a North Vietnamese regimental base, and in the fight that had followed, the enemy, determined to protect its force and supplies, had surrounded the American unit and killed or wounded much of its leadership. Foley's mission was to get the surrounded GIs out.

As Foley's company began its advance early on the morning of November 5, it immediately came under heavy fire from a well-concealed force and suffered several casualties. Because of the location of the besieged unit, as well as the triple-canopy jungle cover and dense vegetation, Foley couldn't call in artillery or air support, so he led two of the platoons in a direct

attack. When two radio operators were wounded in the heavy fire, he helped them to cover where they could get medical aid, then moved back into the center of the action. He was worried that his company would lose momentum and angry that his soldiers were getting hit.

When he saw one of his machine gunners go down, he ran to the gun, picked it up, and draped the ammunition belt over his shoulders. His instinct as an athlete taking over, he charged forward, firing the heavy weapon from the waist. Over the next few minutes, he assaulted the enemy gun emplacements, single-handedly destroying three of them. Penetrating the last bunker complex, he found himself alone for a moment, with perhaps only ten rounds of ammunition left. Then his men caught up with him, and he continued to push them forward for the next several hours. After the encircled American company was finally extracted, Foley was ordered to withdraw.

As a result of recommendations his soldiers had written after this action, Robert Foley was awarded the Medal of Honor on May 1, 1968, by President Lyndon Johnson, who also presented one to Sergeant John Baker, one of Foley's men who had distinguished himself in that engagement.

Foley remained in the Army until 2000, attaining the rank of lieutenant general. He ended his thirty-seven-year military career as the commander of the Fifth Army, then became president of Marion Military Institute in Alabama, the nation's oldest military preparatory school and junior college. Today, he continues to serve U.S. Army soldiers and their families as director of Army Emergency Relief, a private nonprofit organization with headquarters in Washington, D.C.

Going at the Enemy

WESLEY L. FOX

FIRST LIEUTENANT, U.S. MARINE CORPS Company A, 1st Battalion, 9th Marines, 3rd Marine Division

EIGHTEEN-YEAR-OLD WESLEY FOX THOUGHT HE WAS enlisting in the Marines for four years in 1950, but he wound up staying for forty-three. Rising through the enlisted and officer ranks to become a colonel, he claims that he never would have left the Corps had it not been for mandatory retirement.

Fox spent the Korean War lugging a Browning automatic rifle from one battle to another and was wounded in action in 1951. For the next fifteen years, he continued to earn promotions. He was a first lieutenant in 1967 when he went to Vietnam as an adviser to the South Vietnamese Marines; he stayed with them through the Tet Offensive of 1968. He liked the indigenous troops but felt that their idea of warfare tended to be "search-and-avoid," so he signed on for another tour of duty in Vietnam with the 9th Marines in hopes of "getting something done."

In late February 1969, Fox was the commander of a Marine rifle company that was part of Operation Dewey Canyon in the A Shau Valley near the Laotian border. He and his men had been in the area for more than a month, sporadically engaging North Vietnamese troops, when, on February 21, the battalion commander ordered Fox to go down into the valley to determine if an enemy force was attempting to recover a pair of 155 mm guns that American forces had captured earlier and, if so, to do something about it.

Around noon the next day, Fox's company, under-strength with only ninety men and lacking a mortar platoon, located a large force of well-concealed North Vietnamese regulars behind strong defensive positions. Fox quickly made a plan "to go right at them." As he was getting ready, a rocket-propelled grenade exploded nearby, its shrapnel hitting him in the shoulder. Though bleeding heavily, he moved forward through heavy machine-gun fire. As he studied the battlefield, a sniper firing from a tree killed one of his Marines, then shot at Fox but missed. Fox picked up the fallen American's rifle and killed the sniper before he could fire again.

Realizing that if he tried to break contact with the enemy, he would expose his men, Fox committed his reserve platoon to support the company's two assault platoons in a do-or-die maneuver. As he gave directions to his reserve platoon commander, a mortar round exploded, wounding Fox and seriously injuring the platoon commander. Fox then directed his executive officer to take the reserve platoon forward. Within five minutes, the executive officer was killed by machine-gun fire. With all company officers now dead or wounded, Fox continued to direct his Marines as they neutralized the enemy force.

The afternoon was dark and overcast, preventing Fox from calling in air support, but when the clouds parted briefly, two planes were able to take out one of the machine guns blocking Fox's advance. Finally, the North Vietnamese troops began to pull back. Refusing medical aid himself, Fox established a defensive position and prepared his casualties for evacuation. Eleven of his men were killed in action, and fifty-eight were wounded. One hundred five enemy dead were counted.

A year later, he was told that he would receive the Medal of Honor. But he waited for more than a year because at that point the administration was trying to de-emphasize the war—even if it meant de-emphasizing the heroism of U.S. forces as well. Fox finally received the medal on March 2, 1971, at the White House.

Fox is the author of *Marine Rifleman: Forty Years in the Corps,* which was published in 2002.

BIOGRAPHY

BORN
September 30, 1931
Herndon, Virginia

ENTERED SERVICE
Leesburg, Virginia

BRANCH
U.S. Marine Corps

DUTY
Vietnam War

CURRENT RESIDENCE
Virginia

"Too Tall"

ED W. FREEMAN

CAPTAIN, U.S. ARMY Company A, 229th Assault Helicopter Battalion, 1st Cavalry Division (Airmobile)

BIOGRAPHY

BORN
November 20, 1927
Neely, Mississippi

ENTERED SERVICE
Hattiesburg, Mississippi

BRANCH
U.S. Army

DUTY
Vietnam War

DIED
August 20, 2008
Boise, Idaho

BY THE TIME THE KOREAN WAR BROKE OUT, Ed Freeman was a master sergeant in the Army Engineers, but he fought in Korea as an infantryman. He took part in the bloody battle of Pork Chop Hill and was given a battlefield commission, which had the added advantage of making him eligible to fly, a dream of his since childhood. But flight school turned him down because of his height: At six foot four, he was "too tall" (a nickname that followed him throughout his military career). In 1955, however, the height limit was raised, and Freeman was able to enroll.

He began flying fixed-wing aircraft, then switched to helicopters. By 1965, when he was sent to Vietnam, he had thousands of hours' flying time in choppers. He was assigned to the 1st Cavalry Division (Airmobile), second in command of a sixteen-helicopter unit responsible for carrying infantrymen into battle. On November 14, 1965, Freeman's helicopters carried a battalion into the Ia Drang Valley for what became the first major confrontation between large forces of the American and North Vietnamese armies.

Back at base, Freeman and the other pilots received word that the GIs they had dropped off were taking heavy casualties and running low on supplies. In fact, the fighting was so fierce that medevac helicopters refused to pick up the wounded. When the commander of the helicopter unit asked for volunteers to fly into the battle zone, Freeman alone stepped forward. He was joined by his commander, and the two of them began several hours of flights into the contested area. Because their small emergency-landing zone was just one hundred yards away from the heaviest fighting, their unarmed and lightly armored helicopters took several hits. In all, Freeman carried out fourteen separate rescue missions, bringing in water and ammunition to the besieged soldiers and taking back dozens of wounded, some of whom wouldn't have survived if they hadn't been evacuated.

Freeman left Vietnam in 1966 and retired from the Army the following year. He flew helicopters another twenty years for the Department of the Interior, herding wild horses, fighting fires, and performing animal censuses. Then he retired altogether.

In the aftermath of the Ia Drang battle, his commanding officer, wanting to recognize Freeman's valor, proposed him for the Medal of Honor. But the two-year statute of limitations on these kinds of recommendations had passed, and no action was taken. Congress did away with that statute in 1995, and Freeman was finally awarded the medal by President George W. Bush on July 16, 2001.

Freeman was back at the White House a few months later for the premiere of *We Were Soldiers*, a 2002 feature film that depicted his role in the Ia Drang battle. As he was filing out of the small White House theater, the President approached him, saluted, and shook his hand. "Good job, Too Tall," he said.

Courage in a Crossfire

HAROLD A. FRITZ

FIRST LIEUTENANT, U.S. ARMY Troop A, 1st Squadron, 11th Armored Cavalry Regiment

HAROLD FRITZ WAS WORKING TOWARD A CAREER in veterinary medicine when he got his draft notice in 1966. After advanced armor training, he was accepted for Officer Candidate School. Graduating as a second lieutenant early in 1967, he was assigned to the 6th Armored Cavalry Regiment. The following year, he was sent to Vietnam and assigned to the 11th Armored Cavalry Regiment.

On January 11, 1969, Fritz was leading a column of seven heavily armored vehicles on a dirt highway near Quan Loi. The mission, billed as a "gravy run," was supposed to have been one of his last before leaving Vietnam. However, it turned out to be anything but routine. At around 10:30 in the morning, while escorting a U.S. truck convoy resupplying American forces with fuel, ammunition, and other supplies, Fritz was suddenly blown out of his armored vehicle by a huge explosion. Climbing back onto his burning vehicle, he saw that the column had been ambushed by a large force of North Vietnamese soldiers with positions on both sides of the road. Fritz's force was caught in a crossfire of automatic weapons, rocket-propelled grenades, and recoilless rifles. The two machine gunners in his vehicle were killed; many others in the twenty-eight-man platoon were wounded. Ultimately, only five men in the unit were still able to fight.

When about twenty North Vietnamese from one side of the road assaulted his force, Fritz jumped into an armored vehicle and took a heavy toll on the attackers with its M-60 machine gun. When a similar enemy force attacked from the other side, Fritz, fighting with a pistol and a bayonet, led his tiny force in a point-blank charge that temporarily drove the enemy back. He was hit several times by shrapnel and small-arms rounds; one particularly heavy blow on the left side of his chest knocked him down.

During the initial ambush, Fritz had tried to call headquarters for assistance, but his radio was damaged and he didn't know if the transmission had been received. As he readied his men for a last stand to protect their wounded, he saw the aerial of a U.S. tank coming down the road. It was part of a tank platoon that had overheard Fritz's call for help.

With the fresh armor force in the battle, the tide began to turn. Eventually, Fritz and his wounded troopers were evacuated by helicopter. Later that day, when he returned to the battlefield, he found a battered cigarette lighter that had been given to him as a going-away present by his wife. It had been in his left breast pocket and had stopped an enemy bullet that would otherwise have killed him.

Harold Fritz returned to the United States in the spring of 1969. He was serving with the 3rd Armored Cavalry Regiment at Fort Lewis, Washington, early in 1971 when a call came from the Department of the Army informing him that he was to receive the Medal of Honor. The White House ceremony was conducted by President Richard Nixon on March 2, 1971. Leaving his infant son at home, Fritz was accompanied by his father and mother, brother, wife, and elder son and daughter. Before placing the medal around Fritz's neck, President Nixon gave the men, including Fritz's son, commemorative tie clasps. The boy looked up at the President and said, "My little brother who's not here didn't get one." The President removed his own tie clasp and handed it to the boy, saying, "Well, then, give him this."

BIOGRAPHY

BORN
February 21, 1944
Chicago, Illinois

ENTERED SERVICE
Milwaukee, Wisconsin

BRANCH
U.S. Army

DUTY
Vietnam War

CURRENT RESIDENCE
Illinois

Protecting the Wounded

CHARLES C. HAGEMEISTER

SPECIALIST FOURTH CLASS, U.S. ARMY Headquarters Company, 1st Battalion, 5th Cavalry, 1st Cavalry Division (Airmobile)

UNCERTAIN ABOUT HIS FUTURE AND BORED WITH academics, Charles Hagemeister left college after a year and a half and was working as a warehouseman when he was drafted in 1966. After finishing basic training, he was chosen to become a medical corpsman; he went to Vietnam in November 1966, assigned to the 1st Cavalry (Airmobile). He flew into Pleiku on a transport plane that had no windows. Coming down the back ramp of the plane, he was hit by a tidal wave of heat unlike anything he had ever experienced in his native Nebraska. It was then that he realized he was truly in a foreign place.

Early in the morning on March 20, 1967, an Army company operating in Binh Dinh Province was involved in heavy fighting with the enemy. The company's officers had been killed or wounded and the force was in danger of being overrun. Specialist Fourth Class Hagemeister's platoon was ordered out on a rescue mission that afternoon. Soon after scrambling out of the helicopters that brought them close to the action, the Americans were moving through the graveyard of a small village when they were ambushed from three sides by a North Vietnamese battalion supported by a Vietcong heavy-weapons company.

Two of his fellow soldiers went down immediately, and Hagemeister had to run through heavy fire to treat them; then he had to order two new recruits who had been in Vietnam for only a few days to protect them. When he went to help his fallen platoon leader, he saw that the man was mortally wounded. Looking around, Hagemeister realized that more Americans were dead or wounded than were able-bodied. He knew that he would have to take charge.

For the rest of the day, Hagemeister moved from one position to another, treating and encouraging his comrades. The fighting was at close range, and he could not call in air support. At nightfall, as he tried to move the most seriously wounded Americans to safety, he and the others came under sniper fire. Hagemeister picked up a rifle and, aiming at the muzzle flash, shot the man out of a tree. He killed three more North Vietnamese silhouetted against the burning village as they ran toward his flank. Using a rifle, Hagemeister took out a machine-gun nest a few yards away from some wounded GIs. He continued to move the injured soldiers out of harm's way until about midnight, when his unit withdrew to a defensive position.

A little more than a year later, Hagemeister was back in the United States, a few days from being discharged from the Army, when he was told that he was to be awarded the Medal of Honor. During the White House ceremony on May 14, 1968, President Lyndon Johnson asked him, "How long do you have left in the service, son?" Hagemeister replied with a smile, "Seventy-two hours, sir." The President turned to a member of the Army brass and said, "I want you to talk to this young man after we're done here and change his mind." The officer did. Hagemeister reenlisted and later became a commissioned officer. He stayed in the Army until 1990, when he retired as a lieutenant colonel.

Charles Hagemeister followed his military service by working as a defense contractor, conducting large-unit computer-training simulations, in which he simulated capabilities a future enemy might present to Americans in battle.

BIOGRAPHY

BORN
August 21, 1946
Lincoln, Nebraska

ENTERED SERVICE
Lincoln, Nebraska

BRANCH
U.S. Army

DUTY
Vietnam War

CURRENT RESIDENCE
Kansas

Unstoppable Force

ROBERT L. HOWARD

SERGEANT FIRST CLASS, U.S. ARMY 5th Special Forces Group (Airborne), 1st Special Forces

ROBERT HOWARD WAS SEVENTEEN YEARS OLD WHEN he joined the Army in 1956. His father and four uncles had been paratroopers in World War II, and he followed in their footsteps, joining the 101st Airborne. In 1965, during the first of his five tours of duty in Vietnam, he was wounded when a ricocheting bullet hit him in the face. While recuperating in a field hospital, he met a patient who was in the Special Forces. When the man's commanding officer visited, he sized Howard up, then talked him into transferring to the Special Forces.

In 1966, after six months of training in the States, Howard returned to Vietnam as part of the 5th Special Forces Group. By late 1968, he had already been recommended for the Medal of Honor on two separate occasions when, on the afternoon of December 28, his unit was ordered to rescue a wounded Green Beret. As the choppers carrying his platoon of American and Vietnamese Special Forces tried to land, the enemy opened fire. It took two hours for Howard and his men to clear the landing zone and get all the troops in. By dusk, as they were moving forward to a hill where they thought the wounded Green Beret might be hiding, a force of about 250 North Vietnamese suddenly attacked.

Howard and his lieutenant were at the head of the platoon when a claymore mine went off nearby. Howard was knocked unconscious; when he came to, he thought he was blind, until he realized that the blood from wounds on his face had gotten into his eyes. His hands were mangled by shrapnel, which had also destroyed his weapon. He could hear his lieutenant groaning in pain a few yards away, and he was almost overcome by a sickening odor: An enemy soldier with a Soviet flamethrower was burning the bodies of Howard's comrades killed in the attack.

Deciding to blow himself up rather than be incinerated, too, Howard struggled to get a grenade off his web belt, then fumbled with the pin. The soldier with the flamethrower watched him for a moment, then walked away. Howard threw the grenade after him, then crawled to his lieutenant and tried to pull him down the hill into a ravine where the surviving Americans and South Vietnamese had taken refuge. When he got the officer down to a large tree root, where another GI had taken shelter, he screamed at the soldier to hand over his weapon. The soldier tossed him his .45 pistol, then opened fire himself with his rifle, killing three enemy soldiers who were trying to capture Howard and his lieutenant.

At that moment an NVA round struck Howard's ammunition pouch, blowing him several feet down the hill. Still clutching the .45, he crawled back to the lieutenant, shooting several North Vietnamese along the way, and finally dragged him down to the ravine.

Howard took charge of the remaining Special Forces troops, then called in U.S. air strikes. For the next two days, the North Vietnamese probed his position. On the morning of December 31, U.S. helicopters were finally able to stage an evacuation.

Two years later, in February 1971, Howard was a captain in charge of a Special Forces company under assault by the enemy when he got a call on a field telephone from General William Westmoreland. "We're in pretty bad shape here," Howard said, thinking the general had called to find out his situation. "Yeah, I know," Westmoreland replied, "but we're going to bring you out and give you the Medal of Honor."

Robert Howard received the medal from President Richard Nixon on March 2, 1971. He retired with the rank of colonel in 1992.

BIOGRAPHY

BORN
July 11, 1939
Opelika, Alabama

ENTERED SERVICE
Montgomery, Alabama

BRANCH
U.S. Army

DUTY
Vietnam War

DIED
December 23, 2009
San Antonio, Texas

To Die Fighting

ROBERT R. INGRAM

HOSPITAL CORPSMAN THIRD CLASS, U.S. NAVY Company C, 1st Battalion, 7th Marines

IN 1963, ROBERT INGRAM ENLISTED IN THE NAVY TO learn aviation electronics. But after he came down with pneumonia and was sent to the dispensary, he witnessed a meningitis outbreak and was touched by the selfless dedication of the corpsmen. He decided to attend Hospital Corps school. Upon graduating, he was assigned to the 7th Marines. He volunteered for C Company, known as "Suicide Charley," because it was always in the middle of things. His unit was ordered to Vietnam in the summer of 1965.

A fully staffed company when it landed, Suicide Charley had 112 men left on March 28, 1966, when Ingram and another Marine followed two North Vietnamese soldiers down a slope toward a rice paddy. They shot and killed the men, only to be fired upon by more than one hundred automatic weapons. They had run into a large force of the enemy readying an ambush.

The other Marine charged the enemy and was hit immediately. By the time Ingram reached him, he was dead. While kneeling over him, Ingram himself was shot through the palm of his hand. Yet, using the fallen Marine's weapon and ammunition, Ingram tried to suppress a North Vietnamese machine gun causing casualties among his company. Then he saw that his platoon leader was down. While trying to reach him, Ingram took a bullet in the left knee. When he reached the officer, the man was dead. Ingram grabbed his weapon and ammunition and limped toward another fallen Marine. As he sheltered the Marine with his body and tried to treat him, Ingram sensed a motion on his right. As Ingram turned, a North Vietnamese soldier fired at close range. The bullet hit Ingram's right cheek below the eye and passed out through the left jaw. Deaf and partly blinded, Ingram killed the enemy.

Ingram was sure that he, too, would die, but he decided that he would die fighting. Seeing one Marine who was alive, he pulled the man back into the protection of a hedgerow and stuck his rifle into the ground to mark his place. Then he moved to the edge of the rice paddy, and picked off North Vietnamese soldiers one by one until he became too disoriented from blood loss. He dragged himself back to the command post, but he would remember little of what happened until he was back in the United States weeks later.

Ingram left the service in 1968, and became a registered nurse in a family practice in Jacksonville, Florida. He had no contact with the men of Charley Company until 1995, when his former platoon leader called him one night. The memories poured out as they talked for hours. Several days later, they met, and the officer asked, "What medals did you receive for 28 March?" "The Purple Heart," Ingram replied. Shocked, his former commander blurted out, "You were put in for the Medal of Honor!"

As a result of this conversation, the men of Charley Company reunited and committed themselves to do whatever it took to make sure Robert Ingram got the recognition he deserved. They gathered the witnesses to Ingram's actions that day in the rice paddy and worked through political channels to revive the Medal recommendation. As a result, bonds between the men were reestablished and deepened, and some of the wounds of Vietnam that had separated them were healed. When Robert Ingram received the Medal of Honor from President Bill Clinton on July 10, 1998, twenty-four of the men he served with were with him at the White House.

BIOGRAPHY

BORN
January 20, 1945
Clearwater, Florida

ENTERED SERVICE
Clearwater, Florida

BRANCH
U.S. Navy

DUTY
Vietnam War

CURRENT RESIDENCE
Florida

Nightmare Mission

JOE M. JACKSON

LIEUTENANT COLONEL, U.S. AIR FORCE 311th Air Commando Squadron

BIOGRAPHY

BORN
March 14, 1923
Heard County, Georgia

ENTERED SERVICE
Newnan, Georgia

BRANCH
U.S. Air Force

DUTY
Vietnam War

CURRENT RESIDENCE
Washington State

JOE JACKSON ENLISTED IN THE ARMY AIR CORPS in 1941 because he wanted to be an airplane mechanic. He was made a flight engineer aboard a B-25; during a training flight, when one of the engines caught fire, it was Jackson who told the pilot what to do. Later, figuring that if he was going to have to give such advice, he might as well be a pilot himself, he went to flight school, became a fighter pilot, and spent the remainder of World War II as a gunnery instructor.

He flew 107 missions in Korea as an F-84 fighter-bomber pilot. After the war, he was one of a select group of pilots chosen to fly the U-2 "spy plane." He was forty-five years old when he volunteered to go to Vietnam, where he flew the C-123, a light transport, as part of the 311th Air Commando Squadron.

On May 12, 1968, Lieutenant Colonel Jackson was recalled from a routine resupply mission. On the ground, he was informed that a U.S. Special Forces camp had been overrun by approximately five thousand North Vietnamese troops. Three men from the Combat Control Team who were members of an elite Air Force special operations team that had just finished overseeing the evacuation of U.S. and South Vietnamese military and their dependents were now trapped on the ground there. Another C-123 had tried to land and extract them, but it had been driven off by enemy fire. Jackson volunteered for what his radio contact at Da Nang was already calling a nightmare mission.

While orbiting over Kham Duc, Jackson saw tracers from the North Vietnamese guns along the airstrip. The camp was engulfed in flames, and ammunition dumps were exploding, littering the runway with debris. Eight American aircraft had been destroyed; a burned helicopter remained on the landing strip. As a result,

the usable length of the runway was only 2,200 feet. Jackson made his approach like a fighter pilot rather than someone flying a transport: He came down at more than five thousand feet a minute, smacked down on the pockmarked runway, jammed on the brakes, and slid to a stop. Under heavy fire, the three Combat Control men ran out of the ditch where they had been hiding. Jackson's crew grabbed them and hauled them aboard. As the C-123 began to taxi for a quick takeoff, the enemy fired a 122 mm rocket at its nose; luckily, it broke up before hitting the plane and failed to explode. Jackson gunned the engines and took off on the shortened runway, passing through a vicious crossfire as he managed to get airborne.

President Lyndon Johnson awarded the Medal of Honor to Jackson on January 16, 1969. At the ceremony, the President had presented the Medal of Honor to a Marine from the same city in Georgia where Jackson had grown up. The President whispered to him, "There must be something in the water down there."

If Not Now, When?

JACK H. JACOBS

FIRST LIEUTENANT, U.S. ARMY U.S. Army Element, U.S. Military Assistance Command

BIOGRAPHY

BORN
August 2, 1945
Brooklyn, New York

ENTERED SERVICE
Trenton, New Jersey

BRANCH
U.S. Army

DUTY
Vietnam War

CURRENT RESIDENCE
New Jersey

IF JACK JACOBS WANTED A CHALLENGE, HE CERTAINLY had one in 1966. He had a bachelor's degree from Rutgers University, a wife and a daughter, and no money. He had been through ROTC, and his plan was to enter active duty to earn a regular paycheck, then attend law school when his three-year Army commitment was finished. He volunteered immediately for airborne duty—paratroopers earned extra pay for the hazardous duty.

A year later, Lieutenant Jacobs was in Vietnam as an adviser to a Vietnamese infantry battalion in the Mekong Delta. He had wanted to deploy with his unit, the 82nd Airborne Division, and when he asked the Army why he had been chosen for the frustrating job of adviser, he was told it was simply because he had a college degree.

On March 9, 1968, Jacobs was with the lead companies of his South Vietnamese battalion as they searched for the Vietcong. Suddenly, a large enemy force, hidden in bunkers only fifty yards away, opened fire with mortars, rifles, and machine guns. With no place to hide, many South Vietnamese soldiers were killed or wounded in the first few seconds.

A mortar round that landed just a few feet away sent shrapnel tearing through the top of Jacobs's head. Most of the bones in his face were broken, and he could see out of only one eye. He tried calling in air strikes, but the intense enemy ground fire drove off the U.S. fighters. Shortly afterward, the lead company commander was badly wounded, and the South Vietnamese troops began to panic. Jacobs assessed the situation and realized that if someone didn't act quickly, everyone would be killed. The words of Hillel, the great Jewish philosopher, jumped into his mind: "If I am only for myself, what am I? And if not now, when?"

He assumed control of the unit, ordering a withdrawal from the exposed position to a defensive perimeter. He dragged a wounded American sergeant, riddled with chest and stomach wounds, to safety, then returned to the fire-swept battlefield to rescue others. Each time he returned, he had to drive off the Vietcong, and single-handedly killed three and wounded many others. Despite being weak from blood loss, he went back time and again, bringing to safety thirteen fellow soldiers before he tried to take a brief rest—and discovered he couldn't get up again.

During the helicopter ride to the field hospital, he lost consciousness several times. Days later at another hospital, doctors pieced his skull and face together. Though he would undergo more than a dozen surgical operations, he never regained his senses of taste and smell.

Back in the United States, Jacobs was assigned to Fort Benning, where he became the commander of an officer candidate company. About a year after the action, he received an order to report to Washington, and on October 9, 1969, at a ceremony at the White House, President Richard Nixon awarded him the Medal of Honor.

After completing graduate school at Rutgers University, where he earned an M.A. in international relations, Jacobs asked to return to Vietnam. The Army granted his request on the condition that he remain out of harm's way. When he returned to Vietnam in July 1972, though, he immediately got himself assigned to the Vietnamese Airborne Division in the thick of fighting in Quang Tri. He walked away unscathed when the helicopter taking him to his unit was shot down, but he was subsequently wounded again.

Ultimately, he retired as a colonel after twenty years on active duty—quite a bit longer than the three years he had originally planned.

Unrelenting Courage

DON JENKINS

PRIVATE FIRST CLASS, U.S. ARMY Company A, 2nd Battalion, 39th Infantry, 9th Infantry Division

BIOGRAPHY

BORN
April 18, 1948
Quality, Kentucky

ENTERED SERVICE
Nashville, Tennessee

BRANCH
U.S. Army

DUTY
Vietnam War

CURRENT RESIDENCE
Kentucky

LIKE MOST OF THE PEOPLE IN QUALITY, THE SMALL Kentucky community where he was born, Don Jenkins went to work in the coal mines after he left school. Having already worked a shift during his last two years of high school, he never expected to leave his job or his hometown. But in the spring of 1968, he received his draft notice and he reported to Fort Campbell, Kentucky, for basic training and then went on to advanced infantry training. By October, he was in Vietnam as part of the 39th Infantry. Upon arriving, the first thing he noted was the slogan painted on the company headquarters: KILLING IS OUR BUSINESS AND BUSINESS IS GOOD.

On January 5, 1969, Private First Class Jenkins drank wine brought to camp by some local Vietnamese women. He became so ill that in the middle of the night a medic was forced to give him mouth-to-mouth resuscitation. The wine turned out to have been poisoned, and the next morning Jenkins was called into the office of his commanding officer, who threatened to bust him back to buck private. That afternoon, Jenkins and the men of his unit boarded helicopters and flew to a site in Kien Phong Province where intelligence had picked up vague reports of an enemy force. In fact, large numbers of North Vietnamese were dug into bunkers directly around the landing zone, and minutes after they were dropped off, the Americans were taking heavy fire.

Jenkins ran to an exposed position in front of his unit and, cradling his M-60 machine gun in his arms, opened fire on the North Vietnamese gathered around log bunkers. Several charged him; he killed them all. When his machine gun jammed, he grabbed a rifle and continued to fire on the enemy while another soldier

fixed the machine gun. Then he repeatedly ran forward through heavy fire to get ammunition from dead GIs. When there was no more ammunition on the battlefield, he crawled to a fallen American with two antitank weapons, grabbed them, and ran forward, enemy shells kicking up the dirt all around him. When he got within twenty yards of the North Vietnamese bunkers, he took out two of them with the antitank weapons.

Then Jenkins found an M-79 grenade launcher and began firing. He was struck in the stomach and legs with shrapnel, but when he heard one of his comrades call out for help, Jenkins crawled through the high jungle grass to get to him. The fallen soldier was a large man, and Jenkins, slightly built and weighing only 130 pounds, dragged him one hundred yards to safety. By this time, night had fallen. Three more wounded Americans called out for help, so Jenkins crawled out into the darkness and, one by one, brought them back to safety. When his unit was helicoptered out the next morning, Jenkins went to the hospital.

Don Jenkins came home late in 1969 and, after his discharge, went back to work in the coal mines. One afternoon in late February 1971, an Army officer arrived at his door to tell him that he needed to get a new suit and a haircut; he was going to Washington, D.C. There, on March 3, President Richard Nixon presented him with the Medal of Honor. After the ceremony, Jenkins returned to Kentucky and worked in the coal mines until 1999, when he was forced to retire because of a disability.

"Let's Go Get Them!"

LEONARD B. KELLER

PRIVATE FIRST CLASS, U.S. ARMY Company A, 3rd Battalion, 60th Infantry, 9th Infantry Division

LEONARD KELLER HAD JUST TURNED NINETEEN when he was drafted in the spring of 1966. He completed basic training at Fort Campbell, Kentucky, went on to advanced infantry training at Fort Polk, Louisiana, then joined the 60th Infantry in Vietnam. When he arrived that summer, he experienced culture shock. The sights, sounds, and smells made him feel that he was on a different planet.

His unit was stationed in the Mekong Delta. Keller's days took on a predictable rhythm: going out "into the bush" by helicopter or boat for several days on a reconnaissance mission, then returning to base for a day of rest and relaxation, then out into the field again. But constant firefights with the enemy kept things interesting.

On May 2, 1967, another U.S. infantry company was ambushed by the Vietcong in an area near the Ap Bac Zone, and Private First Class Keller's unit went to the rescue. Soon after it was dropped off by helicopter, heavy fire erupted from enemy bunkers and snipers in surrounding trees. The killed and wounded from the other American company were sprawled on the ground. His own unit was also taking casualties. As he heard voices yelling, "Retreat!" Keller became angry and called out, "Let's go get them!" to an American named Ray. The two of them charged the enemy.

Carrying an M-60 machine gun and belts of ammunition looped over his shoulders, Keller killed a Vietcong soldier in his path. Clambering up onto a dike with Ray, he began a systematic assault on a series of enemy bunkers. First Keller laid down a base of fire, and then his comrade lobbed grenades into an enemy position. Then it was Keller's turn to throw the grenades while Ray provided him with covering fire.

After they had taken out three more North Vietnamese positions, they continued their ferocious two-man fight against the enemy despite continuous withering fire. They were able to destroy four more North Vietnamese bunkers before their assault carried them into the tree line beyond the bunkers. There, enemy snipers who had been exacting a heavy toll on the American force climbed down from their firing positions and ran away. Eventually, the entire North Vietnamese force broke ranks and withdrew. Out of ammunition, Keller returned to his unit and helped load wounded GIs onto helicopters for evacuation.

In the summer of 1968, Keller, now a sergeant, was back in the United States when he was informed that he was to receive the Medal of Honor. However, he left the Army that August having heard nothing more about the medal. He assumed that there had been a mistake or the brass had changed its mind. Soon thereafter, he was on the West Coast when a team of Secret Service agents contacted him and told him he had to go to Washington, D.C.

Leonard Keller was awarded the Medal of Honor at the White House on September 19, 1968. It was a moving occasion for him and for President Lyndon Johnson as well. Keller noticed that tears coursed down LBJ's cheeks throughout the entire ceremony.

Keller married a woman who had served in the Navy. He himself worked for the Navy in Pensacola, Florida.

BIOGRAPHY

BORN
February 25, 1947
Rockford, Illinois

ENTERED SERVICE
Chicago, Illinois

BRANCH
U.S. Army

DUTY
Vietnam War

DIED
October 18, 2009
Milton, Florida

The Mobile Riverine Force

THOMAS G. KELLEY

LIEUTENANT, U.S. NAVY River Assault Division 152

THOMAS KELLEY WAS ABOUT TO GRADUATE FROM Holy Cross College in Massachusetts in 1960 when his roommates announced that they'd enlisted in the Navy and urged him to do the same. Kelley couldn't think of any reasons not to, so he joined, too. His first assignment after Officer Candidate School was on board an old World War II landing ship in the Caribbean during the Cuban Missile Crisis; he liked the duty so much that he decided to make the Navy a career.

He served in the fleet off the coast of Vietnam in 1966, but he wanted to get closer to the action and, in 1968, volunteered for the Navy's River Assault Division, part of the Mobile Riverine Force operating on the mazelike riverways of the Mekong Delta. It was a new kind of naval warfare. The boats used were modified World War II troop carriers refitted with guns and armor. The lighter ones were called tangos, and the more heavily armed ones were known as monitors because they resembled Civil War ironclads. Their job was to insert Army troops at freshwater beachheads throughout the delta, provide fire support during their operations, and extract them after their mission was completed. Because of their size and slowness, the boats were particularly vulnerable to enemy guns concealed in the jungle along the water's edge.

On June 15, 1969, Lieutenant Kelley was in charge of a group of eight boats in Kien Hoa Province that had been moving Army forces around for several hours. Late in the day, after taking the soldiers back on board, one of the boats experienced a mechanical failure when it tried to retract its loading ramp. Unable to move, it was immediately targeted by rocket-propelled grenades, machine guns, and mortars from the Vietcong on the opposite side of the river. Kelley maneuvered his monitor between the disabled boat and the enemy and opened fire. When a Vietcong rocket hit a few feet away from him, penetrating the armor of the command area and spraying shrapnel in all directions, Kelley was thrown to the deck below, suffering serious head wounds. Another boat came up, and its corpsman courageously jumped onto the deck of the monitor to begin the first aid treatment that saved Kelley's life. Unable to stand and struggling to remain conscious, Kelley continued to command the battle until the damaged troop carrier was repaired and the squadron was able to get out of harm's way.

He was helicoptered to a field hospital, where he lay in a coma for several days. Having lost an eye and portions of his skull, he underwent reconstructive surgery for his head wounds and was fitted with a prosthetic eye. The Navy declared him unfit for duty and was about to release him when he appealed directly to Admiral Elmo Zumwalt to stay on active duty. His request was accepted.

President Richard Nixon awarded Thomas Kelley the Medal of Honor on May 14, 1970. During some small talk after the ceremony, the President, noting that Kelley was from Boston, asked if this meant he ate baked beans every night. Kelley was momentarily taken aback by the question. "No, sir," he finally replied, "only on Saturdays." Kelley retired as a captain in 1990.

BIOGRAPHY

BORN
May 13, 1939
Boston, Massachusetts

ENTERED SERVICE
Boston, Massachusetts

BRANCH
U.S. Navy

DUTY
Vietnam War

CURRENT RESIDENCE
Massachusetts

No Pretend Marine

ALLAN J. KELLOGG, JR.

STAFF SERGEANT, U.S. MARINE CORPS Company G, 2nd Battalion, 5th Marines,
1st Marine Division

BIOGRAPHY

BORN
October 1, 1943
Bethel, Connecticut

ENTERED SERVICE
Bridgeport, Connecticut

BRANCH
U.S. Marine Corps

DUTY
Vietnam War

CURRENT RESIDENCE
Hawaii

AT THE END OF HIS SOPHOMORE YEAR IN HIGH
school, seventeen-year-old Allan Kellogg told his
parents that he was bored and wanted to drop out. His
father gave him permission. But the boy couldn't just
find some meaningless job; he had to join the military.
Kellogg signed up with the Marines in the fall of 1960.

In his first few years, the closest he came to seeing
action was the 1962 Cuban Missile Crisis, which he
spent with his unit on alert at Camp Lejeune. In 1966,
he was approaching the end of his enlistment, and
many of his friends were going to war. Kellogg asked
himself, Am I really a Marine or just a pretender? He
answered by reenlisting and volunteering for Vietnam.

In the spring of 1970, Kellogg, by then a staff
sergeant, was on his second tour of duty in Vietnam.
On the morning of March 11, the fourteen-man
squad he commanded was in an overgrown valley in
Quang Nam Province, serving as a blocking force for
a company of Marines trying to push the enemy in
their direction. The day was uneventful, and by late
afternoon, Kellogg was getting ready to pull out the
squad. However, he received a radio message that one
of the tanks attached to the approaching company had
hit a mine. The squad had to wait while it was repaired.

As darkness fell, Kellogg could feel the enemy
closing in. He decided it was time to move out. At that
moment, one of his men inadvertently tripped over a
howitzer shell, detonated it, and was killed instantly;
three others were seriously wounded, including the
radio operator. Kellogg called in a medical evacuation
helicopter and tried to hurry the squad toward the
extraction zone a half mile away.

As he moved his men along, Kellogg could make
out columns of Vietcong troops in pursuit. His men

began to take heavy fire. When his squad came to a
narrow and rickety footbridge extending over a rice
paddy, Kellogg crossed first, passing through enemy
machine-gun fire, and showing the men that the
obstacle could be negotiated. As he was beckoning the
others to follow, an enemy soldier suddenly emerged
from dense foliage and threw a grenade that bounced
off Kellogg's chest. With his foot, he jammed the
grenade into the mud and then fell on it. The explosion
knocked his .45 pistol out of his hands and detonated
the ammunition in his belt.

Bleeding heavily from his chest and arms, Kellogg
nonetheless stood up and reassumed command,
leading his men forward. Finally, he and his squad
made contact with the Marine company they had
been waiting for. He was evacuated with his wounded.
While he was hospitalized in Japan, an officer
informed him that he was to receive the Navy Cross.
Kellogg wisecracked, "Just get me out of here, and
we'll call it even."

Upon his recovery, he was assigned to duty at
Camp Pendleton. Early in 1972, his commanding
officer there told him that his award had been upgraded
to a Medal of Honor and that he would be going to
the White House. The medal was presented to him by
President Richard Nixon on October 15, 1973.

Allan Kellogg retired from the Marines in 1990 as
a sergeant major. For a few years, he did the things he
imagined he might have done back in 1960 if his father
hadn't told him that if he left school, he had to join the
military. Eventually, he took a job with the Department
of Veterans Affairs in Honolulu, where he has worked
for more than thirteen years.

A Tribute To All Who Have
rved And Continue To Serve
Our Great Nation

Kerrey's Raiders

JOSEPH R. "BOB" KERREY

LIEUTENANT JUNIOR GRADE, U.S. NAVY Sea, Air, and Land Team (SEAL)

BIOGRAPHY

BORN
August 27, 1943
Lincoln, Nebraska

ENTERED SERVICE
Omaha, Nebraska

BRANCH
U.S. Navy

DUTY
Vietnam War

CURRENT RESIDENCE
New York

GROWING UP IN LINCOLN, NEBRASKA, JOSEPH Kerrey—"Bob" since he was a kid—had an "all-American" childhood: He worked a newspaper route and helped out in his father's lumberyard, then attended the University of Nebraska with the intention of becoming a pharmacist. When he graduated in 1965, he decided to enlist in the Navy rather than wait to be drafted. After Officer Candidate School, he volunteered for Underwater Demolition Training and was eventually selected for a SEAL platoon, where he learned to set up ambushes, abduct enemy personnel, and gather intelligence. He was assigned to SEAL Team One.

Lieutenant Kerrey arrived in Vietnam late in 1968. His SEAL squad, which called itself Kerrey's Raiders, included Kerrey, six enlisted men, and a Vietnamese frogman who served as interpreter. Early in 1969, the team was working in the Mekong Delta, trying to ambush Vietcong cadres and kidnap high-ranking officers. Kerrey sometimes went up in a plane to make his own aerial reconnaissance of the villages before these actions.

On March 14, naval intelligence briefed Kerrey and his men on information received from a deserter that a Vietcong sapper unit had infiltrated a village on an island in the area near Nha Trang Bay and was killing civilians. Kerrey led his men on a midnight mission to neutralize the enemy unit, arriving by water in Zodiac boats and scaling a 350-foot sheer cliff so that they could approach from high ground. At the top, Kerrey split his men into two teams and moved down to the enemy's camp. Suddenly, the area erupted in intense small-arms fire. A grenade, exploding right next to Kerrey, knocked him down. Bleeding badly from a gaping wound that left his foot

dangling from his calf, he called in the second team's fire support, which caught the Vietcong in a crossfire. After applying a tourniquet to his knee and giving himself a shot of morphine, he continued to organize his team's defense. His men, using a trail of tracer bullets to direct their fire in the darkness, routed the enemy and took several prisoners.

The helicopter sent to extract the SEALs and their captives couldn't land on the island, so Kerrey was placed in a sling and pulled up to the hovering craft. He was treated first in Japan, and then in Philadelphia. Doctors were unable to save his leg when gangrene set in, and it was amputated at the knee.

Wearing a prosthetic, Kerrey was awarded the Medal of Honor on May 14, 1970, by President Richard Nixon. He later recalled trying—unsuccessfully—to flirt with the President's daughter Julie during the ceremony.

Kerrey was elected governor of Nebraska in 1983 and U.S. senator in 1989, and was a presidential candidate in 1992. In 2001, he became president of the New School University in New York City. After 9/11, he served as a member of the National Commission on Terrorist Attacks upon the United States. He is the author of *When I Was a Young Man: A Memoir by Bob Kerrey,* which was published in 2002.

A New Kind of Hazard

THOMAS J. KINSMAN

PRIVATE FIRST CLASS, U.S. ARMY Company B, 3rd Battalion, 60th Infantry, 9th Infantry Division

BIOGRAPHY

BORN
March 4, 1945
Renton, Washington

ENTERED SERVICE
Seattle, Washington

BRANCH
U.S. Army

DUTY
Vietnam War

CURRENT RESIDENCE
Washington State

THOMAS KINSMAN WAS WORKING IN THE FORESTS OF Washington State in the timber industry when he received his draft notice and was then sent to Vietnam in 1967. His new occupation as an Army rifleman would expose him to new hazards he had not experienced before.

By early 1968, Kinsman, then twenty-three years old, was a private first class with the 60th Infantry stationed in South Vietnam's Mekong Delta. Over a period of several weeks, his unit was ferried up the Delta in armored barges, trucked by troop carriers, or dropped by helicopters into areas where Vietcong movements had been reported. Sometimes the unit stayed in the field for several days in a reconnaissance-in-force designed to provoke firefights, which would determine the location of the enemy and how many of them there were. These encounters, against a hidden force that never really showed itself, were usually brief and violent. Like most of his comrades, Kinsman found that the nature of the conflict made him feel "jumpy." He kept promising himself that if he found himself in a critical situation he would "pull his weight."

On February 6, 1968, as Kinsman's company was being ferried up a narrow canal in a smaller version of a World War II landing craft, the enemy attacked with rockets and automatic weapons. The craft headed for shore and dropped its front ramp. The Americans splashed out and took cover along the muddy bank before beginning an assault on the well-camouflaged Vietcong bunker complex. In the fighting, Kinsman and seven other soldiers became cut off from the rest of the company. When a hidden enemy fighter lobbed a grenade at them, Private Kinsman immediately alerted his comrades and then threw himself on it, absorbing the explosion and saving their lives.

Although seriously wounded in the head and chest, Kinsman never lost consciousness while being carried back to the landing barge on a stretcher; however, he had such difficulty breathing that a medic was forced to cut a hole into his windpipe. Soon afterward, a helicopter arrived to evacuate him to a field station. After about three months in an Army hospital in Japan, he finally returned home to Washington for additional months of treatment at the Madigan Army Hospital at Fort Lewis, Washington.

Leaving the Army in 1970, Thomas Kinsman was able to return to his old job felling timber. He was working once again in the forest when he saw someone in uniform approaching. It was an officer sent from Fort Lewis to tell Kinsman that he would be receiving the Medal of Honor. While he thought all those who had answered their country's call to serve were heroes, he didn't think of himself as someone special.

On May 17, 1969, President Richard Nixon presented Kinsman with the Medal of Honor at a White House ceremony with his mother and father, his three brothers, and his two sisters and their husbands looking on with pride.

Fighting Red Ants and Vietcong

GEORGE C. LANG

SPECIALIST FOURTH CLASS, U.S. ARMY Company A, 4th Battalion, 47th Infantry, 9th Infantry Division

BIOGRAPHY

BORN
April 20, 1947
Flushing, New York

ENTERED SERVICE
Brooklyn, New York

BRANCH
U.S. Army

DUTY
Vietnam War

DIED
March 16, 2005
Seaford, New York

IN 1967, GEORGE LANG WAS WORKING IN A NEW York defense plant making 750-pound bombs for the military—a job that carried a deferment from the service, although he didn't know that at the time. He was transferred to another department and soon after got his draft notice.

Army Specialist Fourth Class Lang arrived in Vietnam in the fall of 1968. By the following spring, his infantry company was part of the Mobile Riverine Force, living on Navy transport ships and cruising the waterways in tangos armed with .50- and .30-caliber machine guns and automatic grenade launchers.

On February 22, 1969, intelligence reports indicated that enemy troops had concentrated in an area within Kien Hoa Province. After American guns had laid down an artillery barrage, the boats carrying Lang's platoon landed them on shore

Lang, a squad leader, was walking point on the reconnaissance-in-force mission when he saw several enemy bunkers. None appeared to be occupied, although all were connected by communications wires, indicating a relatively sophisticated defensive position. Continuing on, he saw a small house in a clearing with several Vietcong nearby. He and another soldier armed with an M-79 grenade launcher opened fire on them, then hit the ground—and were instantly covered by red ants unearthed by artillery shells. As they jumped into an irrigation canal to get the stinging ants off their bodies, a scout dog was brought up to follow a trail of blood leading away from the house; it ended at the bodies of the Vietcong Lang had hit, who had staggered off into the bush to die.

The Americans advanced another hundred yards in two columns to an area overgrown with palms and banana trees and interlaced with irrigation canals.

Suddenly the enemy opened fire from a concealed bunker, wounding several Americans in the left column. Lang, who was leading the right column, saw where the fire was coming from. With bullets snapping past his head, he sprinted toward it and eliminated the enemy with his rifle and hand grenades. Then, when a machine gun from another bunker opened up about fifty feet directly in front of him, he eliminated it as well. It held a large cache of ammunition, and as he motioned his squad forward to secure it, yet a third bunker began firing. Lang took that one out, too.

The Americans were under heavy rocket and automatic-weapons fire. Lang felt a powerful blow on his back and was knocked off his feet. He had been hit by a large piece of shrapnel. Still trying to direct his men, he was hit again by a bullet that struck his elbow and exited his shoulder. When a medic reached him and asked where he had been hit, Lang answered, "I don't know, but I can't move." The medic made his way back to the American position for help, returning with GIs who dragged Lang to the command post to be evacuated.

The evacuation area was just large enough for small helicopters to land. Once aboard, Lang was conscious until he got to the field hospital; the next thing he remembered was waking up from anesthesia and seeing a priest standing above his bed telling him that he was about to receive last rites before he underwent a second operation.

Lang's spine had been severed by the shrapnel, leaving him a paraplegic. After two months in a hospital in Japan, he returned to the United States, where he was hospitalized for another ten months. He was awarded the Medal of Honor on March 2, 1971, by President Richard Nixon.

Determined to Hold

HOWARD V. LEE

CAPTAIN, U.S. MARINE CORPS Company E, 2nd Battalion, 4th Marines, 3rd Marine Division (Reinforced)

AS A SENIOR IN COLLEGE IN 1955, HOWARD LEE joined the Marine Reserves and, after completing the required Officer Candidate program, became an officer. Finding that he liked the military, he transferred to the regular Marines. When he was given command of his first infantry platoon, he decided to make the Corps a career.

He was sent to Vietnam in the spring of 1966 as a captain in charge of a company in the 4th Marines. On August 8, his company was providing security for the American base at Dong Ha when one of his platoons on a reconnaissance mission near the village of Cam Lo was surrounded by a large North Vietnamese force. The first helicopter sent to extract the trapped Marine platoon picked up about half of them. A second helicopter was hit by enemy fire and crashed. Listening to the operation unfold back at Dong Ha, Lee convinced his battalion commander to let him go forward to provide leadership for the sixteen men left on the ground.

Captain Lee had an aerial view of the Marines' precarious position at the top of a hill as he arrived by helicopter. They were surrounded by what turned out to be North Vietnamese regular forces. On the ground, he and the two men with him were moving up the hill in the middle of heavy fire when the sergeant of the battered platoon, who had been wounded in the head and was bleeding profusely, came running down. Lee thought that the sergeant was intending to report to him, but the soldier ran right by without a word and managed to jump into the departing helicopter as it lifted off.

Once at the American position, Lee went from one foxhole to another to reassure the men. But the U.S. troops were going through ammunition at a rapid rate in their effort to keep the enemy at bay; Lee called for resupply and fire support. One of the helicopter pilots who responded was over the American position when an enemy rocket tore off the tail of the craft and it crashed. Fortunately, the three-man crew survived and, with the helicopter's machine guns, augmented Lee's beleaguered force.

At dusk, the NVA staged an attack that lasted through the night. Although Lee was hit with shrapnel several times in the face and his right side—doctors would later extract fifteen pieces, ranging in size from an aspirin to a quarter—he continued to direct the defense, calling in artillery and concentrating the Marines' firepower. The enemy came so close that he could hear them talking. But they never penetrated the Marines' perimeter, and at daybreak they retreated. That morning Lee collapsed due to blood loss from his many wounds and had to relinquish command. His actions saved his men from capture, minimized the loss of life of his fellow Marines, and dealt the enemy a severe defeat.

Captain Lee spent three weeks on a hospital ship in Da Nang bay and was then sent home. On October 25, 1967, he was at the White House to receive the Medal of Honor. While President Lyndon Johnson was reading the citation, Lee's three-year-old son, Michael, was on the floor squirming. Frustrated, Lee reached down and picked the child up by the collar. That scene became the photo that made the newspapers the next day.

Howard Lee retired as a lieutenant colonel in 1975 after returning to Vietnam in 1970 for a second tour of duty. His son Michael is now a career Marine who has served three tours of duty in Iraq.

BIOGRAPHY

BORN
August 1, 1933
New York, New York

ENTERED SERVICE
New York, New York

BRANCH
U.S. Marine Corps

DUTY
Vietnam War

CURRENT RESIDENCE
Virginia

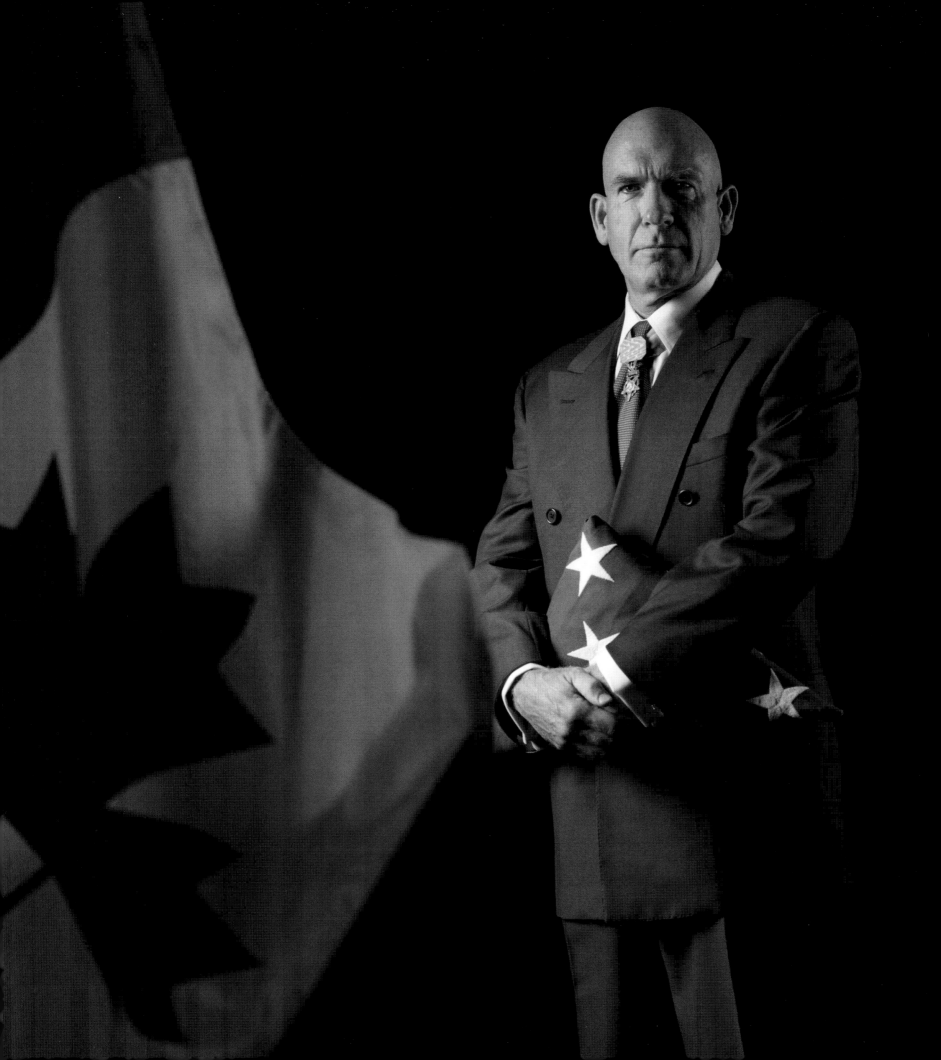

Outnumbered Twenty to One

PETER C. LEMON

SPECIALIST FOURTH CLASS, U.S. ARMY Company E, 2nd Battalion, 8th Cavalry, 1st Cavalry Division

CANADIAN-BORN PETER LEMON CAN REMEMBER observing his British mother and Canadian father study for their U.S. citizenship. It became a defining moment for this eleven-year-old when he and his family were sworn in as American citizens.

In 1969, Lemon enlisted in the Army and volunteered for Vietnam and the 75th Rangers, where he served in a five-man reconnaissance team stalking North Vietnamese Army units.

Early in 1970, nineteen-year-old Lemon requested to be assigned to E Company (RECON) 2/8th Cavalry, 1st Cavalry Division, commanded by the legendary warrior Lieutenant Gregory Peters. The unit was stationed in Tay Ninh Province in a no-man's-land on the Cambodian border called the "Dog's Head." The NVA used the territory as a major supply route for its forces operating inside South Vietnam. To stall the enemy's effort, the 1st Cavalry established two fire support bases, "Jay" and "Illingworth." After NVA troops overran Jay in late March, Lemon's seasoned unit was immediately assigned to reinforce the two hundred men stationed at Illingworth.

They found the firebase had been hastily constructed in a large dry pond bed. Its sooty dust made it difficult to breathe. The berm in areas on its perimeter was only two feet high, and no barbed wire had been strung out beyond the base to slow attacking forces.

Lemon's light seventeen-man platoon was given the most vulnerable sector of the base to defend—only about fifty yards from the wood line where the enemy could mass. At approximately 1:00 on the morning of April 1—April Fools' Day—the NVA launched a forty-five-minute mortar and rocket barrage, followed by a horrific attack in which seemingly endless waves of enemy soldiers assaulted the Americans over the next three and a half hours.

Specialist Lemon's sector was outgunned at least twenty to one by the enemy. He knew that if his unit didn't hold, the entire base would be overrun. He strategically moved between positions, throwing grenades and firing his rifle as the enemy tried to penetrate the berm. Lemon was hit by shrapnel twice, once while dragging a wounded comrade to safety.

Again, as their location seemed likely to be breached, he stood on top of an embankment, fully exposed, desperately trying to operate a .50-caliber machine gun so clogged by dust it fired only one round at a time, before being rocked to the ground by an explosion. In one skirmish, he eliminated all but one of the enemy, then killed the remaining NVA soldier in hand-to-hand combat. As the attack gradually subsided, Lemon, badly injured, continued to aid his wounded comrades and refused to be evacuated until the other more seriously wounded were medevaced to safety.

The bodies of sixty-seven NVA soldiers lay in front of the sector that Lemon's seventeen-man platoon had defended. Three of his comrades—Casey Waller, Nathan Mann, and Brent Street—died during the battle. Lemon would be presented the Medal of Honor; two men in his unit would receive the Distinguished Service Cross, five would accept the Silver Star, and valorous awards went to the remaining soldiers.

Lemon went on to be a successful entrepreneur. For many years he kept the medal in a shoebox in his closet, until he was reunited with his comrades. It was then that he understood that displaying the medal gave him an opportunity to represent what they had all achieved that day in a forgotten place in a distant corner of the world.

BIOGRAPHY

BORN
June 5, 1950
Toronto, Canada

ENTERED SERVICE
Tawas, Michigan

BRANCH
U.S. Army

DUTY
Vietnam War

CURRENT RESIDENCE
Colorado

Saving Spooky 71

JOHN L. LEVITOW

AIRMAN FIRST CLASS, U.S. AIR FORCE 3rd Special Operations Squadron

JOHN LEVITOW DECIDED TO JOIN THE NAVY AFTER high school because the Army and Marines required a lot of walking, and to him that seemed like too much work. But when he showed up at the Navy recruiting office and had to wait because the recruiters were busy, he went next door and joined the Air Force.

Levitow was sent to Vietnam as a loadmaster for C-130s. On the night of February 24, 1969, he was asked to fill in for the regular loadmaster on an AC-47 called Spooky 71. An adaptation of the famous DC-3 airliner, the specially outfitted gunship carried three 7.62-mm mini guns that could accurately spray up to six thousand rounds a minute. It could also, in a few seconds, light up the darkness for GIs below—each of its MK-24 flares burned at three thousand degrees and provided two million candlepower intensity.

After cruising for more than four hours, Spooky 71 received orders to go to the Bien Hoa area, where North Vietnamese troops had come out of their jungle sanctuaries under the cover of darkness to launch attacks on U.S. troops. Banking in tight circles about one thousand feet above the ground, the plane dropped several of its twenty-seven-pound flares out of the open cargo door, then raked the enemy with bursts from its mini guns that sounded like loud zippers.

Suddenly, Spooky 71 was rocked by a violent explosion. The plane had flown directly into the path of an enemy mortar round, and shrapnel had ripped holes in its wings and body. As the aircraft lurched wildly, the pilot struggled to keep control. The five crewmen in the hold were all wounded. Airman First Class Levitow had been struck by more than forty shell fragments on his right side just as he was arming a flare. The crew member who had been about to throw the flare out of the plane was on his back, and the flare was bouncing wildly through the hold.

With the plane gyrating in a 30-degree turn, Levitow, despite the numbness overtaking his body, got to one of the gunners who was about to fall out of the open cargo door and dragged him back from the bay by his uniform. Then he went after the flare; he knew it would detonate within about twenty seconds, burn through the metal floor of the cargo hold, explode the ammunition, and destroy the plane.

The plane pitched and bucked, throwing Levitow from side to side. Twice the smoking flare rolled just beyond his grasp. Then he fell on top of the two-foot canister and trapped it. Hugging it to his body, he crawled toward the cargo door and heaved the canister out. It exploded a split second later. The pilot of Spooky 71 later reconstructed what had happened in the hold by the pattern of the blood Levitow had left on the floor.

John Levitow recovered from his wounds after a brief hospital stay. He flew twenty more missions in Vietnam before being discharged in 1969. On May 14, 1970, he was awarded the Medal of Honor by President Richard Nixon. He was the first enlisted man in the Air Force to receive this honor. The Air Force later named its outstanding graduate award, given by each enlisted professional military education class, the John L. Levitow Award.

BIOGRAPHY

BORN
November 1, 1945
Hartford, Connecticut

ENTERED SERVICE
New Haven, Connecticut

BRANCH
U.S. Air Force

DUTY
Vietnam War

DIED
November 8, 2000
Glastonbury, Connecticut

Adviser in Command

GARY L. LITTRELL

SERGEANT FIRST CLASS, U.S. ARMY Advisory Team 21, II Corps Advisory Group

BIOGRAPHY

BORN
October 26, 1944
Henderson, Kentucky

ENTERED SERVICE
Los Angeles, California

BRANCH
U.S. Army

DUTY
Vietnam War

CURRENT RESIDENCE
Florida

GARY LITTRELL WAS NINE YEARS OLD WHEN HIS UNCLE took him to Fort Campbell to watch the 101st Airborne Division make parachute jumps. He always remembered watching the men floating down and saying to himself, Someday I'll be doing that. In 1961, on his seventeenth birthday, he joined the Army—once the recruiter guaranteed that he could go to jump school.

After graduating from jump school, Littrell was assigned to the 503rd Regiment, which was reorganized as the 173rd Airborne Brigade (Separate). This brigade was stationed on Okinawa. His next assignment was to the 82nd Airborne Division. He then attended Ranger School, where he did well enough to be made an instructor. During his two years there, the "war stories" he heard from returning Vietnam veterans whetted his appetite for combat, so in 1969 he volunteered to go to the war zone. He learned to speak Vietnamese at the Army Language Institute at Fort Bliss and became an adviser to the 23rd South Vietnamese Ranger Battalion, whose dedication and bravery impressed him.

In the early spring of 1970, Littrell was one of four American advisers assisting the 23rd Battalion of the South Vietnamese Army as it looked for North Vietnamese Army units that had been harassing U.S. Special Forces camps in Kontum Province. On April 4, after 473 South Vietnamese Rangers ran into a concentration of approximately 5,000 enemy troops, they established a defensive perimeter on a hill against a ferocious mortar attack. The battalion commander and one of the American advisers were killed in the first day of the fighting. Then two other advisers were wounded, leaving Sergeant Littrell in command.

Over the next four days, Littrell exhorted the South Vietnamese troops not to give up, despite their heavy losses. Moving along the defensive perimeter, he distributed ammunition and tried to help the wounded. Repeatedly abandoning positions of relative safety, he continually called in air support and artillery fire on the advancing enemy. At times he directed the American air strikes to within a few yards of his own position.

On April 8, 1970, Littrell's commanding officer radioed him to attempt a retreat. Littrell moved out with what was left of the battalion. With helicopter gunships guarding his flanks and Air Force fighters clearing a corridor to his front, and by fighting off constant enemy ambushes, he moved the men five miles to link up with "friendlies." Of the South Vietnamese Rangers who had begun the battle, forty-one walking wounded came out—but the enemy had been virtually annihilated.

Littrell was ordered home a few months later. At his going-away party, his commanding officer told him that he had been recommended for the Medal of Honor, but nothing happened and he soon forgot about it. Three and a half years later, he was serving with the 101st Division when he was informed that he was to receive the medal. President Richard Nixon made the presentation at the White House on October 15, 1973.

Command Sergeant Major Littrell retired from the Army ten years later. After retirement, Littrell served for many years with the Veterans Administration. In recent years, he has been very active with the Congressional Medal of Honor Society, serving as its president for two consecutive terms.

Staying Alive

JAMES E. LIVINGSTON

CAPTAIN, U.S. MARINE CORPS Company E, 2nd Battalion, 4th Marines,
9th Marine Amphibious Brigade

THE BATTLE OF DAI DO BEGAN WHEN MAJOR elements of the North Vietnamese 320th Regiment infiltrated the area near the 3rd Marine headquarters in Dong Ha, Quang Tri Province. The command center was defended by an understrength Marine Corps battalion landing team that would find itself in one desperate situation after another during the next three days.

At the heart of it all was James Livingston, once a free-spirited student who, on receiving his Army draft notice after finishing college, decided to take what he later called "the path of greatest resistance" by enlisting in the Marines.

Captain Livingston had been in combat since 1967, most recently as the commander of Echo Company.

On April 30, 1968, Echo Company was sent to defend a key bridge near Dong Ha on the Cua Viet River. The next day it became clear that another company, Golf Company, was having trouble in its assault of Dai Do, so Echo was sent to join it. Charging with his men through a rice paddy raked by extremely heavy fire from .50-caliber machine guns and rocket-propelled grenades, Livingston found the enemy heavily dug in. After his first two platoons stalled, he ordered the reserve platoon to attack. Carrying an M-2 grease gun, Livingston personally led the assault. He was wounded twice by grenade blasts but refused treatment. Once he and his men had broken through the enemy trench line, they went from bunker to bunker, destroying the North Vietnamese troops. Livingston himself killed fourteen of the enemy. When Echo Company finally secured Dai Do, it was left with only thirty-five able-bodied men out of the more than one hundred who had commenced the action.

As the medevacs loaded up the dead and wounded, Livingston heard, over the radio, desperate pleas for help and sounds of fighting in the background. It was Hotel Company, which had attacked the nearby hamlet of Dinh To and encountered heavy opposition from snipers, machine guns, and rockets. After its assault bogged down, it had been put on the defensive by a numerically superior North Vietnamese force dug in behind bamboo hedgerows. "I could tell those young guys were in a world of hurt," Livingston said later. He told what was left of Echo Company to get ready to go to the rescue.

After he reached Hotel Company through a hail of fire, Livingston merged it with Echo and led an attack on the North Vietnamese. At one point, when his submachine gun jammed, he gestured for a Marine to toss him an M-14. He killed another eleven North Vietnamese over the next hour of hand-to-hand fighting.

By late in the day, the battlefield situation was briefly stabilized, but then the reinforced North Vietnamese attacked again. Livingston ordered smoke shells and all available supporting fire in order to bring the survivors of the two companies out in a phased withdrawal. He was hit in the thigh by an enemy machine-gun round and went down. Unable to get back on his feet, he continued to fire from a prone position. When he ordered his men to go on without him, telling them he would cover them, two Marines disobeyed. They picked him up and dragged him to safety.

Livingston was awarded the Medal of Honor on May 14, 1970, by President Richard Nixon. He retired from the Marine Corps as a major general in 1995. After retirement, he served as chairman of the board of the National D-Day Museum. Currently, he is a trustee and board member of that museum.

Pulling the Men to Safety

ALLEN J. LYNCH

SPECIALIST FOURTH CLASS, U.S. ARMY Company D, 1st Battalion (Airmobile), 12th Cavalry, 1st Cavalry Division (Airmobile)

ALLEN LYNCH WAS BULLIED THROUGHOUT HIS school years. A loner, he was a poor student who had few friends. When he graduated from high school in 1964, he felt that he had to get away from Chicago and build a new life. He enlisted in the Army that November.

After three weeks of basic training, he was invited to attend Officer Candidate School at Fort Benning, Georgia. After four weeks, he dropped out and was reassigned to a unit in Germany. A year later, he volunteered to serve in Vietnam.

Upon arriving in Vietnam in the fall of 1966, Lynch was assigned to the 12th Cavalry, where for several months he served as a rifleman, then became his platoon's radiotelephone operator. In December 1967, his company was in the Bong Son area of the Central Highlands. The unit had been in almost daily contact with the enemy for a month and a half, and, on December 14, it was ordered to the rear for rest and recuperation. But another company in the battalion was ambushed, and the next morning Lynch's unit was quickly reassembled and inserted during an air assault against a large force of North Vietnamese regulars and Vietcong who were massing for the Tet Offensive, which erupted two months later.

The fighting was heavy throughout the morning. Early in the afternoon, Lynch saw three wounded soldiers out in the open who were under intense enemy fire. He dropped his radio and went to help. Despite heavy enemy fire, he reached the men and carried them one by one to a trench that offered some protection.

The Americans were separated from the enemy by a large hedgerow of bamboo. Lynch fired at the sound of the enemy's voices and over the next few hours killed several of them.

Lynch's company temporarily pulled back because of the intensity of the enemy fire. Then he located counterattacking friendly forces and assisted in evacuating their wounded. He was in action for several more weeks before he was ordered to the rear. In June 1968, he was sent to Fort Hood, Texas, where he was discharged in April 1969.

One year later, one day before he was to be married, he was returning home from his job as a UPS deliveryman when he saw that he was being followed by a policeman. Lynch feared he would be receiving a ticket, but the officer handed him a note with a telephone number on it and told him to call it. When he called, he was informed that he was to receive the Medal of Honor. President Richard Nixon presented it to him on May 14, 1970. A few months later, Lynch took a job with the Veterans Administration.

Lynch graduated from Southern Illinois University with a degree in health care administration. He also completed twenty-one years of service in the Army Reserve and National Guard. In November 2005, he retired as chief of the Veterans Rights Bureau for the Illinois attorney general. Lynch now volunteers as the chief service representative for the Illinois State Council of the Vietnam Veterans of America. He is also active in a men's Bible study and ministry at the county jail.

BIOGRAPHY

BORN
October 28, 1945
Chicago, Illinois

ENTERED SERVICE
Chicago, Illinois

BRANCH
U.S. Army

DUTY
Vietnam War

CURRENT RESIDENCE
Illinois

They Were Soldiers

WALTER J. MARM, JR.

SECOND LIEUTENANT, U.S. ARMY Company A, 1st Battalion, 7th Cavalry, 1st Cavalry Division (Airmobile)

BIOGRAPHY

BORN
November 20, 1941
Washington, Pennsylvania

ENTERED SERVICE
Pittsburgh, Pennsylvania

BRANCH
U.S. Army

DUTY
Vietnam War

CURRENT RESIDENCE
North Carolina

WHEN WALTER MARM GRADUATED FROM COLLEGE with a business degree in 1964, Vietnam was a distant place that didn't figure in his personal geography. He enlisted in the Army, graduated from Officer Candidate School a second lieutenant, and attended Ranger School. But the Army needed junior officers for a new unit being formed, the 1st Cavalry Division, and he was reassigned. This airmobile division was to test the theory that helicopters could function as the modern equivalent of the horse, carrying men quickly into the heart of a battle. Marm was assigned to the division's 7th Cavalry—George Armstrong Custer's old unit. By September 1965, he was in Vietnam.

At noon on November 14, the 7th Cavalry's 1st Battalion was on a sweep through the Ia Drang Valley when Company B suddenly came under heavy fire. It was the beginning of the first large-scale pitched battle between American and North Vietnamese troops, which would later be dramatized in the film *We Were Soldiers*.

Company A was ordered to relieve the isolated troops and moved out quickly through the thick underbrush. Lieutenant Marm's platoon assumed the lead but was forced to take cover as it came under intense fire from the well-disciplined enemy. When Marm saw four North Vietnamese soldiers trying to outflank his unit, he moved toward them through a hail of bullets and killed all four. And when he saw his men under siege from a well-concealed machine gun, he stood up to draw its fire so he could determine its location. The gun was behind a large, anthill-shaped berm; Marm aimed a bazooka at it and shot. The explosion, though dislodging some of the North Vietnamese soldiers hiding behind the berm, failed to

destroy the machine gun. Marm charged over the open ground toward the mound and threw a grenade behind it, killing eight of the enemy. Marm went around to the left side of the berm, killing the remaining enemy with his M-16 rifle. Turning to motion his men forward to relieve the trapped platoon, he was shot by an enemy soldier in the left jaw; the bullet exited on the right side of his neck. Two of his soldiers rushed to treat him, then escorted him to the battalion command post. He was medevaced out of the battle zone by nightfall.

The Medal of Honor was presented to Marm by Secretary of the Army Stanley Resor at the Pentagon on December 19, 1966. In 1969, Marm asked to go back to Vietnam for a second tour; he was allowed to return only after signing a waiver stipulating that going back into harm's way was his own choice.

Marm retired from military service as a colonel with thirty years of service. He now raises pigs in North Carolina.

A Formidable Enemy

JOHN J. MCGINTY III

STAFF SERGEANT, U.S. MARINE CORPS Company K, 3rd Battalion, 4th Marines, 3rd Marine Division

BIOGRAPHY

BORN
January 21, 1940
Boston, Massachusetts

ENTERED SERVICE
Laurel Bay, South Carolina

BRANCH
U.S. Marine Corps

DUTY
Vietnam War

CURRENT RESIDENCE
California

JOHN MCGINTY ALWAYS LIKED THE RECRUITMENT slogan "Join the Navy and See the World," but he wasn't fond of Navy uniforms, so right after high school he joined the Marines. It was 1957, and over the next few years, besides doing a stint as a drill instructor at Parris Island, South Carolina, he got to see varied and exotic places, including having a posting in the Far East, and another as a military policeman in Kodiak, Alaska.

By the summer of 1966, McGinty, a staff sergeant in the 3rd Battalion, 4th Marines, was in Vietnam. On July 15, the battalion was helicoptered into an area along the demilitarized zone where infrared photos taken by air reconnaissance showed enemy activity. Coming into the landing zone, the choppers came under heavy fire; three were lost off-loading the Marines.

Once he was finally on the ground, McGinty saw that the enemy was not the pajama-clad Vietcong guerrillas the Marines were used to fighting, but rather, for the first time, uniformed and well-supplied North Vietnamese Army soldiers. U.S. intelligence had drastically underestimated their numbers: The Marines were facing an entire NVA regiment.

That first day, the Americans captured a 250-bed enemy hospital dug into a hill under the heavy jungle canopy. For the next two days, the North Vietnamese tried to dislodge the Marines from that position. On the morning of July 18, during a pause in the fighting, the battalion was ordered to withdraw, with McGinty's company acting as the rear guard. The previous day, U.S. troops had been heavily resupplied with ammunition; the other two platoons in the company took some of it and moved out. McGinty ordered the men in his platoon to pick up the remaining ammunition. They grumbled, but this decision would save their lives.

McGinty's was the last platoon out, staying behind to cover the Marine engineers as they destroyed the downed American helicopters in order to keep sensitive equipment aboard out of enemy hands. The North Vietnamese attacked again; only the fifty or so men in the platoon stood between the enemy and the rest of the Marine battalion, vulnerable in its withdrawal.

McGinty and his men opened fire and held back the first wave of North Vietnamese. The second wave was stopped by U.S. fighter planes dropping napalm before it could charge. For the next six hours, McGinty rallied his men repeatedly, receiving wounds in his legs and left eye. The ammunition he had earlier forced his men to carry out allowed them to fight off the enemy.

Seeing two squads cut off from the rest of the platoon, McGinty ran to them through intense machine-gun and mortar fire. Finding twenty men wounded and the corpsman dead, he reloaded weapons for the injured men and organized a defense. He killed five enemy soldiers at point-blank range with his pistol. Then, as North Vietnamese troops again threatened to overrun his position, he called in air strikes to within fifty yards of his men.

As night fell, the enemy withdrew. When choppers arrived to evacuate the Marines, only nine of the fifty were still able-bodied. There were more than five hundred enemy dead left behind.

McGinty received a commission as second lieutenant. One day in 1967, when he was back at Parris Island working as a drill instructor, he learned that he was receiving the Medal of Honor. President Lyndon Johnson presented it to him on March 12, 1968.

Bullets Buzzing Like Bees

DAVID H. McNERNEY

FIRST SERGEANT, U.S. ARMY Company A, 1st Battalion, 8th Infantry, 4th Infantry Division

BIOGRAPHY

BORN
June 2, 1931
Lowell, Massachusetts

ENTERED SERVICE
Fort Bliss, Texas

BRANCH
U.S. Army

DUTY
Vietnam War

DIED
October 10, 2010
Crosby, Texas

DAVID MCNERNEY ALWAYS FELT THAT THE military was in his DNA. His father had volunteered for World War I and fought in Europe, receiving a Distinguished Service Cross, a Silver Star, and two Purple Hearts. His sister was an Army nurse in World War II; his elder brother served aboard the submarine USS *Dace,* which stalked Japanese ships throughout the Pacific. Later on, when McNerney himself was fighting in the jungles of Vietnam, his younger brother was in the skies above, flying combat missions in an F-100.

McNerney joined the Navy in 1949, right after graduating from high school in Houston, Texas. In 1953, when his enlistment was over, he enrolled at the University of Houston. But after six weeks, he saw a recruitment poster for the paratroopers and joined the Army the next day. For the next few years, he was stationed in Korea, Okinawa, and other foreign postings. Then, in 1962, he volunteered for Special Warfare School and became one of the first five hundred advisers sent to Vietnam. His second tour came in 1964 and his third in late 1966, when he was assigned to the 8th Infantry.

In the early spring of 1967, McNerney's unit was stationed in the Central Highlands near the Cambodian border. On the afternoon of March 21, his company was helicoptered into Polei Doc to look for a missing U.S. reconnaissance team. The Americans arrived near dark and set up a defensive perimeter. Moving out the next morning, they ran into fire from a North Vietnamese force that outnumbered them three to one. Sergeant McNerney told his company commander that he would go to the front of the action to get a clearer picture of what they faced. He still remembers the sound of the bullets all around him: like angry bees. Hitting the dirt, he opened fire on the North Vietnamese and killed several of them. Then he saw, as if in slow motion, a grenade sailing through the air toward him. The concussion lifted him in the air and thumped him down.

Learning that his commander and forward artillery observer had been killed, McNerney took over command of the company. Sensing that the enemy was about to envelop his unit, he called in artillery fire to within about sixty-five feet of his position. Having run out of smoke grenades, McNerney moved into a nearby clearing to mark the location for U.S. planes. In plain view of the enemy and under constant fire, he climbed a tree and tied the unit's brightly colored identification panel to the highest branches so that friendly aircraft would know where the Americans were.

Still under heavy fire, McNerney crawled into no-man's-land to collect demolition materials from the rucksacks of the men who had dropped them when the fighting began. He used the explosives to blow up large trees and clear a landing site so that helicopters could begin evacuating his hard-hit unit. Disregarding the pain of his injuries and refusing medical evacuation, McNerney remained with his unit until the next day, when a new commander arrived.

He returned to the United States in August and was sent to Fort Dix as a trainer. On September 19, 1968, he went to the White House to receive the Medal of Honor. President Lyndon Johnson met him in the Oval Office before the ceremony and told him, "You're a good Texan."

David McNerney later volunteered for another tour of duty in Vietnam, his fourth. He left the Army in December 1969 and worked for the U.S. Customs Office until his retirement in 1995.

The Clarity of Engagement

ROBERT J. MODRZEJEWSKI

CAPTAIN, U.S. MARINE CORPS Company K, 3rd Battalion, 4th Marines, 3rd Marine Division

BIOGRAPHY

BORN
July 3, 1934
Milwaukee, Wisconsin

ENTERED SERVICE
Milwaukee, Wisconsin

BRANCH
U.S. Marine Corps

DUTY
Vietnam War

CURRENT RESIDENCE
California

ROBERT MODRZEJEWSKI WAS A STUDENT AT THE University of Wisconsin when he joined the Marine Corps Platoon Leaders Class, the Corps's version of the ROTC. He was commissioned a second lieutenant after graduating in 1957.

By 1966, he was in Vietnam, a captain commanding a company in the 3rd Battalion, Fourth Marines. On July 15, 1966, his unit was involved in Operation Hastings, an effort by Marines and South Vietnamese troops to block North Vietnamese units from infiltrating into the south through the demilitarized zone and Laos. After months of fighting a shadowy guerrilla enemy using booby traps and ambushes, Modrzejewski looked forward to what he thought would be the clarity of a larger engagement.

His company, which was to function as a blocking force for the other battalions involved in Operation Hastings, landed by helicopter and moved to their assigned objective in the dense jungle. Coming upon a well-entrenched North Vietnamese platoon, his men routed it and seized large quantities of ammunition and medical supplies. That night, a significantly reinforced enemy force counterattacked. It was so dark that Modrzejewski had to request that flares be sent up so he could get a sense of what was happening. In a chaotic three-hour battle, the Marines managed to fight off the North Vietnamese. This was the beginning of a two-and-a-half-day siege in which Modrzejewski's dwindling force would have to keep repelling an enemy that was growing in strength.

The second night of the battle was fought at close quarters against a North Vietnamese force that was now battalion-size. Modrzejewski was wounded by shrapnel, but he managed to run and crawl two hundred yards

to retrieve ammunition and provide it to a vulnerable part of his force. He later called in artillery strikes, which came within a few yards of the Marine positions.

By the third day, his unit had sustained many casualties, was surrounded, and was running out of ammunition. The enemy, now grown to the size of a regiment, attacked just before noon amid the noise of bugles and whistles and the explosions of mortars and automatic weapons. Facing more than one thousand soldiers, Modrzejewski reorganized his men for close combat. He called in air strikes again, calibrating them to hit so close that some of his men had to jump into a stream to keep from being roasted alive by napalm. Then, sometime before dark, for reasons Modrzejewski never fully understood, the North Vietnamese force broke off its assault and withdrew into the mountains.

After his tour of duty in Vietnam ended, he was assigned as the commanding officer of the Marine barracks at the Naval Academy, where he was informed that he would receive the Medal of Honor. It was presented to him on March 12, 1968, by President Lyndon Johnson, shortly before his announcement that he wouldn't run for reelection.

Never Give Up

THOMAS R. NORRIS

LIEUTENANT, U.S. NAVY SEALS Adviser, Strategic Technical Directorate Assistance Team, Headquarters, U.S. Military Assistance Command

BIOGRAPHY

BORN
January 14, 1944
Jacksonville, Florida

ENTERED SERVICE
Silver Spring, Maryland

BRANCH
U.S. Navy

DUTY
Vietnam War

CURRENT RESIDENCE
Idaho

THOMAS NORRIS GRADUATED FROM THE UNIVERSITY of Maryland in 1967. He had studied criminology with the hope of joining the FBI, but knowing that he had to satisfy his military obligation, he enlisted in the Navy, eventually joining the SEALs.

On April 2, 1972, a U.S. electronic surveillance aircraft was downed by an enemy surface-to-air missile. Lieutenant Colonel Iceal Hambleton was the sole crew member to eject safely—but he parachuted into the middle of some thirty thousand North Vietnamese troops. Over the next several days, during an extensive rescue effort, four aircraft were downed, ten Americans were killed, two were captured, and another two were trapped behind enemy lines.

Lieutenant Norris volunteered to go after the survivors. On April 10, his five-man team was inserted into a forward operating base (FOB). That evening, Norris led his team through enemy positions to a predetermined interception point deep in enemy territory. One of the downed airmen, Lieutenant Mark Clark, had been informed over his survival radio to work his way to the river and to float downstream. Hiding on a riverbank, Norris heard Clark approaching, but he had to let the American pilot float by because of a nearby North Vietnamese patrol. Once the enemy had passed, Norris slipped into the river and swam after Clark, locating him and returning him to the FOB.

Then the FOB came under heavy attack, resulting in the loss of half of the personnel there. During this attack, Norris saved numerous South Vietnamese soldiers, directed counterfire, and treated the wounded at the base.

On April 13, a forward air controller pinpointed Lieutenant Colonel Hambleton's whereabouts, and Norris and one of his South Vietnamese commandos made a third attempt to rescue him. At nightfall, the two men, dressed like the enemy, got into a sampan and began paddling upriver through enemy positions. They managed to locate Hambleton, but fearing that he was too badly injured to wait for the cover of darkness to bring him out, they put the airman in the bottom of the sampan, covered him with vegetation, and started back downriver. Nearing the FOB, the boat came under heavy machine-gun fire. Norris called in an air strike and, as American planes dropped bombs and smoke, they brought Hambleton to safety.

Several months later, Norris was leading a SEAL patrol on a reconnaissance mission when his team was ambushed by a large enemy unit. At the end of a long firefight, Norris ordered his men to head for the water and the boat waiting to pick them up, while he provided cover. When he was shot in the head, another SEAL, Michael Thornton, charged back to save him, killing two North Vietnamese about to dispatch Norris. For his action, Thornton would be awarded the Medal of Honor in October 1973. Norris, who was hospitalized for three years, defied doctors' orders and attended the White House ceremony.

Norris heard that he, too, might be recommended for the medal, but he didn't feel worthy of it. However, in 1975, when the rescue of Clark and Hambleton was finally declassified, Navy investigators talked with those involved and submitted the action for review. On March 6, 1976, with Michael Thornton in the audience, Thomas Norris was awarded the Medal of Honor by President Gerald Ford. In 1979, after leaving the military, Norris picked up his dream of joining the FBI. He retired in 1999.

Dustoff Pilot

MICHAEL J. NOVOSEL

CHIEF WARRANT OFFICER, U.S. ARMY 82nd Medical Detachment, 45th Medical Company, 68th Medical Group

BIOGRAPHY

BORN
September 3, 1922
Etna, Pennsylvania

ENTERED SERVICE
Kenner, Louisiana

BRANCH
U.S. Army

DUTY
Vietnam War

DIED
April 2, 2006
Enterprise, Alabama

MICHAEL NOVOSEL'S MILITARY CAREER SPANNED three wars. He enlisted in the Army Air Corps ten months before Pearl Harbor, completed the Aviation Cadet program, and by 1945 was a captain flying B-29 bombers in the air campaign against the Japanese. He was a test pilot until 1950, when he was forced to leave the service as a result of a postwar reduction in force. He joined the Air Force Reserve, served in the Korean War, attended the Air Command and Staff School, and left the service again in 1953. He was promoted to lieutenant colonel in the Air Force Reserve in 1955. In 1963, he was working as a commercial pilot and was deeply affected by the assassination of John F. Kennedy. He recalled Kennedy's appeal to patriotic sacrifice and decided to go back on active duty and serve in Vietnam. He was forty-two.

Since the Air Force was over strength in its senior grades, it wouldn't accept him—but Novosel had qualified to fly helicopters when he was a civilian, and the Army accepted him. He had to give up his rank as a lieutenant colonel, becoming a chief warrant officer with the elite Special Forces aviation section. He served his first tour in Vietnam flying a medevac helicopter ("dustoff") with the 283rd Medical Detachment.

His first tour ended in 1967, and Novosel was ready to return to the airlines, but his separation physical indicated that he had glaucoma, a condition that disqualified him from all flying, military and civilian. With the help of some conniving friends, regulations were ignored and a general officer signed a waiver for the eye disease. He returned to Vietnam for another dustoff tour, this time with the 82nd Medical Detachment.

Novosel's mission on the morning of October 2, 1969, was to evacuate a group of South Vietnamese soldiers surrounded by the enemy near the Cambodian border, with all of their ammunition expended and radio communication lost. Novosel and his crew entered the battle area alone, without air cover or fire support. They flew at low altitudes under constant enemy fire, maneuvering to attract the attention of the wounded soldiers and to get them to assemble for evacuation. As he skimmed over the ground, Novosel's medic and crew chief yanked the wounded men on board.

He left the battle area three times to take the wounded to medical care and to refuel. Returning again toward dark, he spotted a South Vietnamese soldier near an enemy bunker. As he maneuvered his helicopter backward to reach the man, an enemy soldier emptied his AK-47 directly at him. Bullets caused the windshield to disintegrate, fragments hit Novosel in the leg and hand, and a bullet glanced off the sole of his boot; he momentarily lost control of the helicopter, then recovered and lifted off under continuous enemy fire. Novosel saved twenty-nine South Vietnamese soldiers that day. (In his two tours of duty in Vietnam, he evacuated more than five thousand wounded.)

Novosel's eldest son, Michael, Jr., a recent graduate of Army flight school, arrived in Vietnam in early 1970 and got assigned to his father's unit. They were the only father and son aviators ever to be assigned to the same unit, fly combat missions as pilot and copilot, and rescue each other when downed by enemy fire.

Novosel completed his tour in March 1970. The following spring, he was notified that General Creighton Abrams had recommended him for the Medal of Honor. The presentation was delayed so that Michael, Jr., could finish his tour and be present at the White House, where President Richard Nixon put the medal around the forty-eight-year-old Novosel's neck on June 15, 1971.

Into the Trenches

ROBERT O'MALLEY

CORPORAL, U.S. MARINE CORPS Company I, 3rd Battalion, 3rd Marine Regiment, 3rd Marine Division

BIOGRAPHY

BORN
June 3, 1943
Woodside, New York

ENTERED SERVICE
New York, New York

BRANCH
U.S. Marine Corps

DUTY
Vietnam War

CURRENT RESIDENCE
Texas

ROBERT O'MALLEY WAS ONE OF FOUR BROTHERS, all of them two years apart in age and two years apart in joining the Marine Corps. Like his brothers, he enlisted after graduating from high school. He was stationed for a time in Okinawa, and in May 1965 went to Vietnam with the 3rd Marine Division.

Late in the summer, U.S. intelligence learned that the Vietcong was planning an attack on the American base at Chu Lai. The Marines designed Operation Starlight, an offensive in which three Marine battalions would block the assault. It was the first major engagement between the Americans and the Vietcong, and the Marines weren't yet familiar with the enemy's guerrilla tactics.

At dawn on August 18, Corporal O'Malley's 3rd Battalion made an amphibious landing near the village of An Cu'ong 2. Almost immediately, more than 1,200 Vietcong hidden in the ridges began to mortar the Marines, knocking out three tanks that were part of the operation. When O'Malley saw that the enemy was firing from a trench line beyond an open rice paddy, he charged toward it. Leaping into the trench line, he killed eight soldiers with his rifle and hand grenades, then ran back to his squad. After aiding in the evacuation of several wounded Marines, he returned to the area of heaviest fighting and helped repel another assault.

O'Malley was finally ordered to evacuate his battered squad. As he led the way to a helicopter landing zone, he was hit by mortar shrapnel in his legs, arm, and lung and began coughing up blood. Despite his wounds, he moved to an exposed position so he could lay down suppressive fire as his men boarded a chopper. Only after they were all safely aboard did he allow himself to be removed from the battlefield.

It took more than four months for the shrapnel in his lungs to stop shifting so that O'Malley could be operated on. After undergoing surgery in Japan, he was sent back to Camp Pendleton and finished out his tour there, leaving the service in April 1966. Late that fall, he was informed that he was to receive the Medal of Honor. He was flown on Air Force One to Austin, Texas, where President Lyndon Johnson was meeting with the Joint Chiefs of Staff. The President presented the medal to O'Malley on December 6, 1966.

O'Malley was the first living Marine from the Vietnam War to receive the medal. Both the Marine Corps drill team and the Marine Corps band took part in the Texas White House ceremony, which included the dedication of a new federal office building. As the President tried to get the medal around O'Malley's neck, O'Malley heard him mumble, "How do you put this darned thing on?"

Charging Through Enemy Fire

ROBERT M. PATTERSON

SPECIALIST FOURTH CLASS, U.S. ARMY 3rd Platoon, Troop B, 2nd Squadron, 17th Cavalry

BIOGRAPHY

BORN
April 16, 1948
Durham, North Carolina

ENTERED SERVICE
Raleigh, North Carolina

BRANCH
U.S. Army

DUTY
Vietnam War

CURRENT RESIDENCE
Florida

WHEN HE WAS A SENIOR IN HIGH SCHOOL IN 1966, Robert Patterson had an argument with his girlfriend and decided to get even by joining the Army. After basic training, he was assigned to the 82nd Airborne Division at Fort Bragg, North Carolina. However, in December 1967 he got orders to go to Vietnam and was transferred to the 17th Cavalry. After being stationed at a former rubber plantation in Song Bay for several months, Patterson's unit moved to Hue. Early on the morning of May 6, 1968, Patterson and his fellow soldiers were moved to La Chu, a farming area of rice paddies and hedgerows, where they were sent on a mission to sweep out what they were told was a small force of Vietcong. The men had just finished eating lunch and were starting to move out when they came under fire—not by a few Vietcong, but by a battalion-size force of North Vietnamese Army regulars that outnumbered them three to one.

Specialist Fourth Class Patterson, a fire-team leader, saw that another squad of his platoon was pinned down by heavy small-arms fire and rocket-propelled grenades. With two of his men, he moved toward the enemy's left flank, but they couldn't make any headway. As bullets churned the ground around him, Patterson climbed up to the second floor of a pagoda and used that vantage point to take out two North Vietnamese bunkers with grenades and his machine gun.

The Americans were taking fire from another bunker and a web of one-man "spider holes" dug into the hedgerows when Patterson saw his platoon sergeant go down. Although he would not himself remember the action clearly, he charged through heavy enemy fire and single-handedly destroyed five North Vietnamese positions while killing eight of the enemy. The isolated squad was then reunited with the rest of the platoon, which pushed forward to continue the attack. Late in the afternoon, Patterson came to in a huge bomb crater, his unit still involved in a firefight that would continue until they were relieved the next morning.

Robert Patterson remained in the Hue area for the rest of his time in Vietnam, taking part in the fighting, some of the heaviest of the war, that broke out in the "second Tet Offensive" later that summer. He rotated back home to Fort Bragg in December 1968. In September of the following year, his sergeant took him aside one day and told him that he was going to Washington, D.C., to receive the Medal of Honor. "You're pulling my leg" was Patterson's response.

President Richard Nixon presented the medal to Patterson on October 9, 1969. Almost as memorable as the ceremony itself was the advice he received from World War II Medal of Honor recipient Rufus Geddie Herring not long afterward: "Young man, let me tell you something right now. It will be much harder to wear that ribbon than it was to earn it." More than twenty-five years later, Patterson said, "Geddie was right. Scarcely a day goes by that I don't think of the responsibilities of this medal."

Moving from Rear to Front

RICHARD A. PITTMAN

LANCE CORPORAL, U.S. MARINE CORPS Company I, 3rd Battalion, 5th Marines, 1st Marine Division (Reinforced) FMF

RICHARD PITTMAN WAS FIFTEEN YEARS OLD WHEN he heard John F. Kennedy's "Ask not what your country can do for you" speech and decided that he would do something for his country when he got out of school. After graduating from high school in 1963, he tried to enlist in the Army, the Navy, and the Air Force, but he was turned down by each because he was legally blind in one eye. However, he managed to get accepted by the Marine Reserve. Then, at one meeting during his Marine recruit training, an officer asked if anyone present wanted to go on active duty. Pittman immediately raised his hand.

In the spring of 1966, Lance Corporal Pittman went to Vietnam as part of the 5th Marines. By midsummer, his unit was involved in search-and-destroy operations in the northern part of South Vietnam near the Demilitarized Zone (DMZ), which separated the South from the North. On July 24, Pittman was at the rear of his company column near the DMZ when heavy gunfire erupted ahead. His company had been ambushed by elements of the North Vietnamese Army in one of its first major incursions into South Vietnam.

As Pittman and a Navy corpsman started forward, he almost collided with a Marine standing in the trail holding an M-60 machine gun. "You going to use this weapon?" Pittman asked. The Marine stared back blankly. Pittman grabbed the gun and several belts of ammunition and moved toward the heaviest fighting. He was surprised by the number of dead and wounded Marines littering both sides of the trail. When his helmet was shot off his head, he hit the dirt. He saw the corpsman get up and try to go to a wounded man, but he was hit and went down. As Pittman continued on, he quickly destroyed the two positions that shot

at him. Then, standing up, cradling the machine gun in the crook of his arm and firing as he went, Pittman moved to the head of the column where the North Vietnamese regulars were rushing his beleaguered comrades. As he reached the position where the leading Marines had fallen, he was suddenly attacked by thirty to forty of the enemy. He calmly established a position in the middle of the trail and, with bullets whizzing past his head, raked the advancing enemy with devastating machine-gun fire. He continued firing until he felt a concussion on his side. At first he thought he had been wounded, but his gun had been struck by enemy fire and disabled. He dropped it and picked up an AK-47 that one of the enemy soldiers had left; he continued firing until he was out of ammunition. Next he picked up a .45 pistol left by a fallen Marine and used it to kill two enemy soldiers as they were almost on top of him. Finally out of ammunition altogether, he threw his only grenade. Inexplicably, the remaining North Vietnamese retreated. Back at his own lines, he discovered that two-thirds of his company had been killed or wounded in the intense engagement.

Richard Pittman was discharged from the Marines in 1968. He was back home in Stockton, California, looking for work, when he learned that he was to receive the Medal of Honor. It was presented to him by President Lyndon Johnson at a White House ceremony on May 14, 1968. Pittman reenlisted in the Marines in 1970 and retired for good in 1988, having served for a total of twenty-one years.

BIOGRAPHY

BORN
May 26, 1945
French Camp, California

ENTERED SERVICE
Stockton, California

BRANCH
U.S. Marine Corps

DUTY
Vietnam War

CURRENT RESIDENCE
California

American by Choice

ALFRED V. RASCON

SPECIALIST FOURTH CLASS, U.S. ARMY Reconnaissance Platoon, Headquarters Company, 1st Battalion (Airborne), 503rd Infantry, 173rd Airborne Brigade (Separate)

BIOGRAPHY

BORN
September 10, 1945
Chihuahua, Mexico

ENTERED SERVICE
Los Angeles, California

BRANCH
U.S. Army

DUTY
Vietnam War

CURRENT RESIDENCE
Maryland

AT THE AGE OF FOUR, ALFRED RASCON CAME TO the United States from Chihuahua, Mexico, with his parents. He became a legal resident a few years later and would always think of himself as "an immigrant by birth, an American by choice." Growing up near California's Port Hueneme Naval Station during the Korean War, he was fascinated by the military; he made parachutes out of old sheets and staged imaginary combat jumps off the roof of his house. At seventeen, he enlisted in the Army and became a medic in the 173rd Airborne Brigade.

In the spring of 1966, Specialist Fourth Class Rascon's reconnaissance platoon was part of a major operation in the jungles of Long Khanh Province. His battalion had been running into resistance from small units of North Vietnamese troops for a few days and, more ominously, finding large caches of weapons and supplies, which suggested that an offensive was being planned.

Early in the morning on March 16, the 1st Battalion's sister battalion a mile away came under a severe North Vietnamese attack. Shortly after Rascon's unit moved to reinforce it, its point men came upon the enemy setting up an ambush. A firefight broke out, beginning what Rascon would later recall as "ten minutes of hell."

Ignoring orders to stay sheltered, "Doc" Rascon ran forward to tend the wounded, who were lying along a narrow trail that was exposed to devastating fire from in front. He made his way to a badly hurt machine gunner; as he crouched over him, Rascon was hit by shrapnel from grenades and a bullet that entered his hip and exited at his shoulder blade. He dragged the man back, but by the time they reached cover, the gunner was dead.

When a second wounded machine gunner yelled, "Need ammo!" Rascon crawled through heavy fire to bring him bandoliers of ammunition. Then, fearing

that an abandoned machine gun could fall into enemy hands, he crawled back and retrieved it. Again, a grenade exploded, spraying shrapnel in his face. Later he used his body to shield another downed GI from fire as he administered treatment to him, saving his life.

Out of the corner of his eye, he saw a grenade land near a sergeant who had already been hit; he jumped up and threw his body over the man. The explosion blew the helmet off Rascon's head and the rucksack off his body. He lay there for a moment in the midst of all the fighting, bleeding from his ears, mouth, and nose. He refused morphine because he didn't want to be incapable of treating his wounded comrades. When he began drifting in and out of consciousness, he was taken to a field hospital. When he came to, the clean sheets made him think he was back home—until he saw that the patient in the next bed was a North Vietnamese soldier.

Rascon heard that he had been recommended for the Medal of Honor but didn't pay any attention to the rumor. He spent three months in a hospital in Japan, then was sent home. Upon his discharge from the Army in 1966, he joined the reserves, went to college, and finally became a naturalized citizen. In 1969, he returned to active duty and was commissioned a second lieutenant. He then returned to Vietnam in 1972 for another tour.

In 1993, some of the men whose lives Rascon had saved in 1966 heard that the recommendation for his medal had gotten lost in red tape. Without Rascon's knowledge, they asked the Army to reopen the files. They took the case to Illinois representative Lane Evans. On February 8, 2000, with the men he had saved looking on, Alfred Rascon received the Medal of Honor from President Bill Clinton. He retired from active duty in 2006, after serving tours of duty in Iraq and Afghanistan.

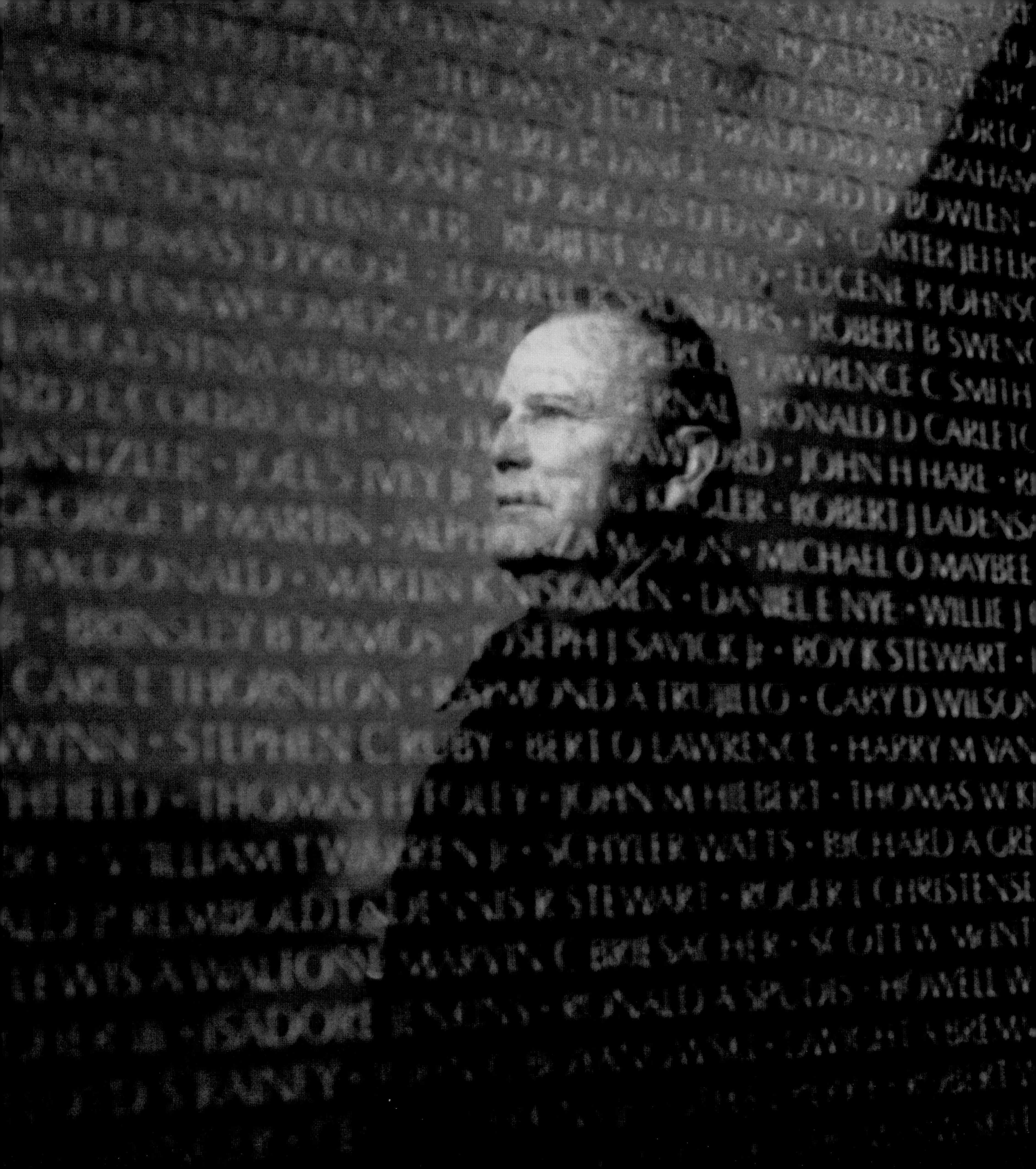

JOHN H HARE
DANIEL E NYE
ROY K STEWART

The Listening Post War

RONALD E. RAY

FIRST LIEUTENANT, U.S. ARMY Company A, 2nd Battalion, 35th Infantry, 25th Infantry Division

RONALD RAY WAS ONE OF FIVE BROTHERS, THREE of whom served in the military. In 1959, he left high school to enlist in the Army. Discharged after serving three years, he came home for two months, then reenlisted in the Special Forces. There he excelled in training activities such as HALO (high-altitude, low-opening) parachute jumps, which involved diving out of a plane at such high altitudes that oxygen was required and free-falling to 1,500 feet before opening the chute. His battalion commander recommended him for Officer Candidate School.

On June 19, 1966, two weeks after arriving in Vietnam, Lieutenant Ray was in charge of a platoon of the 35th Infantry in the Ia Drang Valley, part of an operation to cut off elements of the North Vietnamese Army entering Vietnam from Cambodia. A few days earlier, his company commander had split the unit into two parts, ordering Ray's platoon to cover a large area where enemy troops might try to infiltrate. Ray located a knoll to use as a base of operations and set up listening posts near approaches he thought the North Vietnamese might use.

Early on the afternoon of June 19, ten men in one of these listening posts came under intense fire. Convinced that they were being encircled by a large enemy unit, Ray radioed them to move back, but by this time they were cut off by enemy gunners. When Ray called his company commander for reinforcements and was informed that there was no other unit close enough to help, he told the trapped men that he would come get them.

He and the rest of his unit pushed through more than a mile of dense jungle until the listening post was in sight, then began throwing grenades and firing their weapons in small, frequent bursts to make the North Vietnamese think they were a larger force. The ruse was momentarily successful, and the enemy pulled back long enough for Ray's men to join the others. But the North Vietnamese quickly regrouped and began to pour heavy fire at the Americans.

A squad that Ray sent to try to silence one of the enemy positions was immediately pinned down. Fearing that the men would be annihilated, he charged the position himself and killed the four enemy gunners with grenades and his 12-gauge shotgun. Nearby, a medic and the badly wounded man he was trying to evacuate came under fire. Ray went to their rescue, killing several more North Vietnamese. A few moments later, when he saw a grenade land near two of his men, he dived over them to shield them from the blast. He was badly wounded by shrapnel. Although he was shot in the legs by a machine gun, he managed to silence it with his last grenade.

Ray was momentarily paralyzed in his lower body by the trauma, but he continued to direct his men. During a lull in the fighting, he ordered his sergeant to prepare a withdrawal. He was planning to stay behind to cover his men, but once they left, his sergeant hoisted him on his back and took him to an evacuation zone.

Ray was medevaced to Pleiku and operated on there, then sent to Fort Bragg, where he spent six months in the hospital. In 1970, he was at Fort Benning, Georgia, when the commanding general told him that he was to receive the Medal of Honor. It was presented to him by President Richard Nixon on May 14, 1970. Ray was retired from the military for medical reasons in 1980 and served as an assistant secretary for the Department of Veteran Affairs from 1989 to 1993.

BIOGRAPHY

BORN
December 7, 1941
Cordele, Georgia

ENTERED SERVICE
Atlanta, Georgia

BRANCH
U.S. Army

DUTY
Vietnam War

CURRENT RESIDENCE
Florida

A SHAU VALLEY, SOUTH VIETNAM, 1969

Battle for Hamburger Hill

GORDON R. ROBERTS

SPECIALIST FOURTH CLASS, U.S. ARMY Company B, 1st Battalion, 506th Infantry, 101st Airborne Division

BIOGRAPHY

BORN
June 14, 1950
Middletown, Ohio

ENTERED SERVICE
Cincinnati, Ohio

BRANCH
U.S. Army

DUTY
Vietnam War

CURRENT RESIDENCE
North Carolina

HIS TWO OLDER BROTHERS WERE ALREADY IN THE Navy when Gordon Roberts enlisted in the Army three days after graduating from high school in 1968. He became part of the 101st Airborne, the same unit his father had served in during World War II.

Specialist Fourth Class Roberts arrived in Vietnam in May 1969, and a few days later found himself in the middle of the battle for Hamburger Hill, a week-and-a-half-long struggle with North Vietnamese Army troops in the A Shau Valley. For the next several weeks, his battalion attempted to block the enemy's main resupply route from Laos.

At midday on July 11, Roberts heard the sound of heavy fighting about three and a half miles away, where another U.S. infantry company, badly outnumbered, had lost its battalion commander and was surrounded by the NVA. Roberts's company boarded helicopters and went to relieve them.

After landing, Roberts's platoon was maneuvering along a ridgeline to attack the heavily fortified enemy position that had the American company pinned down. Suddenly, the platoon was hit by fire coming from camouflaged North Vietnamese bunkers on a hill overlooking them. Roberts dived for cover with the rest of the men, but then, seeing that the platoon was likely to take serious casualties, he got to his feet and charged the closest enemy position, firing as he ran. He killed the two North Vietnamese manning the gun, then continued on to a second bunker. When a machine-gun round knocked his weapon from his hands, he grabbed another rifle from the ground, took out the second bunker, and destroyed a third with grenades.

As he charged a fourth enemy position, Roberts was now in a no-man's-land, cut off from the rest of his platoon. With shells snapping past him, he fought his way to the company his unit had been trying to relieve when attacked. There he worked to move wounded GIs from exposed positions to an evacuation area, later returning to his own unit.

Roberts was back home, stationed at Fort Meade early in 1971, when he was informed that he was to receive the Medal of Honor. With his family looking on, he was presented with the medal by President Richard Nixon on March 2, 1971.

Three weeks later, Roberts was discharged from the Army. He graduated from college and pursued a career in social work for eighteen years; during that time, he joined the National Guard and became an officer. He decided to go back on active duty in 1991 and served a tour of duty in Iraq in 2005 as the commander of a logistics battalion.

From the Barrio to Vietnam

LOUIS R. ROCCO

SERGEANT FIRST CLASS, U.S. ARMY Advisory Team 162, U.S. Military Assistance Command

BIOGRAPHY

BORN
November 19, 1938
Albuquerque, New Mexico

ENTERED SERVICE
Los Angeles, California

BRANCH
U.S. Army

DUTY
Vietnam War

DIED
October 31, 2002
San Antonio, Texas

LOUIS ROCCO GREW UP IN THE BARRIO OF EAST LOS Angeles. A high school dropout and a gang member, he was frequently in trouble with the law; he later said that he often stole so his family could eat. In 1954, while still a teenager, he was arrested for armed robbery. During a break in his trial, he met an Army recruiter and told him his life story. The recruiter convinced the judge to drop a prison sentence for Rocco if the boy quit his gang, went back to school, and entered the military when he turned seventeen. Rocco complied with the judge's order. He enlisted in the Army and joined the Special Forces.

During his first tour of duty in Vietnam in 1965, Rocco suffered nothing more serious than a poisonous snakebite. His second tour was another story. On May 24, 1970, hearing that several soldiers in a South Vietnamese Army camp had been badly wounded in an area northeast of Katum, Rocco, now a sergeant first class and medic with Advisory Team 162, volunteered to fly in with a medevac crew to evacuate them. Their helicopter came under intense enemy fire from every direction as it dropped into the landing zone. As the pilot tried evasive maneuvers, Rocco leaned out of the craft to identify enemy positions and poured suppressive fire from the door gun into them. But with its hydraulics badly damaged by enemy fire, the helicopter crashed in an open field.

The pilot was hit in the leg, the copilot's arm was almost severed, and the South Vietnamese couldn't come out to help because they were afraid of being cut down by the enemy, who had pinned them down for several hours. Although his wrist and hip were fractured and his spine was badly bruised, Rocco managed to pull the unconscious pilot, copilot, and

crew chief out of the flaming wreckage, severely burning his hands in the process. He carried each of the wounded men to a protected area fifty yards away, returning each time through heavy fire a little weaker. He administered first aid to them until he collapsed from his own wounds and lost consciousness.

Over the next two days of fierce fighting, two more helicopters were shot down trying to save Rocco and the others. Finally, gunships cleared the area well enough to allow medevac choppers to land and evacuate the men.

Rocco was treated in an American field hospital. While there, he was told by his commanding general that he had been recommended for the Medal of Honor, but he didn't hear anything more for four years. He discovered later that the recommendation was stalled because he was Special Forces and didn't belong to a regular unit. His comrades continued to pressure the Pentagon, and in 1974, Rocco received a call ordering him to go to the White House. On December 12, President Gerald Ford presented the medal to him, his hands shaking during the ceremony. "Sorry," the President said to Rocco. "I'm nervous. Yours is the first one of these I've given out."

Medic on a Mission

CLARENCE E. SASSER

PRIVATE FIRST CLASS, U.S. ARMY Headquarters Company, 3rd Battalion, 60th Infantry, 9th Infantry Division

BIOGRAPHY

BORN
September 12, 1947
Cherango, Texas

ENTERED SERVICE
Houston, Texas

BRANCH
U.S. Army

DUTY
Vietnam War

CURRENT RESIDENCE
Texas

WHEN CLARENCE SASSER WAS DRAFTED IN 1967, HE assumed that he would be just another GI. After a battery of tests indicated he should be trained as a medical aidman, he was surprised that the Army thought he might have the ability to save lives.

By the fall of 1967, Sasser was in Vietnam with the Army's 9th Infantry Division. He didn't experience a heavy firefight until January 10, 1968. Early that morning, his company was flown out toward the Mekong Delta on a reconnaissance-in-force operation to check out reports of enemy forces in the area. At about 10:00 A.M., the dozen helicopters carrying the undermanned company of slightly more than one hundred soldiers swooped down onto a large rice paddy near where the Vietcong had already been sighted. As the formation descended, the U-shaped wooded area nearly enclosing the landing zone erupted with small arms, recoilless rifle, machine-gun, and rocket fire. The mission might have been aborted, but the lead helicopter was hit and crashed, so the others immediately followed to protect it.

With the shallow water of the rice paddy roiled by enemy fire, the Americans tried to get out of the helicopters as quickly as possible and head for the mounded levees that offered them their only cover. In the first few minutes of the engagement, more than thirty men went down. The air was already filled with screams of "Medic!" when Sasser scrambled out of his helicopter. Running across the open rice paddy, he didn't have time to set medical priorities; he could only "go to the one who was calling the loudest." He slithered through the muck to get from soldier to soldier, working on his belly because standing upright meant certain death. Bullets chopping the water would sometimes trace a swift path toward an American

infantryman and hit him. Sasser couldn't keep up with the casualties.

As he picked up a wounded GI and dragged him to cover against the embankment of a dike, Sasser was hit by shrapnel from an exploding rocket. Although it didn't have the energy of a bullet, the red-hot metal fragment burned itself into his shoulder. He pulled it out himself, waiving off help from medics from the other platoons.

Rushing back to the rice paddy to aid more wounded, he was hit in both legs by machine-gun fire and knocked down. He used his arms to pull himself through the mud to help a wounded soldier calling out from a hundred yards away. Close by, he saw a group of GIs huddled together, disoriented by the heavy fire; he managed to talk them into action, getting them to crawl toward the protection of a dike where they could begin to fire back at the enemy. "I felt that if I could get the guys up and fighting," he said later, "we might all get out of there somehow."

By afternoon, the enemy began to pull its main force back but left enough fighters behind to keep the Americans pinned down. Although faint from blood loss and in agonizing pain, Sasser continued to treat the wounded. Finally, at 4:00 the next morning, eighteen hours after the battle had begun, the area was sufficiently pacified for U.S. helicopters to arrange an evacuation. American troops had suffered thirty-four dead and fifty-nine wounded.

It took several months of rehabilitation in Japan before Sasser could use his legs again. While recovering, he was called into the hospital commander's office and told that he was to receive the Medal of Honor. It was presented to him by President Richard Nixon at the White House on March 7, 1969.

NOT FORGOTTEN

Like Fighting in Braille

JAMES M. SPRAYBERRY

FIRST LIEUTENANT, U.S. ARMY Company D, 5th Battalion, 7th Cavalry, 1st Cavalry Division (Airmobile)

JAMES SPRAYBERRY WAS BORN IN GEORGIA AND grew up on a family farm in Alabama. He was attending college in 1966 when he decided that he needed more excitement in his life and enlisted in the Army. After basic training, he went to Officer Candidate School, graduating early in 1967 as a second lieutenant. Assigned to an armor battalion at Fort Benning, Sprayberry wanted to be in action and volunteered for Vietnam.

In the spring of 1968, Lieutenant Sprayberry was in the A Shau Valley of Vietnam, serving as an executive officer with a company of the 7th Cavalry. Late in the afternoon of April 25, the day after his twenty-first birthday, his company was ambushed by a large North Vietnamese force. Within minutes, Sprayberry knew that this enemy force was more disciplined than any he had yet seen—fully controlling the forbidding terrain of mountains and heavy undergrowth, and carefully targeting the Americans with interlocking fields of fire from well-protected bunkers.

Sprayberry's company commander had taken a platoon and tried to flank the enemy, but the unit was hit hard, suffering eleven wounded and four dead in the first few minutes of fighting. The commanding officer went down and so did the medic accompanying him; the platoon's lieutenant was killed instantly. Sprayberry realized that the enemy was using the pinned-down Americans as bait to draw others into the kill zone, yet he asked for volunteers and set off to rescue his comrades.

At nightfall, under cover of darkness, his twelve-man patrol moved toward the isolated platoon. Receiving fire from an enemy machine gun, Sprayberry crawled toward the bunker from which the fire was coming and took the gun out with a grenade. He killed several more enemy soldiers with grenades,

then charged three other North Vietnamese bunkers, eliminating each of them. It was like fighting in Braille: He could gauge the enemy positions only by muzzle flashes. Making his way back, Sprayberry killed an enemy soldier who popped up from concealment. Soon he made radio contact with the other Americans and began directing their withdrawal.

After eight hours, the long rescue was finally completed. Although Sprayberry had single-handedly killed twelve of the enemy, eliminated two machine guns, and destroyed several bunkers, he felt that his mission was not yet complete. He had been unable to bring out the bodies of three Americans killed in the action. The next day the company tried again, but enemy fire was too heavy. When the weather cleared, a helicopter crew volunteered to try to locate the bodies, but the helicopter was immediately shot down, and the three-man crew was killed. Now he would have to leave the bodies of six Americans behind.

Sprayberry was back home in 1969 with orders to leave the military when he walked into an antiwar demonstration at Fort Lewis. He was so angered by what he saw that he decided to make the Army a career. He was awarded the Medal of Honor by President Richard Nixon at the White House on October 9, 1969, and retired from the Army as a lieutenant colonel in 1988.

He went back home to Alabama to run the family farm, yet he continued to regard finding the remains of those six Americans in the A Shau Valley as unfinished business. Over the years, he worked with a team that included a former medic and a forensic archaeologist to solve the puzzle of the exact whereabouts of the bodies left behind nearly forty years earlier. In 2006, Sprayberry traveled to Vietnam to continue the search.

BIOGRAPHY

BORN
April 24, 1947
Lagrange, Georgia

ENTERED SERVICE
Montgomery, Alabama

BRANCH
U.S. Army

DUTY
Vietnam War

CURRENT RESIDENCE
Alabama

Unbroken Spirit

JAMES B. STOCKDALE

CAPTAIN, U.S. NAVY Senior Officer, 4th Allied Prisoner-of-War Wing

JAMES STOCKDALE ENTERED ANNAPOLIS IN 1943, hoping to get into action in World War II. But by the time he graduated, the war was over. He spent the Korean War stateside as a Navy air instructor. It wasn't until the war in Vietnam that he finally saw action as a fighter pilot.

By the fall of 1965, Captain Stockdale was commander of Air Wing 16 on board the USS *Oriskany* and had flown some two hundred missions over North Vietnam. On the morning of September 5, his A-4E Skyhawk jet was hit by antiaircraft fire during an attack on a railroad facility near the city of Than Hoa. Unable to control the plane, he had no choice but to eject. The force of the ejection broke his left knee and left shoulder. As he floated down in his parachute, he saw his plane explode in a rice paddy. When he landed in the street of a small village, a group of North Vietnamese peasants were waiting. They clubbed him until North Vietnamese soldiers arrived to pull them off.

What followed was eight years of imprisonment for Stockdale, three of them in solitary confinement, where he was repeatedly subjected to brutal treatment ranging from beatings to agonizing rope torture and near asphyxiation. Eventually, he was moved to the "Hanoi Hilton," where he was senior officer among the American POWs. He organized the men to keep their captors from breaking their spirit and using them for propaganda. He established a command structure among the prisoners and set up a "tap code" so they could communicate with one another from within their isolated cells. When one seriously ill officer was refused medical care, Stockdale led a prisonwide hunger strike. He made the men aware that they would inevitably

"break" under torture but that they should hold out as long as possible and do their best.

Stockdale set an example of this himself. In 1969, when the North Vietnamese indicated that they planned for him to appear in a propaganda film, he beat his own face bloody with a piece of wood and cut up his scalp with a dull razor blade. When guards identified him as the organizer of resistance and threw him into solitary, he feared that he would name his collaborators under torture. So he hobbled in his leg irons to the windows of his cell, broke the glass, and used the jagged pieces to slit his wrists. The guards found and treated him before he bled to death. After this show of defiance, the torture abated.

On February 12, 1973, Stockdale, along with all the other POWs, was released and sent home. Three years later, on March 6, 1976, President Gerald Ford presented him with the Medal of Honor. Stockdale served as president of the Naval War College and, in 1977, retired from the Navy as a vice admiral after thirty-seven years of service.

BIOGRAPHY

BORN
December 23, 1923
Abingdon, Illinois

ENTERED SERVICE
Abingdon, Illinois

BRANCH
U.S. Navy

DUTY
Vietnam War

DIED
July 5, 2005
Coronado, California

The Weight of the Wounded

KEN E. STUMPF

SPECIALIST FOURTH CLASS, U.S. ARMY Company C, 1st Battalion, 35th Infantry, 25th Infantry Division

BIOGRAPHY

BORN
September 28, 1944
Menasha, Wisconsin

ENTERED SERVICE
Milwaukee, Wisconsin

BRANCH
U.S. Army

DUTY
Vietnam War

CURRENT RESIDENCE
Wisconsin

EARLY IN 1967, THE COMMUNISTS' CONTROL OF Vietnam's Quang Ngai Province was so complete that many villagers had never seen any troops other than those of the Vietcong. The U.S. command decided to try to break this stranglehold on the area through a series of company-size search-and-destroy missions.

On April 25, Ken Stumpf was on one of these missions. A U.S. helicopter gunship orbiting the area had killed one Vietcong fighter in one of the small villages and wounded another. Around noon, Specialist Fourth Class Stumpf was ordered to investigate with his six-man squad while another squad, including the platoon's radio operator, followed behind.

Stumpf was on point about fifty feet ahead of his men when he came to a chest-high dry irrigation ditch. He stopped, unable to see much ahead because of a maze of bamboo and palm trees, and ordered his men to wait while he returned for the field radio and to report to his captain. He had gone about fifty yards when he heard gunfire. Running back, he found that three of his men had gone to check out the area beyond the ditch and been hit by a Vietcong machine gun.

Stumpf took cover with the remaining three men, and another squad joined them. The Vietcong began to pour out a torrent of fire, and for the next hour the GIs shot blindly into the heavy foliage. When three or four enemy soldiers camouflaged by clumps of grass on their uniforms suddenly attempted to flank their position, the Americans shot them.

In a momentary lull in the battle, Stumpf heard the cries of the three men who had gotten cut off from his squad. With the other GIs laying down covering fire, he charged forward and stumbled onto them in heavy undergrowth. He put the most seriously wounded man on his back and carried him to the ditch, blue tracer bullets streaking past them. Then he returned for another wounded soldier and brought him out. Exhausted, he lay panting on the ground for several moments, then went back one more time and carried out the third GI.

At about two in the afternoon, American artillery blew away the thick vegetation, and it became clear that the Vietcong were concealed in a series of bunkers. Stumpf, who always carried a sandbag full of grenades, ran forward with one of his men to assault the VC positions. He destroyed the first bunker. As they approached the second, four enemy soldiers suddenly appeared; Stumpf opened fire, and the VC fell. So did Stumpf's backup, killed by a bullet in the chest. One more bunker remained. Armed with extra grenades, Stumpf ran to it over open ground and threw a grenade through the aperture. When the VC managed to throw it back out, Stumpf hit the ground in a fetal curl as it exploded; then he stood, pulled the pins on two more grenades, held them for an extra second, and tossed them in, this time destroying the gun emplacement.

Weeks after the battle, Stumpf was waiting in a chow line when he overheard a couple of GIs whispering that he was being recommended for the CMH. It really confused him, since in basic training a drill sergeant had told Stumpf's group of recruits that if they fell on a grenade and saved their comrades, they'd get a CMH—"Casket with a Metal Handle." Standing in line waiting for his meal, Stumpf couldn't figure out why he was being recommended for a casket with a metal handle. He soon discovered, though, that it was the Medal of Honor he was being recommended for. It was awarded to him by President Lyndon Johnson on September 19, 1968.

Single-handed Rescue Team

JAMES A. TAYLOR

FIRST LIEUTENANT, U.S. ARMY Troop B, 1st Cavalry, Americal Division

JAMES TAYLOR SERVED IN THE ARMY AS AN enlisted man for ten years before being selected for Officer Candidate School and becoming an officer. After graduating as a lieutenant, he was assigned to the 1st Squadron, 1st Cavalry. In 1967, he was the executive officer of B Troop in Vietnam.

On November 8, 1967, Taylor was at his base camp when he was notified that his commander had been wounded in action and was being evacuated from the battle area. Taylor was ordered to fly out to the combat zone by helicopter to assume command of B Troop. At that time, B Troop was under the operational control of the 3rd Brigade of the 1st Cavalry Division. After arriving in the combat area, a decision was made to consolidate the troop, evaluate the situation, and attack the enemy at first light the next day.

Prior to launching the attack, Taylor was replaced as troop commander and resumed his duties as executive officer. As the battle began the next morning, Taylor's priorities were to coordinate the evacuation of the wounded, to call in air and ground support, and to arrange for additional supplies, including ammunition and fuel.

On the morning of November 9, the troop's armored personnel carriers were pushing through an overgrown area near Que Son on a search-and-destroy mission. Early in the day, they approached a hillside, which suddenly erupted with enemy machine-gun, recoilless rifle, and mortar fire. Taylor and the other officers realized they had stumbled onto a regimental-size North Vietnamese force.

One of the armored cavalry assault vehicles was hit immediately by recoilless rifle fire, wounding all but five crew members. Lieutenant Taylor rushed through heavy enemy fire and the detonating ammunition that was stored in the burning vehicle to pull each of the wounded men to safety. Moments later, the vehicle exploded.

Within minutes, a second armored vehicle was hit and caught fire. Once again, Taylor moved forward on foot to pull the wounded to the safety of a nearby dike just before the vehicle exploded. This time he was knocked down and injured by a mortar round, but he managed to get to his command vehicle and began to establish a medical evacuation site for his men.

Suddenly, his vehicle was raked by machine-gun fire. He began firing his own machine gun and killed the three-man North Vietnamese crew. As he was approaching the evacuation site, yet another U.S. assault vehicle was hit. Again he dismounted and ran forward to pull out the wounded. After loading them into his vehicle, he drove them to the evacuation site to get them aboard the medevac helicopters.

Taylor reorganized his unit and briefed the new commander when he arrived. Then he participated in another attack that eventually overran the North Vietnamese position.

Early in 1968, he received a letter from his wife in which she said that members of her family had heard he was being recommended for the Medal of Honor. He assumed it was merely a rumor until he was pulled back from the front lines—despite his protests—and made company commander of Headquarters Company, 123rd Aviation Battalion at Chu Lai, South Vietnam.

At the White House on November 19, 1968, Taylor was nervous and worried about embarrassing his family. But it was President Lyndon Johnson who became emotional. He had tears in his eyes as he shook Taylor's hands, and embraced him after awarding him the medal.

BIOGRAPHY

BORN
December 31, 1937
Arcata, California

ENTERED SERVICE
San Francisco, California

BRANCH
U.S. Army

DUTY
Vietnam War

CURRENT RESIDENCE
California

Eight Days in the Forest

BRIAN M. THACKER

FIRST LIEUTENANT, U.S. ARMY Battery A, 1st Battalion, 92nd Artillery

SON OF A CAREER AIR FORCE OFFICER, BRIAN Thacker graduated from Utah's Weber State College and was commissioned in the Army through the ROTC program. After a tour in Germany, where he was "allowed to make a lot of second lieutenant mistakes," he was sent to Vietnam in the fall of 1970, serving with the 1st Battalion, 92nd Artillery.

He was first assigned to a battery of guns that provided support for combat engineer operations. Then, in the spring of 1971, he took charge of a six-man observation team organized by the battalion. Along with an interpreter, the team was ordered to a hilltop in Kontum Province called Fire Base 6. There they supported South Vietnamese (ARVN) artillery in firing down on North Vietnamese units operating in the valley below.

On the morning of March 31, when the enemy launched a coordinated attack along a sixty-mile front, Fire Base 6 was among the positions hit. Thacker was asleep when he heard sounds of the heavy machine guns, rocket-propelled grenades, satchel charges, mortars, and recoilless rifles. The North Vietnamese had penetrated the South Vietnamese perimeter; three of Thacker's five men were killed as the American and ARVN force retreated from bunker to bunker in hand-to-hand fighting throughout the morning and early afternoon. Calling in air support, Thacker rallied his forces to hold on against the superior North Vietnamese.

The first U.S. helicopter trying to resupply Fire Base 6 was shot down; its crew climbed out of the wreckage and joined what was left of the U.S. team. When a second chopper trying to rescue the first crew was shot down as well, Thacker knew his beleaguered force couldn't hold out.

The nearest extraction point was another firebase six miles away along the ridgeline. During a lull in the fighting, as the enemy prepared for a final assault, Thacker organized a withdrawal of the remaining friendly force, lingering behind to provide covering fire before joining his comrades. He called in U.S. artillery on his own position in a desperate effort to keep the enemy at bay, but in the ensuing chaos, he became cut off. Finding himself alone, he ran for cover deep in a heavily overgrown bamboo forest. He stayed there for the next eight days without food or water. The North Vietnamese were often so close around him that he could hear—and even smell—them. The bamboo canopy kept him cool during the hot days; his wool nightshirt protected him during the cold mountain nights. Several days after the ARVN ranger unit retook the firebase, Thacker decided he could move to safety. Over a period of several hours, he slowly crawled from his bamboo refuge back to the firebase. He was medevaced out the next day, given medical treatment in Pleiku, and sent to Japan for hospitalization.

By May, Thacker was back home. His father, who was stationed at an Air Force base, told him of rumors that he had been recommended for the Medal of Honor, but Thacker didn't think it was possible. Two years later, however, he received a phone call inviting him to the White House, where President Richard Nixon presented him with the medal on October 15, 1973.

BIOGRAPHY

BORN
April 25, 1945
Columbus, Ohio

ENTERED SERVICE
Salt Lake City, Utah

BRANCH
U.S. Army

DUTY
Vietnam War

CURRENT RESIDENCE
Maryland

Hero Saves Hero

MICHAEL E. THORNTON

PETTY OFFICER, U.S. NAVY Navy Advisory Group

BIOGRAPHY

BORN
March 23, 1949
Greenville,
South Carolina

ENTERED SERVICE
Spartanburg,
South Carolina

BRANCH
U.S. Navy

DUTY
Vietnam War

CURRENT RESIDENCE
Texas

ALTHOUGH HE CAME FROM THE LANDLOCKED HILLS of South Carolina, the idea of being in the Navy seized Michael Thornton's boyhood imagination when he saw movies such as *The Fighting Sullivan Brothers* and *Frogmen*. He enlisted in the Navy shortly after graduating from high school, went through Underwater Demolition Recruit Training, and became a member of the elite SEALs.

In the fall of 1972, with the U.S. involvement in Southeast Asia winding down, there were only three officers and nine enlisted SEALs left in Vietnam. Thornton was one. Their primary missions were rescuing downed American airmen and doing "sneak and peek" reconnaissance on the North Vietnamese Army's inexorable advance into the south.

On October 31, a five-man SEAL patrol was ordered to gather intelligence about enemy activity at the Cua Viet River Base. The patrol was made up of three South Vietnamese SEALs, Lieutenant Tom Norris, and Petty Officer Thornton. Both of the Americans were experienced combat veterans. Earlier that spring, in fact, Norris had led a similar team on a heroic mission to rescue a pair of U.S. airmen who had been shot down in enemy territory, an action for which he would be recommended for the Medal of Honor.

Launched in a rubber boat at dusk by a Vietnamese junk, the SEAL patrol paddled toward the beach in the gathering darkness. About a mile offshore, the men left their small boat and swam to shore. Then they moved inland, passing silently beside numerous enemy encampments. They patrolled all through the night, gathering important intelligence. As daybreak approached, seeing no identifiable landmarks, they realized that they had come ashore too far north; in fact, they were in North Vietnam. As they moved back toward the beach, Lieutenant Norris established radio contact with the fleet. However, they were soon spotted by the enemy and began to take heavy fire. More than fifty enemy soldiers attacked, closing to within five yards.

During a five-hour firefight, Thornton was wounded in his back. Norris ordered Thornton and two of the South Vietnamese SEALs to fall back to a sand dune to the north and provide covering fire. Not long after, the Vietnamese SEAL who had stayed behind arrived at Thornton's position and told him that Norris had been killed. Thornton charged back over five hundred yards of open terrain to Norris. When he got there, he killed two enemy soldiers standing over the lieutenant's body. He lifted Norris, barely alive and with a shattered skull, and began to run back toward the beach, enemy fire kicking up all around him.

The blast from an incoming round fired by the USS *Newport News* blew both men into the air. Thornton picked up Norris again and raced for a sand dune and then retreated three hundred yards to the water. As he plunged into the surf, Thornton lashed his life vest to the unconscious officer's body. When another SEAL was hit in the hip and couldn't swim, Thornton grabbed him and slowly and painfully swam both men out to sea. Despite his wounds, Thornton swam for more than two hours. All three wounded men were rescued by the same junk that had dropped them off sixteen hours earlier.

On October 15, 1973, Michael Thornton was on his way to the White House to receive the Medal of Honor from President Richard Nixon. Lieutenant Norris, still a patient at nearby Bethesda Naval Hospital, had been forbidden by his doctors to go to the ceremony, but Thornton spirited him out the back door of the facility and took him along. Almost three years later, Norris himself received the medal, with Thornton looking on.

Wild Weasel Dogfight

LEO K. THORSNESS

MAJOR, U.S. AIR FORCE 357th Tactical Fighter Squadron

BIOGRAPHY

BORN
February 14, 1932
Walnut Grove, Minnesota

ENTERED SERVICE
Walnut Grove, Minnesota

BRANCH
U.S. Air Force

DUTY
Vietnam War

CURRENT RESIDENCE
Alabama

LEO THORSNESS ENLISTED IN THE AIR FORCE IN 1952 at the age of nineteen, largely because he had a brother serving in Korea. Though he didn't make it to Korea himself, he stayed in the military, becoming an officer and a fighter pilot. In 1966, he went to Vietnam as part of a squadron of F-105s. The "Wild Weasel" was a specially modified two-seat F-105 and had the job of finding and destroying surface-to-air missile (SAM) sites. The Weasels were capable of lingering in target areas longer than other fighters, and as a result suffered a high loss ratio; not many Weasel pilots completed their hundred-mission tours.

On April 19, 1967, Thorsness was on a mission deep in North Vietnam. He and his wingman took out an enemy SAM site with missiles, then destroyed a second site with bombs. In the second attack, the wingman radioed that his plane, hit by intense antiaircraft fire, was going down. "Turn toward the mountains and I'll keep you in sight," Thorsness told him. As the pilot and his backseater ejected from the damaged aircraft, Thorsness circled above to keep them in sight. Suddenly, he saw an enemy MiG-17 fighter setting up a gunnery pass on the parachutes. Although the Weasel was not designed for dogfights, Thorsness attacked the MiG and destroyed it with bursts from his gatling gun.

Dangerously low on fuel, Thorsness quickly air-refueled from a tanker and returned to the MiG-infested area to protect the downed crew from North Vietnamese soldiers. When his rear-seat weapons officer spotted four more MiGs in the area, he turned back through a barrage of North Vietnamese SAMs to engage them. He hit another one (although he never got credit for the kill because his gun camera had run out of film) and drove the remaining enemy planes away.

Heading for Udorn Royal Thai Air Base, the closest U.S. airfield, Thorsness climbed to thirty-five thousand feet. Seventy miles from base, with his fuel tanks on empty, he pulled the throttle to idle, knowing he could glide two miles for each thousand feet he fell. Just as he was landing, the F-105's engine ran out of fuel and shut down.

Two weeks later, he was shot down over North Vietnam on his ninety-third mission. He bailed out and was captured, and wound up a prisoner of war in the "Hanoi Hilton," where he ran into the two F-105 crew members he had tried to rescue. After two years of unremitting torture, he learned, through a secret "tap code" among the prisoners, that his name had been submitted for the Medal of Honor. (The officer in charge of writing Thorsness's citation had been shot down himself and brought to the same prison.)

When the war ended in 1973, Thorsness was released and sent home. He had knee injuries, sustained when he bailed out of his plane at six hundred knots, and back injuries as a result of torture. He received the Medal of Honor on October 15, 1973, from President Richard Nixon. "We've been waiting for you for six years," Nixon told him. "Welcome home."

After retiring from the Air Force as a colonel, Thorsness was an executive with Litton Industries and later served the people of Washington as a state senator. In 2002, he started speaking on his personal mantra, "Do what's right—help others."

Playing Hardball

JAY R. VARGAS

CAPTAIN, U.S. MARINE CORPS Company G, 2nd Battalion, 4th Marines, 9th Marine Amphibious Brigade

THE SON OF IMMIGRANTS—AN ITALIAN MOTHER AND a Hispanic father—Jay Vargas had two older brothers who fought at Iwo Jima and Okinawa in World War II, and a third who fought in Korea. Vargas himself got as far as the Class A Portland team in the Los Angeles Dodgers farm system in the early 1960s before he realized he probably wouldn't make it as a big-league baseball player. He decided to play for the Marines instead.

By 1968, Captain Vargas was in command of Company G of the Fourth Marines in Vietnam. On April 29, his unit, positioned along the demilitarized zone separating North and South Vietnam, was the last American element in the area. It was supposed to be lifted out, but when the helicopters came under heavy fire, Vargas's men had to march to base camp during the night. Along the way, hundreds of enemy artillery rounds burst around them, but the impact of the shells and the spray of shrapnel were partially absorbed by the soft muddy soil of the rice paddies, and everyone made it back to base without serious injury.

The next day, although they hadn't slept for thirty-six hours, Vargas and his men were loaded onto landing craft and taken down the Bo Dieu River to an area around the village of Dai Do where two other Marine companies were in a battle with a North Vietnamese Army regiment. Company G went ashore at about one in the afternoon. Vargas had been ordered to attack across seven hundred yards of open ground; the company made it about one-third of the way before the NVA opened fire. When one of Vargas's platoons was pinned down at a hedgerow by machine guns and mortar and artillery rounds, he hurried toward it with a reserve platoon. Although wounded by a grenade, he took out three machine-gun positions by himself. Company G

finally entered the village in the afternoon and engaged in hand-to-hand fighting with enemy soldiers popping up from spider holes and out of abandoned huts.

Vargas thought he had secured Dai Do when suddenly the NVA launched a massive counterattack. Taking cover in the village cemetery, Company G dug up fresh graves, tossed out the bodies, and used the holes for cover. The fight raged through the night.

The next morning, the bodies of more than three hundred enemy soldiers lay near their position. Vargas's battalion commander arrived on the scene and ordered a renewed assault on the village. Low on ammunition, Company G pistol-whipped, stabbed, and beat the enemy with rifle butts. Vargas killed a North Vietnamese soldier with his knife. He carried to safety a Marine whose arm had been severed, and when the soldier pleaded for his arm, Vargas went back and found it. When the battalion commander, fighting like any other rifleman, was shot in the back three times, Vargas dragged him a hundred yards to an evacuation point, firing at the enemy as he went with an AK-47 he had picked up on the battlefield.

By the end of the third day of battle, the North Vietnamese had melted away and Vargas finally allowed himself to be treated for a bullet wound in his side and shrapnel from mortar blasts.

Jay Vargas received the Medal of Honor from President Richard Nixon on May 14, 1970. After the ceremony, his father struck up a conversation with the President. The next day, the senior Vargas disappeared for several hours. When he returned and his son asked him where he'd been, he replied nonchalantly that the President had asked him to come to the White House and have a sandwich with him.

BIOGRAPHY

BORN
July 29, 1940
Winslow, Arizona

ENTERED SERVICE
Winslow, Arizona

BRANCH
U.S. Marine Corps

DUTY
Vietnam War

CURRENT RESIDENCE
California

Door Gunner

GARY G. WETZEL

PRIVATE FIRST CLASS, U.S. ARMY 173rd Assault Helicopter Company, 11th Combined Aviation Battalion, 1st Aviation Brigade

GARY WETZEL GREW UP AS THE SECOND OLDEST of nine children and joined the Army at the age of eighteen. It was only one month after his nineteenth birthday when he landed in Saigon. With aspirations of being a pilot, he reenlisted to be guaranteed the duty station of his choice. Assigned to the 173rd Assault Helicopter Company, the Robin Hoods, Wetzel served as a door gunner. About ten days before he was scheduled to return home after serving two tours, he was shot down for the fifth time on January 8, 1968.

Wetzel's helicopter, hit by a rocket-propelled grenade, had its left front blown apart and was trapped in the landing zone by intense enemy fire. Two of the crew were killed outright by the hostiles. While going to the aid of his aircraft commander, Wetzel was blown into a rice paddy by a homemade grenade that shredded his entire upper left arm and caused severe wounds to his right arm, chest, and left leg. Without hesitation, and despite profuse bleeding, he staggered back to his gun well, tucked his mangled arm into his waistband, and took the enemy under fire. Wetzel's machine gun was the only weapon placing effective fire on the enemy, and although severely wounded, Wetzel remained at his position until he had taken out the automatic-weapons emplacement that had been inflicting heavy casualties on the American troops and preventing them from moving against the enemy.

Passing in and out of consciousness, Wetzel sustained a stab wound to his right thigh from a bayonet. He disregarded his own wounds and returned to aid his crew chief, who was attempting to drag the wounded aircraft commander to safety. He continued to grab other wounded and pull them across the rice paddy, all the while losing consciousness and blood.

After Wetzel and the other survivors were rescued the next morning, he spent a week on the critical list. His arm was amputated in a field hospital, but he had to undergo another surgery in a Tokyo hospital because of infection. After about five months in hospitals, Wetzel began to learn how to live a productive civilian life with a prosthetic arm.

While working as an expediter in Wisconsin, Wetzel was approached by a colonel, a major, and a first sergeant who told him that he was going to Washington to receive the Medal of Honor. It took the officers two weeks to convince him that they were sincere. Wetzel received the Medal of Honor from President Lyndon Johnson on November 19, 1968, in a ceremony at the White House.

When asked what the medal means to him, Wetzel replied, "When I was in the Tokyo hospital, where the doctors took out more than four hundred stitches, some of the guys I pulled out who were recovering from their wounds found out I was there. They would walk up to my bed and ask, 'Are you Gary Wetzel?' And I'd say, 'Yeah,' and they would pull out pictures of their wives, kids, or girlfriends and say, 'Hey, man, because of you, this is what I've got to go back to.'" And then Wetzel would reply, "I'm not Superman. I was just a guy doing his job." Today, Gary Wetzel lives in South Milwaukee, Wisconsin, and works as a heavy equipment operator.

BIOGRAPHY

BORN
September 29, 1947
South Milwaukee,
Wisconsin

ENTERED SERVICE
Milwaukee, Wisconsin

BRANCH
U.S. Army

DUTY
Vietnam War

CURRENT RESIDENCE
Wisconsin

Portraits of Valor

WAR ON TERROR

The Mission Continues

It is understandable that most people associate the Medal of Honor with America's great conflicts of the twentieth century—World War II, Korea, Vietnam. These were the last times our country fielded massive armies of citizen soldiers in conventional wars whose battles elicited widespread interest (or, in the case of Vietnam, controversy) at home.

These wars have such a hold on our imagination that it is often assumed that bravery stopped then—at that bygone time when our warriors were not part of a professional military and did not have protective armor, night-vision goggles, pinpoint air strikes, and other advantages that make combat less hazardous. Yes, our servicemen and -women today are admirable, such a view acknowledges, but their enemies are merely insurgents, and the conflicts in which they fight are dominated by predator drones, Global Positioning Systems, digitized command and control, and other elements of high technology that make the human element and the willingness, if necessary, to do and die less a factor than in the past.

This is not what Medal of Honor recipients from earlier wars think. Often sent by the Pentagon into the battle zones of the War on Terror to talk about their own past exploits as a way of inspiring our troops, they come back themselves inspired by the spirit of courage and selflessness they have witnessed. They are awestruck by the intricate knowledge and skills our military men and women must master today; by their ability to negotiate complex rules of engagement while moving through war zones defined both by high technology and by improvised explosive devices, suicide bombers, and other primitive and inhuman weapons; and by the fact that today's soldiers must serve with a weapon in their hands and the microphones and cameras of the media in their faces, and thus must be always ready for their every action to be subjected to a scrutiny that was not as readily present in the battlefields of previous wars.

It is true that Medals of Honor are rarer today than in the past when our wars were marked by large unit engagements. To date, only eight medals have been awarded in Iraq and Afghanistan, seven of them posthumously. Three of these went to servicemen (Marine Corporal Jason Dunham, Navy SEAL Michael Monsoor, and Army Specialist Ross McGinnis) who threw their bodies on enemy grenades to save the lives of their comrades—an almost instinctive act in which there is time only for one decision: whether or not to sacrifice oneself so that others will survive and stay in the fight. Another four medals were awarded to men (Army Sergeant Paul Smith, Navy SEAL Michael Murphy, Army Sergeant Jared Monti, and Army Sergeant Robert J. Miller) who died supporting their fellow soldiers in fierce encounters where they all single-handedly engaged the enemy in actions that exemplify the willingness of our soldiers today, as in past conflicts, to step past the boundaries of ordinary bravery when the need for extraordinary courage suddenly arises.

These men and what they stood for will be represented in the future by Army Staff Sergeant Salvatore Giunta and Army Sergeant First Class Leroy Petry, the first living Medal of Honor recipients during a conflict since the Vietnam War, and perhaps others who have yet to be identified. Sergeant Giunta was on patrol with his squad in Afghanistan's Korengal Valley on October 25, 2007, when they were ambushed by an enemy force. During the fight, Giunta ran forward through heavy fire to rescue a wounded comrade being carried away by two Taliban. His comrade was wounded too seriously to survive, but he lived long enough to see Giunta fighting for him. So while Giunta was not able to save his friend's life, he was able to bring him home. Sergeant Petry's platoon was conducting combat operations in Paktya, Afghanistan, on May 26, 2008. Although wounded by a bullet that went through both of his legs, Petry led a comrade to cover. When a grenade landed just a few feet from them, Petry was able to reach it and throw it away from his fellow Rangers, preventing their certain injury or death. While he was releasing the grenade, it detonated and amputated his right hand.

Medal of Honor recipients have always distinguished themselves by such courage and self-lessness, as has our military as a whole—not only during the great conflicts of the last three generations, but also since this country was founded in the blood of the American Revolution. Whether it has been Iwo Jima, the Chosin Reservoir, Khe Sanh, or Fallujah in Iraq and Kandahar Province in Afghanistan, the story is always the same. "The bravest are surely those who have the clearest vision of what is before them," as the Greek historian Thucydides wrote, "glory and danger alike, and yet notwithstanding, go out to meet it."

After President Barack Obama awarded him the medal, Staff Sergeant Giunta said, "If I'm a hero, then every man that stands around me, every woman in the military, everyone who goes into the unknown is a hero." This is exactly the legacy of the Medal of Honor and why it continues to shine brightly today, not only in the deeds of those whose valor is formally celebrated, but also in the daily service of those who may never receive a decoration. These courageous individuals, whose names rarely appear in our newspapers and whose service takes place largely outside our view, call to mind the famous definition of true character: "doing the right thing when no one is watching." They have volunteered to get into a fight that sometimes lacks the clarity of past wars. They willingly engage a new kind of enemy that targets our civilians while hiding among its own. They purchase the normality we enjoy by holding at bay those who would like nothing better than to bring their terror war directly into the American heartland. The meaning our military men and women hold for our country—the ones who receive medals and the ones who do not—can be seen in their willingness to allow the rest of us to take this constant sacrifice for granted and to sleep easily at night because they are on guard.

Saving a Buddy at All Costs

SALVATORE A. GIUNTA

SPECIALIST, U.S. ARMY Company B, 2nd Battalion (Airborne), 503rd Infantry Regiment, 173rd Airborne Brigade Combat Team

BIOGRAPHY

BORN
January 25, 1985
Clinton, Iowa

ENTERED SERVICE
Hiawatha, Iowa

BRANCH
U.S. Army

DUTY
War in Afghanistan

CURRENT RESIDENCE
Colorado

SALVATORE GIUNTA WAS A SELF-DESCRIBED "sandwich artist" working at Subway in late 2003 when he heard a radio commercial for the U.S. Army. About to turn nineteen, Giunta made an appointment with a recruiter. He told himself that he was only interested in the free T-shirt the commercial promised. But he was really looking for a life path. The recruiter's message—that in a time of war, one man can make a difference—resonated with Giunta, and he volunteered.

After basic training and airborne school at Fort Benning, Georgia, he was assigned to the 173rd Airborne Brigade Combat Team and deployed to Afghanistan in the spring of 2005. His first tour there lasted for a year. When he returned to Afghanistan for a second tour in the spring of 2007, he saw immediately that it had become a far more dangerous place: There were more Taliban and more firefights. He was now stationed at Firebase Vegas in the forbidding Korengal Valley, known as "the Valley of Death" because so many servicemen had died fighting there.

On October 25, 2007, Specialist Giunta's company was at the end of a five-day mission to tame the area before winter arrived. Two days earlier, the Taliban had killed a popular staff sergeant and wounded two other men. The company commander now ordered two of the company's platoons to go to a nearby village and retrieve seized equipment, which was being exhibited as "war trophies." Giunta's platoon stayed on an overlooking mountain ridge to provide cover.

Shortly after nightfall, with the mission completed, Giunta's unit was ordered to return to base. Their way lit by the moon, the Americans had walked for about five minutes when rocket-propelled grenades and machine-gun fire began to explode all around them.

Sergeant Joshua Brennan was walking point and went down immediately. He was the leader of the platoon's Alpha Team, while Giunta was the leader of Bravo Team. The two were close friends. They had traveled through Italy when they were stationed at the 173rd Airborne's base near Vicenza and had been together on both Afghanistan tours.

When Specialist Hugo Mendoza, the squad medic, rushed forward to help, he was shot and killed. Giunta braved the heavy fire to pull another American to safety. An enemy round struck him in the chest, but his protective vest stopped it. He was hit again in the rocket launcher he carried over his left shoulder, three to four inches from his neck.

Realizing that the Taliban fighters were trying to surround and overrun the unit, Giunta and two comrades counterattacked, throwing volleys of grenades. Looking for Sergeant Brennan, Giunta moved forward into the darkness. He saw the dim shapes of two Taliban dragging Brennan away. Giunta killed one of the enemy and hit the other. He tried to reassure Brennan, who had eight serious wounds, as he and the other Americans gave medical aid while waiting for a helicopter. His friend died a few hours later.

Several days later, Sal Giunta learned that he had been recommended for the Medal of Honor. In the three years it took for the recommendation to be approved, Giunta sometimes felt a kind of dread—not only because becoming the first living recipient of the medal in nearly four decades would change his life, but also because he believed that all the others involved in the Korengal Valley fight were as worthy of being honored as he was. He felt this more strongly than ever when President Barack Obama fastened the medal around his neck at the White House on October 25, 2010. After the ceremony, Giunta said, "Every single soldier I've been with in two combat tours deserves to wear this just as much as I do. That's something that will always stay with me."

Tossing a Grenade to Save Lives

LEROY A. PETRY

SERGEANT FIRST CLASS, U.S. ARMY Company D, 2nd Battalion, 75th Ranger Regiment

BIOGRAPHY

BORN
July 29, 1979
Santa Fe, New Mexico

ENTERED SERVICE
Santa Fe, New Mexico

BRANCH
U.S. Army

DUTY
War in Afghanistan

CURRENT RESIDENCE
Washington State

SERGEANT FIRST CLASS LEROY ARTHUR PETRY IS the second living, active-duty service member to be awarded the Medal of Honor for actions in Iraq or Afghanistan. He has deployed eight times in support of the War on Terror, with two tours to Iraq and six tours to Afghanistan, totaling twenty-eight months of deployment. He has served as a grenadier, a squad automatic rifleman, a fire team leader, a squad leader, an operations sergeant, and a weapons squad leader. During this time, he has received two Bronze Stars, a Purple Heart, three Army Commendation Medals, two Army Achievement Medals, a National Defense Service Medal, three Army Good Conduct Medals, an Afghanistan Campaign Medal with Combat Star, an Iraq Campaign Medal with Combat Star, and a Global War on Terrorism Expeditionary Medal, among others.

He enlisted in the United States Army from his hometown of Santa Fe, New Mexico, in September 1999. After completing Basic Training and Advanced Individual Training—both at Fort Benning, Georgia—Petry was assigned to the 2nd Battalion, 75th Ranger Regiment at Joint Base Lewis-McChord, Washington.

On May 26, 2008, his platoon was conducting combat operations against an armed enemy in Paktya, Afghanistan. Reacting to the need of another assault squad, he moved to their aid to provide supervision and guidance. He was wounded by one round, which went through both of his legs, but still managed to lead a comrade to cover. When a grenade landed just a few feet from them, despite his own wounds and with complete disregard for his personal safety, Petry risked his life to reach and secure the live grenade and throw it away from his fellow Rangers. As he released the grenade, it detonated and amputated his right hand.

With remarkable presence of mind, Petry assessed his wound and placed a tourniquet on his right arm, while his comrades returned fire and killed the enemy.

Petry is the ninth service member to have received the Medal of Honor for actions in Afghanistan and Iraq. Of these recipients, all but Petry and Army Staff Sergeant Salvatore Giunta were awarded the medal posthumously. The seven men honored posthumously are Army Specialist Ross A. McGinnis, Army Sergeant First Class Paul R. Smith, Navy Petty Officer Second Class Michael A. Monsoor, and Marine Corps Corporal Jason L. Dunham, all for actions in Iraq, and Army Staff Sergeant Robert J. Miller, Army Sergeant First Class Jared C. Monti, and Navy Lieutenant Michael P. Murphy for actions in Afghanistan.

On July 12, 2011, President Barack Obama awarded Sergeant Petry the Medal of Honor. As of this writing, Petry serves as a liaison officer for the United States Special Operations Command Care Coalition-Northwest Region, and oversees wounded warriors, ill and injured service members, and their families.

HONORING
UNKNOWN SOLDIERS

Tomb of the Unknowns

THE MEDAL OF HONOR IS EMBLEMATIC OF ONE individual's willingness to put everything at risk to save a comrade, drive back the enemy, hold a position. Those who wear it emboss the abstract ideal of courage with a specific face, a name and character, a deed that gives momentary clarity to the chaos of battle.

The medal brings immortality to those who live to accept it, and also to the many who receive this honor after their death. The stories of these men and women have become part of the American narrative, yet the recipients are themselves always the first to remember comrades who weren't so honored and to acknowledge all those anonymous and unremembered servicemen and servicewomen who made the ultimate sacrifice.

If the Medal of Honor commemorates the valor of the unique few, the Tomb of the Unknowns symbolizes the service of all the others—those who came back from the foreign battlefields where they served their country and those who died there. This haunting monument was created by Congress in the spring of 1921 to honor all the unidentified soldiers who had fallen in World War I. Four bodies were exhumed from military cemeteries in France and their caskets placed in a hall under an honor guard. Army Sergeant Edward Younger, a highly decorated veteran of the war, randomly selected one of them; the others were reburied. The remains of the Unknown Soldier were brought home to lie in state at the Capitol and were then interred at Arlington National Cemetery on Armistice Day of the same year. As part of the ceremony, President Warren Harding presented the Unknown Soldier with the Medal of Honor.

In 1931 a monument was erected to stand over the simple marble tomb. The design selected was in the form of a sarcophagus, eleven feet tall and eight feet wide at the base. On the panel facing the Potomac River are three carved figures symbolizing Victory, Valor, and Peace. On the back panel is the inscription HERE RESTS IN HONORED GLORY AN AMERICAN SOLDIER KNOWN BUT TO GOD.

In 1956, President Dwight Eisenhower signed a bill to select the Unknown Soldiers of World War II and Korea. In 1958, two sets of unidentified remains from World War II—one from the Pacific theater and one from the European theater—were taken aboard the USS *Canberra*, a guided missile cruiser. Navy Corpsman William Charette, himself a Medal of Honor recipient, selected one of them as World War II's Unknown Soldier; the other was buried at sea. At the same time, in Hawaii, Army Sergeant Ned Lyle made the selection of the Unknown from the Korean War. On Memorial Day 1958, the two caskets were taken to Arlington by caisson. President Eisenhower awarded each soldier the Medal of Honor, and the two caskets were buried.

The Unknown service member from the Vietnam War was selected by Medal of Honor recipient Marine Corps Sergeant Major Allan Kellogg and buried at Arlington on Memorial Day 1984 after being presented with the medal by President Ronald Reagan. (In 1998, these remains were identified by DNA as those of Air Force Lieutenant Michael Blassie, shot down near An Loc in 1972. He was reinterred in a family plot; the crypt of the Vietnam Unknown remains empty to this day.)

The Tomb of the Unknowns is a reminder that no member of the American armed forces, wherever he or she serves or however he or she falls, is forgotten. The profound association of the Medal of Honor with the tomb is a reminder that all who give their last measure of devotion for their country are heroes.

World War II forged an enduring patriotic spirit in our home. I was six years old and those memories are now very faint, except one of a small red, white, and blue service flag that hung in the living room window. It was adorned with three blue stars—representing my brothers Lou, John, and George, who were serving in the Army on foreign soil. To this day, that small service banner still remains seared in my memory.

In January 1999, I embarked on a photographic quest to honor the millions of veterans like my brothers, whose lives, interrupted by war, changed history—the country's and their own. My first images were of aging men and women in veterans' hospitals, but after I discovered that only 155 recipients of the Medal of Honor were still alive, this project clicked into sharp focus. Initially, my goal was to complete all 155 portraits. But the inescapable grip of mortality took its toll in the following years. There are now fewer than 85 living recipients; a few chose not to participate, and some were reluctant to face the camera one more time.

America's most iconic symbols of freedom seemed an ideal backdrop for several of the portraits. Leo K. Thorsness was photographed at the Lincoln Memorial; Hector A. Cafferata and General Raymond Davis at the Korean War Memorial. During his photo session in the Medal of Honor Room at Arlington National Cemetery, former U.S. Senator Joseph R. (Bob) Kerrey revealed that the formal portrait was a first for him. Admiral James B. Stockdale wished to be photographed on the carrier deck of the USS *Constellation,* while Brian M. Thacker wanted his portrait next to the Albert Einstein Memorial sculpture in Washington, D.C. Within hours after being reunited with the nurse whose life he saved thirty-two years earlier, Major Drew D. Dix agreed to be photographed only if the nurse and the other rescue team members were included in the portrait. John L. Levitow, his body ravaged with cancer, graciously consented to sit for what was to be his final portrait.

It's been a rare privilege to be in the company of living history—more than 143 Medal of Honor recipients who put their trust in me. I'm extremely proud of the opportunity to share this photographic experience with you, and my hope is that this body of work will serve as a tribute to all who have worn an American military uniform.

Finally, on a personal note, I wish to thank my family both near and far for their encouraging words and love, and my cherished grandsons, Enzo and Rocco, whose energized spirit and playful innocence serve as daily reminders that life is truly a gift.

Nick Del Calzo

Although they served in a democratic fighting force, the men profiled in this book emerged from what military historians call the fog of war as an aristocracy of valor. What they did in battle was so extraordinary that it raises those questions we ask without expecting an answer: Why do some people rise to the occasion? What is the DNA of courage? Is there something God-given in their willingness to risk their lives for their comrades and countrymen?

Some say a nation is defined by its heroes. If so, we Americans are very fortunate indeed. What the men in this book did to earn the Medal of Honor, and what they have done in the years since then to carry its formidable weight, should give us confidence that this country—which our enemies foolishly underestimate and which we ourselves constantly worry has lost its footing—is in fact a growing ground for character, endurance, determination, and guts.

In talking to the men profiled in this book, I asked them how they were capable of acts of heroism that seem unfathomable to an average person. They all replied in so many words that it was no big deal, that they were just doing their duty. This was no foot-scuffing, aw-shucks false modesty. They truly believe that they are ordinary men called upon to do something extraordinary on a given day—just as firmly as they believe that they merely hold this medal in trust for all those they served with in our time of need, many of whom never came home.

Because these brief profiles are in some sense illustrations of Nick Del Calzo's remarkable photographs—images that show so well the content of the subject's character—I have merely tried to elaborate on the citations that went along with the medals. But I also got a glimpse of rich lives lived after their rendezvous with destiny—lives involving family, community, and enterprise that are part of another, larger story about America and why we went to war in the first place.

I would like to thank my friend Wally Nunn, who made this book happen. Also, Major General Perry Smith, who made a contribution to each of these profiles; Lieutenant General Nick Kehoe, who saw the project to completion; and Laurie Orseck, whose editorial skills made each of these pieces better.

I also want to remember my father-in-law, Louis Giachino, who served in Europe during World War II with the 434th Fighter Squadron of the Army Air Corps. He was a good man.

Peter Collier

ACKNOWLEDGMENTS

There are many individuals who have contributed to bringing this labor of love and commitment to reality. Each, in his or her own special way, has been instrumental in perpetuating the Medal of Honor's legacy of courage, sacrifice, and patriotism.

They include those who worked tirelessly with Nick Del Calzo over several years, such as Jim Gunlock, who was involved from the moment the idea was born; Patricia Germek, Jan Baker, Linda Raper, and Sandra Corriere, whose encouragement and enthusiasm always shined through; and Bruce Marsden and Ron Landucci, whose photographic talents helped the images come alive.

Special acknowledgment is extended to the staff of the Congressional Medal of Honor Society for their extensive research, insights, and support, in particular, making Medal of Honor recipients available for countless photograph and interview sessions. There are others who, convinced of the profound importance of this work, made possible the addition of invaluable substance and dimension; they include Al Hoffman, Jon Reynolds, Orson Swindle, and Doug Sterner.

An extraordinary group from New Orleans deserves special recognition for providing major financial support at a critical time. For their generosity, we are eternally indebted to J. Edgar Monroe, Bruce North, Cokie Rathborne, Thomas Snedeker, Edward Kohnke, JBM Morris, Tidewater Inc., Langston Sweet & Fresses P.A., and the Marine Corps Support Group of New Orleans. Additional donations or in-kind contributions came from Fred and Barbara Kort, Harold and Gerda Seifer, Emil and Eva Hecht, Rhoda and David Chase, Wallace Nunn, the Elizabeth Hooper Foundation, The Barr Fund, Hasselblad USA Inc., and ILFORD Imaging.

Among the many others who gave of their time and talents are Steve Fayne, Bill Grantham, Paul Haring, Kevin M. Kelly, Scott Nickell, Brandt Wilkins, and Nancy Z. Wilson. And, of course, many thanks for the tireless efforts of the Artisan staff.

Without the efforts of these and many others not mentioned, it would not be possible to fully appreciate what these genuine American heroes have given their country so selflessly.

Index

(continued from front endpapers) So many men and women have fought and died for the freedoms we enjoy as Americans . . . those freedoms don't come free. —**THOMAS J. KINSMAN** ✴ It's not the absence of fear that makes you a hero, but knowing what needs to be done and doing it. —**ALTON W. KNAPPENBERGER** ✴ May God bless each of us always and may each of us always strive to be worthy of his blessings. —**GEORGE C. LANG** ✴ Your moral values define you as a person and are the bedrock upon which an honorable and meaningful life is built. —**HOWARD V. LEE** ✴ True heroism is not a matter of chance, it's a matter of choice. —**PETER C. LEMON** ✴ The American flag represents all of us and should be treated with respect. —**JOHN L. LEVITOW** ✴ To our youth, don't give in to peer pressure. If it's wrong, say no. Your peers will respect you for it and you will be my hero! —**GARY L. LITTRELL** ✴ There is no greater honor than the opportunity to serve and help preserve our freedom—it's the essence of humanity. —**JAMES E. LIVINGSTON** ✴ Our freedom allows us to enjoy the sense of honor and pride necessary to be a hero—stay free, be proud, and never cease to do what is right. —**JOSE M. LOPEZ** ✴ "Greater love hath no man than to lay down his life for his friends." From the Revolutionary War forward, our American servicemen and women have done that in the name of the freedom you enjoy today. —**JACK H. LUCAS** ✴ I can do all things through Christ who strengthens me (Philippians 4:13). —**ALLEN J. LYNCH** ✴ A lot of young kids think they're out there by themselves; life is a team effort—you're not alone and you have family and friends to help you. God won't put more in your backpack than you can carry. —**WALTER J. MARM, JR.** ✴ When we respect our flag, we honor our country and those heroes who gave their lives to keep her free. —**ROBERT D. MAXWELL** ✴ My Medal of Honor should be shared with my shipmates—when trouble strikes, one's first impulse must always be to take care of one's shipmates. We all tried to do that. —**RICHARD M. MCCOOL, JR.** ✴ This medal I wear was earned by the Marines and Navy Corpsmen of the First Platoon of Kilo Company, Fourth Marine Regiment. Against tremendous odds, One-Kilo, supported by intrepid Navy and Marine aviators, upheld the honor of the Marine Corps, and I am proud to have been their leader. Semper Fidelis. —**JOHN J. MCGINTY III** ✴ The most important possession you have is your name—never dishonor it. —**DAVID H. MCNERNEY** ✴ To me, patriotism means love of God, country, and freedom—a nation of united people. —**GINO J. MERLI** ✴ If I'm a slave and you're free, will you fight for my liberty? —**LEWIS L. MILLETT** ✴ Always believe in yourself, God, and country. —**HIROSHI H. MIYAMURA** ✴ To all young Americans, place God first, family and country always. —**OLA L. MIZE** ✴ Every day has its test, and every time we fail to do what is right, we weaken our character and the character of this great country. —**ROBERT J. MODRZEJEWSKI** ✴ We live in the best country in the world—it is our duty to love, guide, and protect it. —**RAYMOND G. MURPHY** ✴ It is America's youth on which the future of our great nation depends. We should encourage them to take full advantage of opportunities along the road to become productive citizens through character building, education, and training. —**CHARLES P. MURRAY, JR.** ✴ God bless our corps and country. Semper Fidelis. —**REGINALD R. MYERS** ✴ The victories of yesteryear are just one key to the door of freedom, so that we can all be free today. Education is essential to becoming good citizens and learning to appreciate others. —**ROBERT B. NETT** ✴ Everyone faces seemingly overwhelming odds some time in their life—never give up! —**THOMAS R. NORRIS** ✴ The American flag displayed on one's lapel will never equal carrying it in one's heart. —**MICHAEL J. NOVOSEL** ✴ Treat others as equal and respect divergent views. Nothing is impossible if you seek divine guidance from our heavenly Father, which alone lends the essential fiber to this great nation. —**GEORGE H. O'BRIEN** ✴ No matter how difficult it seems at the time, it's easier to do the right thing than spend a lifetime regretting that you didn't. —**ROBERT O'MALLEY** ✴ Stay in school as long as you can—you can always do more than you think. Without education, life is more difficult. —**NICHOLAS ORESKO** ✴ Since joining the Marines in 1936, my guiding light has always been Proverbs 3:5–6: Trust in the Lord with all your heart and lean not on your own understanding, in all your ways acknowledge Him and He shall direct your path. —**MITCHELL PAIGE** ✴ Your integrity is the most valuable asset you have—never jeopardize it. —**ROBERT M. PATTERSON** ✴ To be an American comes with many rights, privileges, and responsibilities. It is our duty to honor, defend, and preserve them for future generations. —**RICHARD A. PITTMAN** ✴ Those who give up freedom for peace will soon lose both. —**EVERETT P. POPE** ✴ Freedom, patriotism, and choice are